Caste in Half

Susan Robinson

2QT Limited (Publishing)

First Edition published 2018 by
2QT Limited (Publishing)
Settle, North Yorkshire BD24 9RH United Kingdom

Copyright © Susan Robinson

The right of Susan Robinson to be identified as the author of this work has been asserted by her in accordance with the Copyright, Designs and Patents Act 1988

All rights reserved. This book is sold subject to the condition that no part of this book is to be reproduced, in any shape or form. Or by way of trade, stored in a retrieval system or transmitted in any form or by any means, electronic, mechanical, photocopying, recording, be lent, re-sold, hired out or otherwise circulated in any form of binding or cover other than that in which it is published and without a similar condition, including this condition being imposed on the subsequent purchaser, without prior permission of the copyright holder.

Publisher Disclaimer:

The events in this memoir are described according to the Author's recollection; recognition and understanding of the events and individuals mentioned and are in no way intended to mislead or offend. As such the Publisher does not hold any responsibility for any inaccuracies or opinions expressed by the author. Every effort has been made to acknowledge and gain any permission from organisations and persons mentioned in this book. Any enquiries should be directed to the author.

Printed by Ingramsparks

Cover images: shutterstock.com

A CIP catalogue record for this book is available from the British Library

ISBN - 978-1-912014-43-9

My father, Malcolm Robinson.

Chapter One

My Life in the Karasuk Hills

THIS BOOK TELLS the sometimes funny, sometimes tragic story of my life. Having one foot in traditional culture and one foot in colonialism, I struggled to come to terms with the life that was given to me. Through adversity I grew stronger and made a life of my own. It also relates the part that history played in bringing me to adulthood and how my traditional African heritage and my white heritage sometimes have strange parallels.

> What is time? A passing click,
> A clock we watch, a man-made trick.
> Time may go but never comes,
> The hands still move the heart still drums.
> Beauty found and beauty lost,
> Time passes by and at such cost,
> Became complete but no one cared,
> Never would I bend my knee,
> Admit defeat to them or me.
> My strength it comes from deep inside,
> I shall still as myself preside.
> So, what of now to sink or drown?
> I'll show them all I'll wear no frown.

Chapter One

I was born in the Karasuk Hills, at a place called Lomut near the Kerio Valley in Kenya at the escarpment near the peak of the hills. This is where the Cherangani Hills end and the Karasuk Hills begin.

The Marakwet people live here; in many ways they share the same culture with my people, the Pokot, and they intermarry. My native people, the Pokot, built their homes on the escarpment that rises about 3,370 metres (11,057ft) high as a defence against disease and surrounding enemies. The height and the land combine to create an endless landscape that is breathtaking. The air is sharp and cold, especially in the nights and early mornings. The view is wide and one can see the panorama of endless hills; this place gives a person a sense of greatness and freedom. The sky is pale blue and the clouds tower up and sail through it. Some days the winds blow steadily and run through these hills; the slopes would be a perfect place to launch a glider. Sometimes the clouds move with the wind but sometimes they catch on the summits of the hills and break into rain.

The fog comes towards my mother's village early in the morning, a floating mass that moves towards the hills and vanishes in the blue sky. Then we see a beautiful view of the Sigor Valley below, a vast plain of game country that stretches as far as the eye can see. Some days, when the fog vanishes into the blue sky, we can see little maize plantations and native villages below and tiny huts with smoke coming from them.

The trees in the valley are like thorn bushes and cacti grow here and there. The valley is home to giraffe, lion, leopard, cheetah, buffalo, elephants, elands and all sorts of game animals. There are many beautiful springs and wells that make perfect places to camp. The grass is short and green; the natives graze their sheep and cows along this escarpment.

Looking down on these slopes is awesome. One can see deep

into the valley to the brown desert marked by thorn bush trees and winding, dry, seasonal river beds. Sometimes gigantic clouds gather and dissolve over the landscape and a light shower of rain paints a blue, slanting streak across the horizon below the escarpment. Other times, just before sunset, the scenery draws close about you; the hills are close with their deep blue and green colouring. If you go outside before the village sleeps, you can see the stars above burning very brightly.

Some evenings the wind rushes past into the trees beyond and into the maize fields but there is no sign of rain. We know the sound of the approaching rain; it is loud as it comes back to embrace the hills.

The features of the landscape make you feel part of it, as if you have lived in this part of the world for a very long time. Walking and working in these hills, you feel oneness with the long valleys, thickets, the green slopes and rocky crags. High up on the peaks of these hills there are springs and water gushes out and spills down in a sheet of water, forever coming down.

As you walk down these narrow paths, below you can see tracks made by a herd of eland antelopes. As you look down the valley towards Sigor, you can see herds of buffalos or elephants in the distance.

The Pokots live in large extended families. They have many round huts clustered in one place belonging to a particular clan. The huts are thatched with grass; it is mostly the women who build the family home while the men are out herding the cows or hunting. One big hut in the centre belongs to the father of the family; around this hut are many others belonging to his wives and older male children. A store is always built for the foodstuffs, mainly the grain. The space between the huts is a playground for little children; it is also where maize and millet are ground on flat stones to make flour. The goats and cows are milked at the back of the huts

Chapter One

and there is a *boma* made out of long sticks. The Pokots, like the Maasai, believe that cows belong to them and go out to raid neighbouring tribes.

My mother was happy here; she was used to the lifestyle and the surroundings. She told me that she was very frightened to give birth to me in these hills. I always wanted to visit these hills as a grown woman but I never got the chance. Her people lived by harsh laws, and sometimes life and death depended on these laws; they would not have accepted me as one of them as I was born light skinned. In Pokot culture, light-skinned children are believed to be a bad omen, to even bring death to the village. Thus a child born as an albino will be given to the spirits, left in the bushes for the spirits to take. Of course, we know that spirits don't take them, hyenas or wild animals eat them.

My grandmother was a midwife. As soon as she saw that I was light skinned, my mother saved me by telling my grandmother and grandfather the truth, that my father was white. Our people had not seen white people before, only a Catholic priest from a distance at Sigor market place.

A big *baraza* (meeting/gathering) was held, with the native elders and chiefs. My grandfather told the angry people that when I turned three months old, he would take me to my father who worked in the British government as an agricultural officer. He promised that he would not allow me to be seen in the Pokot community again. My mother and I were secluded and given a separate hut, but we were under the protection of my grandfather so no one dared touch me or throw me to their spirits.

My father was a serving officer in the British Army in the Second World War; before that he was a student at Oxford University and got a double first in Classics. After the war, he won a provisional appointment to the Colonial Service. Father did not take the three-month course at the Imperial Institute in London as required in law, culture, surveying and tropical sanitation. He had enough experience from working in the Sudan Defence Forces under the Sudan Plantation Syndicate Ltd. At Barakat, Sudan, in the 1940s he gained enough skills, knowledge and experience the hard way. Sometimes life-and-death decisions had to be made without hesitation. One could not learn these in a classroom.

My father was given a job with the Department of Agriculture in Kenya under the British Colony Protectorate. He was the agricultural officer for Kapenguria and Chepareria, a sub-district in West Pokot. His first wife, Helga, was of German descent. They met after the Second World War. The marriage lasted a long time but went wrong as soon as they got to Kenya. They got their decree absolute at the beginning of 1958.

My father made many government trips to Chepareria. Travel was the most demanding part of his work and he spent most of his time in this district under canvas. He was obliged to journey hundreds of miles every year, usually on foot or horseback, gathering taxes and hearing appeals from local tribunals. He inspected public work projects, supplied seeds for farms and saw to the welfare of the British-protected tribes, whom he simultaneously ruled and served. In his duties he encountered occupational hazards such as black-water fever, malaria, dysentery and other tropical scourges. Most of the time he travelled alone; there was hardship and loneliness and it was rare to meet a fellow European. Food could not be preserved and in some places the soil was not fertile and vegetables were impossible to grow.

Sometime in 1958, my father was asked to temporarily replace the agricultural officer in Sigor District in the West Pokot area. He prepared his provisions and his ammunition and loaded them into the old Land Rover. The cook, Alfred, and one native leader guide accompanied him.

The road to Sigor was bad, deep with dust and barred with

Chapter One

blocks of stones taller than the Land Rover. They drove through bushes, cactus and thorn trees until they reached the flat plain near the border of the Turkana and Pokot areas and were about to branch to the east towards Sigor. They could see fresh spoor of a lion in the dust. The place was parched, arid, and not too different from the desert; very little rain was recorded here.

Father hoped to keep his Land Rover at a steady speed to avoid breakdown, for he had been warned to take care at this junction. Camping would be dangerous for there were many lions roaming about, so Father tried to get through before nightfall. About sunset they had a puncture. Luckily Father normally travelled with two spare tyres.

They arrived late at night and had to occupy the agricultural officer's house. It was made out of corrugated iron sheets and brick walls, not much of a home. Some metres away was another structure with no walls, just a roof made out of iron sheets supported by brick pillars. This was the district officer's court and where Father had to act as the magistrate on behalf of the District Commissioner in Kapenguria, Alexander David Shirreff – he served in Kenya's administration from 1945 till 1963.

My mother was a Pokot of the Simba clan. All Pokots classify themselves according to clan and each clan holds authority and a position in the community. The Simba clan is a ruling clan from which all the leaders are elected. Members of the Simba clan are recognised as the most fearless.

My mother had run away from her first husband in Baringo District with her two sons. Her husband married many wives and, if my mother objected or complained, he beat her. Pokot men have many wives; the more wives, children, cattle, camels, sheep and goats they own, the greater their wealth and position in society. No man can be an elder or a chief in Pokot culture unless he has many wives.

My Life in the Karasuk Hills

My mother ran away to her mother at Lomut in the Karasuk Hills. She knew it would cause problems, and later her parents would pay a penalty for the cows her husband had paid during their wedding day, but she took her chance. She came to stay at her parents' home with her two sons.

My mother, although used to Pokot ways, soon got depressed and came down the Lomut Mountains to the market place at Sigor, leaving her two sons in the care of her mother. This was where she met my father.

It was a big market day; the Pokot barter food for other products. Alfred, my father's cook, was trying to buy a sheep for my father using English money. He happened to come across Mother, who was dressed in her native costume. My mother talks a lot and, with a few Kiswahili words, told the cook that she was looking for a job and willing to work for him since the cook looked different from the other people in the crowd.

Alfred took my mother to my father and persuaded him that the woman would be useful as a cook's helper. At first everything went well but after three months my father had to go back to his post at Chepareria as another officer had come to replace him. He took my mother along with him. No one knew that my mother was wife to a Pokot or was running away and had left her children behind in the Lomut Mountains. All married Pokot women wear a leather bracelet as a sign that they are married but my mother had cut off her bracelet, so that other Pokots would not know that she was married.

Once in Chepareria, Mother replaced another cook's helper by the name of Taprandich who at that time was absent. It was not by accident that Taprandich was missing; she had been gone for a long time and needed to be replaced. Rumour had it that she had gone to the Pokot interior to get her cows back after other Pokots from Karamoja had raided them. Being of Maasai descent, Taprandich

Chapter One

had the courage to get together some young warriors and some of her relatives and retrieve what belonged to her. She had a strong character, a mixture of Tugen and Maasai (Kenyan tribes).

My mother took her position as a cook's helper but she was lazy and untidy and not up to the job. She spent most of her evenings visiting other Pokots and forgot to arrive on time for my father's dinner so the cook had to perform all her duties. At times she went missing at weekends to go to *ngomas* (circumcision festivals).

The only reason she was not sent away was because Alfred the cook did not report her to Father. Alfred had noticed her sneak into my father's bedroom on several occasions. Alfred pretended that my mother performed her duties and covered for her; he never told Father of her late arrivals or her laziness.

Things grew worse when my mother started to be very sick. At first they thought she had malaria but she continued to vomit every morning. Finally, the cook complained to my father about her bad behaviour and laziness. This sealed her fate and she was told to go back to Lomut to her parents' home.

My father gave her enough money to get to Lomut and enough food to last a month or so. My mother was afraid to tell him that she was pregnant and kept it secret. She was offered an escort but she turned down the offer. She was in shock; she thought the medicine women back home in her village had done their job and given her medicine to stop the pregnancy.

When Mother got home my grandmother, on hearing that she was pregnant, chased her away to live with distant relatives. Until she was very heavy with the baby during the seventh month, Mother lived with people who mistreated her and had no sympathy for her. Finally, she decided to go back to her parents' home in Lomut. She started the trek through the bushes towards the hills. The first day was a long, arduous and lonely haul; she was very frightened for the bush was full of wild animals – lion, leopard, cheetah, hyena and herds of buffalo.

Many years after I was born, my mother told me her story. She got a lift from a transport lorry going to Lodwar but she was left at the border of Pokot and Turkana, from where she had to trek through grass country and then thorn bushes. The Karasuk Hills were in front of her but they seemed miles away. The sun was very hot and the air vibrated like the strings of a violin. Mother walked in the burning air and sometimes sat under a tree to rest in its shade, but she knew her life depended on finding a village to retire to for the night for protection. The luggage she carried seemed very heavy and she abandoned her food to lighten the load.

She stopped and looked into the distance, where she saw a herd of some sort moving on the plain ahead of her. At first she thought they were wildebeests, but they looked much smaller; they did not look like gazelles or antelopes. It was difficult for her to tell what they were from that distance, and the quivering air and the monotony of the scenery made it even more so. One could mistake a jackal for an eland or an ostrich for a buffalo.

After a second, it dawned on my mother to stand still behind one of the thorn trees and hope that her scent would not spread towards these animals. A small breeze came across and blew past her. When she looked again, she saw that they were wild dogs. Wild dogs are not as big as hyena, they are about the size of a normal dog, and they are very vicious. They are black with a white tuft at the tip of the tail, have round ears, rough, uneven hair and they smell bad. The Pokots are afraid of wild dogs; they believe that when they run in large numbers they are a portent of war.

My mother was very frightened and stood still. She looked in their direction; they seemed to travel on a track that turned to the side, away from her. Three or four dogs were running alongside each other and it took time before the whole group passed. They looked tired, as if they were running away from something and had

Chapter One

been running for a long time. When they had gone by, Mother felt safe. Exhausted both in body and spirit, she sat down for a while, then got up and started to walk faster to look for shelter for the night.

After some hours, my mother came upon a family that were migrating to join another clan that lived near the edge of the hills a few miles from Sigor. The husband and his three wives welcomed her. There were several grown-up boys and other, smaller children and they all camped in an open place. The husband and the older sons quickly cut thorn bushes to make a *boma* (fence) to protect the few cows and goats and two donkeys they had with them.

The sun went down in its equatorial haste and the bushes were enveloped in the peculiar stillness of a tropical night that is never altogether silent. There was a tree in the centre of the camp that had big branches that spread out like an umbrella, strong enough for two sons to sit on them and watch all night with bows and arrows. Of course, these weren't much use against a lion.

A big fire was lit in the centre of the camp; there was enough firewood to last the whole night. One son and the father stood guard with spears. Everyone in this camp, including my mother, knew their lives were in danger. When a Pokot shoots with his bow and arrow and lets go of the bowstring, you hear the twang of the bowstring and the whistle of the arrow as it speeds towards its target, and they are very accurate.

A quick meal was prepared of milk and *ugali* and everyone slept together round the tree next to the blazing fire that stayed alight the whole night. The night was cloudless, a full moon provided perfect visibility and the ground around the camp place was empty of bush. Suddenly they heard the most terrific roar – a lion was out there! Their blood ran cold. The animals stayed together; they too could sense the danger.

For several hours the father and his adult sons kept an almost motionless vigil, peering intently through the thorn fence. Suddenly they froze as they heard a deep, long, drawn-out sigh – a sure sign of hunger – from the bushes beyond the fence. Rustling sounds told them that the lion was approaching rapidly. Lions can jump around twelve feet high, so the *boma* was not much protection. Then the movement stopped and there was an enraged snarl. Apparently, the lion had sensed and seen the Pokot warriors so he started to back away.

The lion stalked the camp for about two hours, horrifying everyone by slowly edging nearer and nearer. The father expected the lion to rush in at any moment. Everyone kept perfectly still, hardly blinking. If the Pokots were to save their animals, they had to guess the exact place where the lion was and throw their spears at it. The young Pokot boys up in the tree released their arrows and the father threw his spear into the darkness in the direction of the lion.

They heard a terrifying roar and the lion crashed. No one could see him as he ran into the shrubs beyond. There were a series of mighty growls before the sounds faded. They were all convinced that the lion was wounded and had run away with spears and arrows sticking in its body.

No one slept that night; everyone was exhausted and the father ordered them to start moving in the early morning, taking no chances by staying in the vicinity of this wounded lion. If it came back it would definitely make a kill because it was wounded and hungry.

For two more nights my mother was safe in the company of this family until they had to go their separate ways when they reached Sigor. From there, Mother stayed with relatives then went up the hills to my grandmother's village on the escarpment at Lomut. Her family received her until the time of my birth.

After my birth, being half white, it was difficult to persuade the village people that I was not an albino but was born of a white

Chapter One

father. The elders passed judgement that I was to be taken to my father. My grandmother was a hard woman and very traditional; she agreed that I should be returned to my father but not before they had performed a ritual that would bind me to the Lomut hills. Even now, I feel that I am bound to these very hills.

My mother told me about the long journey to Chepareria, to my father's place of work. My grandfather, two Pokot elders and the chief of the area accompanied her. I have tried to imagine what it was like and what the reaction must have been when my father opened the door and saw my mother and me at his doorstep. By all accounts he at first denied a relationship with my mother. The elders, however, were more realistic and decided drastic action was called for.

The small black eyes in their dry, wrinkled faces glittered and their thin lips moved gently as if they were repeating father's words. I was taken from my mother and unceremoniously placed on my father's armchair where, by all accounts, I started to howl and scream. My mother was ushered out of the house by the elders as they left. They told the *muzungu* (boss) that when he was ready to discuss matters, he would find them at Chepareria where the chief and elders of the land met under the tree of Baraza.

The cook was ordered to bring in the cleaning lady to pick me up and calm me down. My father dressed and prepared to go out to Chepareria to meet my mother's father and the elders. He wore a helmet, coloured shirt with silk cravat, calf-length leather boots, and a formidable bowie knife hung in a scabbard from his belt. He rode his horse because of the distance. He found the men sitting underneath the big Baraza tree; they were ready to sit underneath this tree until the case was heard.

My father had lived long enough with these Pokots, so the first thing he did was offer money to buy two sheep to roast and eat. They took this as the first sign of exhaustion in a besieged city and sat down for the night. Father suggested that my mother be allowed to go to me while the case was discussed.

My father's one worry was that the elders would take this case before the District Commissioner in Kapenguria, Alexander David Sherriff, so Father thought it best that he handled the case; he admitted paternity straight away and promised to look after my mother and me.

The elders insisted that he paid a dowry in the form of twenty cows. My father asked if they would take cash instead of cows. They accepted and the deal was done. The elders and my grandfather left me and mother to my father's care and the matter was never discussed again.

During this period, white men and black women were not allowed to marry. My father had to take my mother to Longleat Farm at Kitale, along the Cherangani Road. He gave my mother a two-room house to live in and provided for her upkeep.

Chapter Two

The Man-Eaters of Tsavo National Park

My mother and I had to travel by train to Mombasa from Kitale to meet my father in Lamu. At that time, he worked for the Crown as an agricultural officer. Afraid to travel alone, Mother was accompanied by my father's good friend, a white settler called Mr Alistair Burn, who had bought property in Kitale town and years earlier had run a petrol station and hotel business. He also owned a three-thousand-acre farm on the way to the Pokot and Sabaot tribal border in the Kwanza area. After independence, he sold out because of cattle rustling between the two tribes and moved to Mombasa to start an estate agency business in which he did very well.

The train had a three-class system: first class for whites only; second class for coolies, and third class for Africans. Naturally Alistair had to travel first class. My mother and I were left with a choice of second class – reserved for Asians only – and third class for Africans. Still, it was comfortable. We sat on our narrow, comfortable bunk on the train, which took us to Nairobi before travelling via Mombasa on the branch rail line.

The Lunatic Express was the name given to the railway from Mombasa to Nairobi via Kisumu town. Kitale rail line was a minor rail line for transporting goods and passengers to the main rail lines,

The Man-Eaters of Tsavo National Park

which was joined at Molo then through Nakuru, Naivasha and up the escarpment to Nairobi.

Mother pulled up the window shades and we surveyed the landscape. Africa looked different outside the rail-car window; the country becomes truly dark during the night.

The train arrived at Nakuru in the early morning. My father's friend came through to our carriage and handed my mother some sandwiches, fruit and hot coffee in a thermos. She was grateful for this, as the journey had been quite tiring.

It was quite scary for us as the train chugged through thick forest, bushes and scrub, up the Mau escarpment and the sponge-like morass of swamp and the cotton-soil plain. This rail line was an engineering miracle.

As the train joins the Molo through to the Mau summit in the Londiani area, it reminds you of the Nandi people. The Nandi tribe presented the most serious threat to the railway builders; they occupied vast tracts of country to the north and south of the route. The Nandi were very much like the Maasai in physique, dress, customs and belligerence. They showed no pride in their new status as British Protectorate citizens and nearly a half a decade passed before they were completely subdued. In that time, Nandi spearmen waged relentless hit-and-run attacks on the railway, which they appeared to regard as an inexhaustible source of steel and copper for weapons and ornaments. Stealing rail lines and telephone wires, they made it quite clear that the British were not welcome. They became more hostile in the 1900s, and regarded themselves as the superior force – the victorious ones.

This Nandi resistance was led by Koitalel Arap Somoei. They staged vigorous demonstrations against the administrators and settlers. They did not acknowledge white rule and could put up to 8,000 spearmen into the field. In 1903, it became necessary to defend the railway against Nandi raids. All stations between the Mau

Chapter Two

escarpment and Kisumu were protected by barbed wire and troops of the Third K.A.R who patrolled the line.

The Nandi removed sections of the rail line, which they made into spearheads. Trains were not allowed to travel by night through Nandi territory and armed *askaris* (policemen) escorted the train to its destination. It was like America a generation earlier with the settlers passing through Sioux and Apache territory. The settlers who farmed near Nandi must have had a terrible time. The Nandi created havoc, stealing cattle, refusing to pay their taxes and using poisoned arrows against the settlers.

Chief Laibon Koitalel was a dictator and medicine man. He held meetings with his people, telling them that the British government would be removed from the district. They sprang ambushes and attacked in a full-scale war against a British Colonel officer by the name Richard Meinertzhagen. Finally, the chief was killed by Meinertzhagen himself.

Only then did the Nandi accept British rule, move to the reserved area allocated to them and start to pay their taxes. The colony witnessed no further problem until the Mau uprising half a century later.

We arrived at Nakuru town, past Lake Nakuru, which had a big game reserve. There was a natural forest in the distance. Zebra and *dik-dik*. The train moved up the small escarpment of Kariandusi. Leaving Lake Elementaita, we proceeded up to Gilgil through thick forest to Naivasha town, then the train moved upwards on its way to Nairobi. Glancing back, we saw Lake Naivasha in the distance like a giant sheet of blue paper. All this time the train steadily chugged up to the summit of the Kikuyu Escarpment. The train climbed more than 1,700 feet above sea level and we saw a series of vertical drops to the valley below. From an engineering point of view, fixing the rail to the sharp-pitched escarpment was probably the most intricate and punishing task that the builders had to

The Man-Eaters of Tsavo National Park

undertake because it involved climbing ten miles over eight long viaducts. Ronald O. Preston accomplished this engineering feat.

Cable lines had to be built to lower the goods and wagons. From the top you could gaze down into the rift. The great extinct volcanoes of Longonot and Suswa rise up out of the valley on either end and the terraces that scar the sides of Longonot are distinctly visible.

At the base of Lake Longonot is the grand Lake Naivasha, an expanse of water twelve miles by eleven miles. It looks like a sheet of ornamental water in a park. This used to be Maasai land and still is, although the Maasai have been pushed out now.

The Maasai are a unique people. During the nineteenth century, they were to eastern Africa what the Apache were to the Southwestern United States. A traveller needed only to meet one of their warriors, collectively known as Elmoran, in full battle dress. At first glance, this Elmoran might not seem dangerous; he was not particularly muscular, but he was over six feet tall and had the face of a fiend. His lion-mane headdress, which appeared angrily alive, made you feel like a rabbit in his presence. Even when bare-headed, their coiffure of pigtails, saturated with fat and red ochre, bespoke not of clowns but hellish freaks.

The Maasai Moran's sole garment was a goatskin blanket draped over the shoulder. It extended only to the waist, providing the freedom for him to clout, slash and impale. These actions were performed with a unique weapon, the knob kerrie, a hardwood club that could open a man's skull with a single blow. He carried a double-edged sword called a *simi*, encased in a red-stained ox-hide scabbard, and an eight-foot spear with a two-foot blade. A Moran also carried an enormous fifty-pound buffalo-hide shield emblazoned with chalk devices and emblems that revealed his clan and age group.

A Moran feared only magic, since he had undergone pain on

Chapter Two

the day he was circumcised. He stood erect and watched expressionlessly as his foreskin was cut from his penis in the ceremony that separated him from childhood and made him into a soldier belonging to a military elite. He could run all day while hunting and his reflexes were swifter than a wounded leopard. When entering a hut, he would fix his spear in the ground at the left-hand side of the door so that he could seize it instantly in case of an attack. His regiments went into battle abreast in long lines to form a wall, the warriors' shields overlapping in the manner of the Roman *testudo*. The sun struck the spear blades that levelled out from the advancing walls of gaily coloured shields, while the massed Elmoran took up the war cry that could cause an involuntary bowel movement in the enemy and often ended a battle before it commenced.

Maasai were alien to East Africa, having wandered down from the regions of the upper Nile sometime during the seventeenth century. Ethnically they were Nilo-Hamites, and their slim frames, prominent cheekbones, curved noses and thin lips contrasted sharply with the Negroid characteristics of their Bantu neighbours.

With their light skin colour, pure-blooded Maasai might have passed as Anglo-Saxon or Southern European. There is an opinion that the Maasai are descendants of the lost Roman legion of one of Mark Antony's armies that was never found. Mark Antony's physical characteristics and battle formats are strikingly similar to the Maasai's. The *simi* spears are the weapons of Roman centurions (Roman soldiers).

The crisp, clean air of Limuru, a magical place, produced an ideal climate, cool and refreshing in comparison to the heat of the valley floor. There are temperate juniper-wooded highlands from the Kikuyu Escarpment to Nairobi.

The train was due to arrive in Nairobi at eleven fifteen the following morning, and it came in on time. The train had finished its first leg. We still had 327 miles to go before reaching Mombasa.

The Man-Eaters of Tsavo National Park

Nairobi was known to the Maasai as *Nakunseton* (meaning the beginning of all beauty). Preston, the first railway engineer, described the place as a bleak, swampy stretch of soggy landscapes, where no human lived but thousands of animals of every kind lived. It did not have any trees. Nakunseton had been bisected by a small stream, which the Maasai named Vaso Nairobi (cold water). This was the name most Europeans and Africans later preferred to use and by which it was known by the British in 1899.

Three years later, Ellis G., the royal engineer, established a staging depot on the site for the oxen and mules used as transport animals by the protectorate government; long before that caravans skirted the swamp en route to and from Uganda. But for all practical purposes, Nairobi was no more than a lonely sprawl of papyrus until the railway arrived. The Maasai brought their herds to water there.

Since Nairobi occupied the last stretch of level ground before the Rift Valley, where our train had just ascended, it became the railway's principal nerve centre. Sir Charles Eliot decided to move the Protectorate headquarters from Mombasa to Nairobi. Once the rail construction reached Nairobi, the town grew rapidly.

Today, Nairobi looks much better, with nice buildings and tall shops, Tarmac roads and good drainage. Before 1901, when it rained the place was deep in mud. Indian *duka* were seen everywhere; the Indians built their houses so close together that air and light were scarce and allowed the most disgusting filth to accumulate. Even in modern times, Indians have not improved on this and most Africans live in even worse conditions, creating slum areas. They do not care about the filth around them until the dirt thrown everywhere blocks the water drains, creating a health hazard.

The post office, soda and water factory and a shaky timber structure known as Wood's Hotel, which doubled as a general store, were abandoned as a poor insurance risk. Railway officials used

Chapter Two

corrugated iron but other British residents were happy to use it for housing and their clubs.

Before long, a city government was formed. This was an establishment of an embryonic municipality (council), which was created and presided over by Ainsworth, who had been directed by the Foreign Office to transfer his Ukambani Provincial headquarters from Machakos to Nairobi. Thus, Nairobi became the principal metropolis of all Eastern Africa.

From 1898 to 1900, disease and starvation took at least 25,000 African lives. Rinderpest struck down thousands of livestock and wild game in Ukambani and parts of the Kikuyu land. In April 1898, spring rains failed northwest of the Tsavo, which resulted in drought and a rampant smallpox epidemic. Porters on Uganda-bound caravans also experienced hunger.

As the train passes through this part of Ukambani, you wonder what happened when the rail line was constructed. When starvation was at its highest level, the bodies of the starving and sick were left to rot and no proper burials were performed in the wilds and villages of Ukambani. Game and wild beasts faced the same fate – survival of the fittest.

While part of the railway was being constructed, work must have been delayed by the poisoned arrows from Wakamba natives as they launched attacks on the construction workers to take their food to avoid starvation themselves. Food was needed for the coolies and the natives who worked for the British; twenty-one tons had to be sent up daily from Mombasa by rail, as no food could be produced locally.

Luckily for those Kikuyus who lived in the highlands, owing largely to their altitude and temperate climate, they escaped the worst blight and had enough maize, millet, sweet potato, yams, cassava, beans, bananas, sugarcane, sheep and goats.

Before the train builders arrived on Kikuyu land, during the

The Man-Eaters of Tsavo National Park

time of the caravans crossing the fringes of their country, the leaders were reluctant to sell their food to travellers, Swahili slave and ivory traders, and the early missionaries like Thomson, Lugard and Jackson. Kikuyu land served as a kind of storehouse where a food supply was available. Now the Kikuyu had started to become hostile to foreigners because of the railway and government; it was one thing to barter a little maize flour or a few sheep with the occasional party of transients, but by 1898, the white man had made it clear his intention was to stay.

'The Iron Snake will one day cross our land,' ran the ancient tribal prophecy. Now the 'snake' had arrived and the Kikuyu were ready to resist its invasion with ferocity that could only be matched by the Maasai.

As the train approached the Kapiti and Athi plain, blazing showers of red-hot embers that poured from the locomotive smokestack could be seen, while passengers clung to the roofs of their carriages. This gave them an unobstructed view of the most varied collection of game species anywhere on earth. To an English country squire, whose estate might have been stocked with a few dozen deer, it was a revelation to look out on an ocean of zebra, giraffe, impala, Thomson gazelle, Oryx, kob, hartebeests, wildebeests – an endless sea of ruminants as far as the eye could see. The gently undulating prairies were nearly invisible beneath their living carpet of animals, oblivious to the fire-breathing engine; the herds grazed and gambolled as if men had never contaminated their placid lives with their presence. The zebras nearest the road might raise their heads momentarily as the train thundered by but returned to munching the grass, unperturbed. The government had marked off the Kapiti and Athi plains as a game reserve and, by unfathomable intuition, the animals knew that rifles would not molest them here.

During the 1900s, the grand tour became popular among the world's white upper class and furnished Kenya with one of its prin-

Chapter Two

cipal sources of revenue. Vast expanses of the protectorate were set aside for hunting for the world safari, which lured affluent tourists. Cost seemed no object; big game hunting was big business.

Hunters were allowed to carry at least three rifles and a thousand rounds of ammunition, plus an assortment of coloured rockets for signalling at night. These were packed and shipped to Mombasa for clearing and given specially issued permits. Porters were hired, then a headman, gun bearers, askaris, cooks and personal servants.

Safaris also needed tents, blankets, groundsheets, mosquito nets, water filters and medicine bags. Provisions included tinned foods, preserves and other delicacies. Substantial supplies of salt, mal killers were needed to preserve the skin. Very few visitors could cope with these details, so Kenya rapidly developed a modest but thriving safari industry.

Visitors could telegraph ahead and arrive in the knowledge that everything would be ready for them. They booked into capacious, canvas, double-roof ridge tents, which could be collapsed and carried. Hired African labourers carried around bathtubs.

The hunters had to go through grass or dense bush and sometimes thick indigenous forest. Skilled Africans tracked and virtually coaxed animals within rifle range. Trophies were skinned, salted and cured on the spot by expert skinners then taken by runners to Nairobi, by train to Mombasa and shipped onwards to London. Champagne, armchairs and seven- or eight-course dinners were prepared by Goanese cooks.

Harassment by lions did not cease beyond the perimeter of Tsavo. At Simba, it was almost as if the man-eaters were seeking to cut the railhead off from its source of supplies. Trains were frequently held up for the better part of the day as lions sprawled across Simba's tracks at sunset and kept Indian point-men from lighting the signal lamp. Rhinoceros sometimes charged supply trains and approached the railhead, throwing themselves against

The Man-Eaters of Tsavo National Park

the locomotive wheels and nearly derailing the engines until a well-placed rifle bullet dispatched them. Derailments were common on sections of the line supported by wooden sleepers; despite their coating of creosote, they were often eaten away by white ants. The Indian coolies were stricken with malaria until fifty percent of them were sick. When malaria put down a hundred percent of the coolies, replacements were needed from Mombasa.

No new country is a place for weaklings and the Britons who went out to tame Kenya were frontiersmen of the best kind. Delamere took the lead in adding the province to the British Empire.

The *pièce de résistance* on the final hundred miles from Nairobi was ahead. Flanked on the north by the broken-toothed peak of Mount Kenya, the train was now clattering to Ukambani's eroded half-desert.

The first stop was usually Simba Station at eight o'clock, where everyone stumbled to the platform bleary-eyed and ready for the ceremony of morning tea or cocoa. Soon enough, the train swayed out of Simba Station on its way through Tsavo. Refreshments were served with lunch: brandy, coffee and cigars for first class. Second-class passengers were given simple meals, good enough for Mother and me, as we were not used to good food.

As the train moved swiftly over Tsavo Bridge, the movement of water in the river below was invigorating. Before 1898, travellers used this place as a stopover. Caravans halted here to rest their porters and replenish their water supplies. Although the place had a charm about it, it was not altogether wholesome. The river name was Tsavo – the Kamba word for 'slaughter'. This spot was a war area before the rail line was built; the Maasai and the Wakamba people fought here often and dead bodies were left to rot. Lions probably roamed the place and grew used to eating people who were not dead; in this way they got the taste for human flesh.

Natives believed that the place had an evil spirit, which enticed

Chapter Two

men away at night, led them to the river and made away with them. All traces of missing people disappeared, although sometimes an odd sandal or cap was found.

In 1898, when the railway line reached this area, the coolies paid little attention to these myths. The engineer, Preston, observed that they would desert if they believed these stories. He hoped that work would proceed quickly, giving the coolies little time for thought.

Hardly had the coolies laid the first plate of the railway when disaster struck – it was reported that one coolie had vanished. A search party found the skull and feet of the missing man and lion tracks were seen around the remains. Thorn bomas were built around the coolie tents as a defensive measure. Preston went out with his Winchester rifle and a few brave men to track the lion but it was in vain; all they found was an old skull and bones.

A week later, early in the morning, the whole camp was awakened by men yelling. Others were beating drums and banging empty kerosene-oil tins. Panic-stricken, Preston grabbed his Winchester, ran towards the noise. He was told that a lion's growl had been heard near a tent and a coolie had disappeared.

They abandoned their search after an hour; by then the lion would have killed the coolie with a single blow of its forepaw. After sun up, the man was found dead. His face had been eaten clean of skin and flesh, leaving him a skeleton.

Preston was replaced by an engineer who took charge of building a permanent bridge over Tsavo. Lieutenant Colonel J.H. Patterson, an Indian Army officer with long experience in railway building, was confident he could build the railway within four months.

Tsavo was an accursed spot and the lions were dreadful monsters. Normally lions do not attack humans without provocation; probably this is due in part to the smell of a man, which most undomesticated animals find repugnant. Faced by an approaching human, the lion is more likely take to its heels. In fact, nearly all

The Man-Eaters of Tsavo National Park

dangerous African game species will flee; an unarmed man can often walk across miles of lion-infested bush in perfect safety. Only if there were no wild animals for the lion to hunt would it go for the man.

Most lions find human flesh revolting but if they are hungry enough to go for it would most likely attack a weak person, not a strong one who has weapons and could fight back.

The man-eaters at Tsavo were very rare. These lions had wits, big claws and animal cunning. Seldom have any man-eaters demonstrated the gifts of this pair that committed an act of sabotage at Tsavo. In 1898, before the railway and during the rail construction, there were other man-eaters in the area. Drought and plagues wiped out the game in the region, so the lions resorted to humans for food. Man-eaters in other places hunted in large groups.

Lions attacked Voi and Makindu Stations; this was how the name Simba came about. The place alongside the railway station was called 'samba'. Simba is a Kiswahili name for lion. These man-eater lions attacked neighbouring camps and killed, but were nothing in comparison to Tsavo, which was a place under siege.

The first few days' rail construction went smoothly. This bridge was the first major river crossing, apart from the one built at Makupa, which was slightly smaller. The plan for the structure demanded lots of materials as it would be three hundred feet above the river, with rails laid down on four sixty-foot iron girders supported by three stone piers rising at least fifteen feet above the river to ensure it was secure when the river flooded. This spot was the worst for floods, during the rainy season; African rain fell in sheets and in minutes flooded the area.

Patterson went to work quickly, measuring the riverbank, allowing for flood levels, calculating water levels, marking the position of the abutment and piers, surveying the alignment and estimating the required materials. After a short period, all that was needed was

Chapter Two

brought in from Kilindini Harbour.

Coolie labourers had knowledge of iron work, so soon the noise of hammers, drilling and blasting echoed throughout the district. The noise from the site would have been enough to frighten off a normal predator. Patterson had been briefed about the death of the coolies in Preston's gang but, because of the large number of coolies working under Preston, he thought they had died in quarrels over money or religion.

On the third week of March, a servant awoke Patterson before dawn and told him a *Jemadars* (powerful Sikh) by the name of Ungan Singh had been dragged away from his tent and was nowhere to be seen.

Patterson went to the tent and found everyone panic stricken. Trails were followed into the nearby bush and a dreadful spectacle of flesh, bone and a head was found. The poor fellow's eyes were still open with a startled, horrified look in them. The remains of his body were buried quickly and medical officers took the head to the hospital for examination.

What was astonishing about the place where the lion had mauled Ungan Singh was that two lions' paw marks seemed to indicate a violent struggle for the body. It seemed that the lions would terrify the coolies and affect the work on the bridge over River Tsavo, which was of great importance. Patterson made a solemn promise to himself that he would hunt down and kill the two lions.

The hunt began that night. Patterson took his .303 rifle and a twelve-bore shotgun up a tree to a perch that allowed him to see for eight miles. He hoped that the lions would return to the same spot. There were more coolies up the tree that night too because they were frightened to remain in their tents. At midnight they heard a roar and fear gripped every human soul. The African black night made it even more frightening. The sound came nearer. Patterson, although frightened, still hoped that he would kill the lions. When

The Man-Eaters of Tsavo National Park

the roaring stopped more than an hour later, there was only stillness.

These lions roamed in absolute silence. Patterson was alert, his fingers still on the trigger as he tried to look into the black night. Suddenly an explosion of roars shattered the night, and then came screams in the distance.

The lions could feel Patterson's presence but never came close to him; they made their kill at the far end of the camp two miles away. Patterson was very disappointed in himself.

The next night he tied a goat to a tree, hoping it would act as bait. He stayed silent and watched but this night was also in vain, as were many nights. At midnight, screams and shouts filled the air as the man-eater dragged another victim away – but it was always elsewhere in the camp, never near Patterson.

These lions continued to harass the camp. It was frustrating because they did not strike every day. Word went out that they had attacked a nearby Wakamba village (a Kenyan tribe who lived near Tsavo). A week passed and everyone was tense at the prospect of a surprise attack; no one could rest or relax.

During the day, work proceeded satisfactorily as the lions never attacked during daylight. Also, there was safety in numbers – in 1898, about 2,000 labourers were needed to work on the vastly expanding railhead station.

A month went by and more railhead gangs were to be moved to other sections of railway line a long distance away. The five hundred coolies that remained were panic stricken and most wanted to leave. Permission was given and work was suspended on the bridge until reinforcements came for security.

Huge *bomas* made out of thorn bushes were put in place to protect the few coolies that remained with Patterson. Fires blazed through the night. The number of night watchmen was doubled and empty oil tins were suspended from trees to produce a clat-

Chapter Two

tering noise in the hope of frightening away the two man-eaters. But the lions continued to break in each night, always finding weak spots in the fence and silently making their way into the *bomas*. It seemed that nothing could stop them. They prowled the camp and Patterson was totally frustrated.

Tsavo policemen and their deputies were called to help. Other English supervisors, including Dr Brock, the medical officer, were also present. Even the Jemadars were allowed to carry rifles.

The lions always killed in places away from Patterson, as if they sensed his presence. They seemed to have human intelligence. Around mid-April the beasts became audacious enough to attack the camp in daylight and were seen on occasion.

At the hospital, some coolies who were sick with malaria were easy prey for the lions. Although the *boma* around the hospital tents was much thicker and higher, this did not stop the lions. They tore the tents to shreds and broke bottles with blows from their paws. Another hospital was quickly constructed nearby.

Patterson had never seen these lions, only heard their growls. He knew they liked to visit vacated campsites so he lay in wait for them in the abandoned hospital. That night, the lions went to the new hospital and devoured the sick; next morning skulls and fingers were found.

Patterson still did not give up; he ordered that the hospital be moved again and kept watch over the abandoned one. That night, Dr Brock joined Patterson on the night watch at the wagon near the vacated hospital. After several hours, the silence was broken by a snapping of dry twigs and an inexplicable dull thud. Something was moving very stealthily towards them. Patterson didn't trust his eyes, which by then were strained from prolonged staring through the dark night. He whispered to Brock and asked if he could see anything but Brock was silent. Suddenly, something huge sprang at them. Patterson shouted 'Lion!' and they both fired their rifles

The Man-Eaters of Tsavo National Park

simultaneously.

The gunshots burst like dynamite. The two lions panicked and fled. This saved Brock and Patterson – and the lions as well.

The next morning, a bullet was found in the dirt less than two inches from paw marks. This was Patterson's first close encounter with the man-eaters. He was used to hunting tigers in India and they were more dangerous than these African lions; in normal circumstances, he would have killed these lions but they proved difficult opponents. The lions showed a complete contempt for human beings; nothing frightened them away.

The lions attacked for pleasure and ate coolies while a Jemadar in a tree nearby emptied the magazine of his rifle at them half a dozen times. One particular night, a coolie was attacked and dragged from the railway station then brought near to the camp where he was devoured. The crunching of bones and the chilling and dreadful purring filled the air and rang in everyone's ears for days afterwards. It was dangerous to go out; one could do nothing but sit and watch.

To keep up the workers' spirit, and for work to proceed, Patterson decided to hunt the lions down. During the day the lions hid in tall savannah grass or dried-out water courses; they came out only after dark. The lions had every chance against the hunter in the open tall grass and bushes, and tracking them was very difficult.

Patterson moved into quarters with Brock. A thorn *boma* two hundred feet in diameter encircled the house and a big bonfire was kept ablaze all night. The officer's personal servants, who lived inside this secure barricade, were at hand to help with meals and laundry. The hut had a small veranda where Patterson studied Kiswahili grammar after dinner, drank whisky or brandy and enjoyed the breeze. Both Patterson and Brock kept their rifles within reach and cast anxious glances at the inky darkness beyond the circle of the firelight. Both were as afraid as the coolies.

Chapter Two

Weeks went by and work progressed slowly. Preston's temporary diversion was steadily and slowly being replaced with better permanent rail structures. Rock blasting and cutting had to be undertaken by the railhead labourers to allow the locomotives passage. There was a dried-up water course between the cutting and the river and there was insufficient time to bridge it. Earlier Preston had simply laid rails down the shallow but sharply sloped banks; when daily supplies came from Kilindini Harbour by train, they swayed slightly while negotiating this diversion.

Eventually these were levelled with iron girders across the gulley. Sinking the foundation of the piers beneath the river beds was difficult because of the strong currents in the river. Two dams were built before work could continue then the foundation of the piers started sinking. Frustrated, they nearly resorted to pile-driving, when they struck solid rock. Another problem emerged: where to find stones to build the piers themselves? The stones they found were too hard to be chipped into stone blocks. Search parties went into the bushes to look for better rocks. Luckily, they came upon a better stone quarry several miles from the bridge construction site. A railway was needed to transport these rocks to the building site and a shaky, groaning narrow-gauge trolley line was built. Owing to the nature of the terrain, it had to cross the river twice on flimsy viaducts of felled trees, which sagged alarmingly whenever the heavily laden wooden hand carts passed over them.

The weight of these trolleys was so heavy that the makeshift rails collapsed. Luckily none of the workers were injured or killed when these accidents occurred. Patterson narrowly escaped death when his cart jumped the track and plunged into the river. So, the transportation of the stones proceeded slowly; it was not until early August that the huge piers of Tsavo Bridge began to rise from the river bed.

The coolies were not happy. The lions' presence made everyone nervous and jumpy. The coolies' wages did not cheer them, as they knew that each day could be their last day on earth. These Indians were used to hardship and were miles away from home. There was no guarantee of ideal working conditions – but neither did their contract include being shredded into strips of bloody meat!

They started to blame Patterson for their predicament. They were expected to be obedient to their white masters from the British Empire but their masters had an equal obligation to uphold safety and, when necessary, to defend the lives of their charges. The coolies looked to Patterson for protection but the two lions continued to prey on them as if Patterson was not doing his duty to protect them.

Patterson was the coolies' judge and had a notebook in which to write down all their wrongdoings, but in truth he was more of a hunter than a disciplinarian. The coolies were low-caste Indians; if they had been in India, Patterson playing the small tyrant would have been acceptable, but not in Tsavo.

Fear increased every day. Skilled masons were needed to dress the stones and a request to Kilindini was made for skilled stonemasons. These masons were paid forty-five rupees ($15.00) monthly in comparison to the fifteen rupees received by the unskilled coolies. Some coolies were given the task of dressing the stones; they knew nothing about the masonry, they were simple coolies masquerading as craftsmen in order to get a higher pay.

Patterson tested them on some stonemason work; they failed and their wages dropped to the level of other coolies. The imposters attempted to intimidate the few true masons into lowering their working standards in a bid to frustrate Patterson into abandoning his tests to find out the true masons from the false ones. The scheme failed, but the imposters did not forget it.

The masons' free time was occupied by religious discussions that became so heated that Patterson frequently had to calm them

Chapter Two

down and separate the Hindus from Mohammedans. The coolies liked to avoid work and fight one another with knives. They tended to gossip or doze under the shade of trees, and work slowed down. Patterson noted their names with a view to reducing their wages but this created more enmity between him and the coolies. Their resentment simmered and the coolies plotted to kill him.

One morning Patterson was still in his tent. An informer came running to warn him that during the previous night, all the workers had secretly planned to kill Patterson while he was on his regular inspection of the quarry. Patterson's corpse would be thrown into the bushes, where it was assumed the man-eaters would quickly devour it; that would turn the suspicion away from the coolies. All the men in the meeting agreed and as a binding token, they all wrote their names on a piece of paper.

Patterson dismissed the threat and marched out on his normal morning patrol. He was again warned by his head mason, Heera Singh, who crept out of the bush and told him not to proceed. Singh said that twenty masons had not reported to work that day, as they did not want to be part of the evil plan.

Patterson started to believe the story but he continued to the quarry. The faces of the treacherous men gave them away; they exchanged stealthy glances. One, by the name of Jemaders, reported to Patterson that two men were fighting in the narrowest part of the ravine. Without hesitation, Patterson went to see if these workers were fighting. When he reached the spot, the two culprits were pointed out to him and, as always, he took out his notebook and wrote down their names.

Suddenly he heard yelling all around him. About two hundred men carrying hammers and crowbars surrounded him in a circle. One man rushed in Patterson's direction to seize his wrists, shouting that he should hand over his gun. Patterson wrenched his arms free and threw the man to the ground. He stood still, waiting for

The Man-Eaters of Tsavo National Park

them to act again. The circle of men around him grew tighter and all their faces showed murderous intent.

A man pushed another man at Patterson because he was afraid to deal the first blow. Patterson quickly stepped aside. This man rushed past him, tripped over a big stone and fell down. Luckily, he did not hit Patterson.

Everyone looked confused. Patterson stood on a big stone and talked over their noise furiously and loudly. He said that their plot to murder him was known, and that the *sirkar* (government) would soon find out the truth; they would not believe that man-eating lions had killed him. Patterson told them that he knew there were only one or two scoundrels among them who had persuaded the rest to do this evil deed. Even if they got rid of him, another sahib English engineer would be sent out to supervise them and he would probably not be kind. They had nothing to fear if they abandoned their plot.

The coolies appeared to respect Patterson's authority. When asked if they were prepared to go back to work, the vote was unanimous. Patterson had narrowly escaped death. He jumped down from the rock and continued his rounds. The workers remained behind with sullen faces in an uncertain mood.

Unknown to everyone, the caravan master in charge of transporting water and supplies to the gangs was working in front of the railhead. He had observed the whole incident from a distance, concealed in the bushes with a rifle. He would have opened fire to disperse the mob but all went well. Patterson had shown courage.

The threat to Patterson's life did not end there; the same workers continued to plot to kill him that same night. Taking no more chances with his life, Patterson reported the matter to the protectorate authorities at Tsavo Station. The ringleaders were arrested, put on the railway and taken under guard to Mombasa for trial. This put an end to such homicidal plots and no more trouble ensued.

Chapter Two

The problem with the lions remained, although the lions had stopped attacking for a while. The only report of killings was along parts of the rail lines ahead; this gave a false sense of security to all the Tsavo coolies, who thought the lions would never come back to Tsavo Bridge. The coolies soon started sleeping outside their airless cramped tents.

One night, familiar terror-stricken screams awoke the camp. Heaps of flesh were brought outside Patterson's tent that next morning. The following night another coolie was taken away. This repeat of the siege by the lions enraged Patterson and he went berserk, raging like an animal. He did not bury the fragments of the bodies but used them to bait the lions for he was sure they would come back to the same place that night. The final months of the year were frustrating and a reign of terror began.

The government offered £100 to the person who killed the lions. Posters were put up at Mombasa and along the railway line. Navy, Army and civil service officers on local leave, together with wealthy sportsmen from England, came to Tsavo to hunt the lions but it was all in vain. The lions continued to kill coolies. The place was crowded and there were too many suggestions about how to kill the lions. Patterson knew these hunters had no experience in how to hunt down big cats.

Patterson then produced the biggest rat trap in the world: an iron cage welded from discarded iron. The trap had two compartments, separated by a thick grille of steel bars. Volunteers armed with rifles served as bait and sat in one section. The other cubicle was for the lion; once the lion was in it, it would lock itself in by releasing a complicated spring mechanism. A *boma* was built around the cage and a weak spot left on one side, covered with a tent as a disguise.

As no one else was willing, Patterson acted as bait for several nights. Mosquitoes kept him awake but no lions came near the

The Man-Eaters of Tsavo National Park

cage. It was as though they were cunning enough to know that Patterson was waiting for them.

The coolies had started to believe that these were not real lions but devils in lions' shape; angry spirits of departed tribal chiefs had taken the lions' form to protest against a railway being built on their land. Others saw these beasts in different manifestations, such as hyenas, donkeys, goats and dogs, and transformed them into lions, right before their very eyes at night. They were so superstitious that they imagined human beings changing into a form of a lion, and they were very afraid.

During the height of panic, people were nearly killed because they were mistaken as evil spirits. John Boyes, a mechanic and advisor, while returning after dinner to his tent, was one such victim.

The administrator, Hobley, came to Tsavo at this time and noted the gloom and terror in the place. Everyone was jumpy; they needed more guns and protection. All night guns went off at intervals in the coolie camps. It was a disturbing night for Hobley, who returned to Mombasa a few days' later making promises for protection.

The coolies had reached breaking point. Some moved into Patterson's campsite; they left a sick man behind and when they came to fetch him they found he had died of shock. Patterson himself was on the verge of collapse. During the day he supervised the work and at night he was up in the trees watching out for lions, or walking endless miles searching for them.

The lions still attacked the camp but passed him unnoticed at night. They were very clever creatures, as though they sensed him, and attacked different places every night so he had no chance of getting a shot at them.

The lions had a habit of approaching with great roars but once they were within the circumference of the camp, they went silent. Shouts could be heard from camp to camp, '*Khabardar, Bhaieon,*

Chapter Two

Shaitan ata! (Beware, brothers, the devil is coming!). This warning was no use because sooner or later shrieks would break the silence and another man would be missing from the roll call the next morning. Even Patterson started to believe that they could be devils.

Around December 1st, late in the afternoon, Patterson was returning to his camp from the bridge. He was confronted by a massive strike around his *boma*; the coolies announced that they would remain in Tsavo no longer for anything or anyone. They had come from India with an agreement to work for the British government, not to be food for the devil lions. There was no way Patterson could persuade them to stay.

At that moment the locomotive's whistle announced the approach of the daily materials train through Tsavo en route to Mombasa from the railhead. The whistle seemed to act as a signal. Five hundred men rushed to the station and threw themselves on the tracks. Frantically, the engine driver applied the brakes. He was unable to reduce the speed below five miles an hour but that was all the workers needed to jump onto the locomotive and its four goods wagons. The driver was anxious to cross Taru Desert before dark, so he opened the throttle. Tsavo was left behind with only Patterson and four-dozen coolies who refused to abandon work on the bridge.

Work came to a complete halt. The remaining labourers moved closer together and built stronger barriers against the man-eaters. Huge *bomas* were reinforced and some coolies dug pits under their tents. Others placed thorns on the roofing. Sleeping cribs were thrown on top of the elevated water tanks. But all these measures could not stop the man-eaters' attacks at night. Some coolies started to stay in treetops for protection but still screams were heard in the night as branches gave way. Outside help would take some time to arrive. Patterson telegraphed the protectorate administration for armed manpower. The local district officers arrived at Tsavo with

The Man-Eaters of Tsavo National Park

a detachment of askaris, followed by the railway police superintendent and twenty sepoys (Indian police), who were promptly installed in trees.

Patterson's trap was brought out again. Two sepoys were ordered to volunteer as bait, while Patterson joined the visiting officers in a sleeping crib, waiting for nightfall and hoping his trap would work.

It was exactly nine o'clock when the intense stillness was broken by the noise of the door of the trap clattering down. At last one brute was done for, they thought!

These two sepoys proved to be unreliable; they were frozen with terror as the maddened lion hurled itself at the bars of the cage. They forgot their instructions to open fire and it was only after several minutes of encouragement and threats from the officer that they regained their composure. When they did fire, they were so frightened that bullets whizzed around until a direct hit was scored on the door lock. This opened the trap and the lion jumped off into the night.

Very downhearted next morning, Patterson went out hunting with groups looking for the lion's tracks, but they were unsuccessful. After some days, the officers who had come to help at Tsavo had to go back to their post and once again Patterson was left alone to sort out the man-eaters.

At six o'clock on the ninth of December, Patterson went out to hunt and track down the lions by himself. Minutes later, as he was about to leave his compound, a Swahili man ran in his direction shouting, '*Simba, simba*' (lion, lion). Shaking with fright, he hurriedly told Patterson that a lion had tried to snatch a man from the workers' camp, but luckily ended up killing one of the donkeys and was now devouring it. Without wasting a second, Patterson rushed to his tent and grabbed a hunting rifle that had been given to him by a police officer because it was long-range and better for dealing

Chapter Two

with the lions.

Patterson followed the Swahili man through the thorn bushes towards the man-eater. As they approached, Patterson could see the outline of one of the lions through the dense bushes but unfortunately the Swahili man stepped on a branch on the ground, which snapped. The beast must have heard the sound because it growled and disappeared in the thick savannah and then into the nearby jungle.

Patterson quickly went back to camp; the only way to flush out these giant lions from the jungle was to use his Indian tiger-hunting skills. Men were ordered to collect drums, horns, tins, pots and anything that could make a noise. They formed a wide semi-circle around the thicket where they believed the lions had taken cover. Beating the instruments continued while Patterson hid behind a seven-foot anthill to wait for the lion to come out.

A huge lioness came into the open. This was the first time that Patterson had seen the man-eater. He was spellbound just looking at her; he had never seen such a big lion before. Thanks to the noise made by the beaters, the lion did not sense his presence and it came close, within fifty feet of the anthill. Patterson raised his rifle but at that moment the lion sensed his presence and caught sight of him. She seemed astonished at Patterson's sudden appearance; she stuck her forefeet into the ground, threw herself back on her haunches and growled savagely.

It seemed impossible to miss the shot. Pointing the rifle at her head, Patterson was confident that he would not miss. He pulled the trigger – but to his horror, he heard a dull snap signalling a misfire. Patterson was so confused that he forgot he was carrying a double-barrelled weapon and could have fired the second shot.

That split second was all the lion needed to attack Patterson and open his skull with her powerful paws. But luck was still on Patterson's side because she was more confused than he was. Patterson

The Man-Eaters of Tsavo National Park

regained his senses and fired again; this time he heard the thudding sound of a bullet striking home.

The lion was only wounded and plunged quickly into the bushes. Patterson ran after it but the trail vanished into the thick bushes. Furious and frustrated with himself, Patterson regretted having borrowed a weapon with which he was not well acquainted. What bad luck!

He returned to camp and decided to go back to the donkey's carcass. He discovered that the lions had hardly touched it. They had not had chance to eat; perhaps they would return when it was dark to finish the meal.

Patterson looked around for a large tree; finding none he built a *machan*, a rickety wooden scaffold about twelve feet high. The dead donkey was secured by a steel wire to an ancient stump. At sundown, Patterson climbed onto his flimsy perch three yards from the dead donkey, hoping to get a good target although he knew he was in a dangerous position. The lions were capable of crushing the *machan* as if it were a cricket wicket.

The sun goes down quickly in Africa since it is in line with the equator. For an hour or so Patterson sat very still, peering into the night, and then suddenly he froze. A sound came from the bushes; it told him that the lion was approaching. It stopped and he heard an enraged snarl. The lion had seen or sensed Patterson and started to back away – then it stopped. It did not go for the bait or run away but started to stalk him. For about two hours, Patterson heard it slowly creep round the structure, edging nearer and nearer. Every moment he expected the lion to rush in. He could not fire at it because the night made the lion all but invisible. Patterson kept perfectly still, hardly daring to blink.

Suddenly Patterson felt an object strike the back of his neck. There was a flutter of wings and he almost toppled from the *machan* in fright. An owl had mistaken him for a tree. The momen-

Chapter Two

tary noise drew a short rasp from the lion; it was so close that its shape could be seen. For a few seconds, Tsavo's peril was forgotten. If Patterson was to save his own life, he had to squeeze the trigger.

The sound of the shot was followed by a terrific roar and the lion leapt about in all directions. No longer able to see it, Patterson kept blazing away into the thick bush. After a period of silence, there was a series of mighty groans that gradually subsided into deep sighs and finally ceased altogether. Patterson was convinced that finally one of the devils would no longer trouble the Tsavo camp. The silence ended as a tumult of enquiring voices was heard across the dark jungle from the men in the camp. Patterson shouted back that he was safe and sound.

Everybody was cheering. Scores of hurricane lamps twinkled through the bushes. Men turned up, some beating tom-toms, others blowing horns, some walking, others running to the scene. Patterson ordered them to go back to camp at once because the second lion might be lurking nearby. There was also the possibility the first lion might not be dead and the bullet wounds would enrage him.

In the morning, the truth of the matter was known: the lion was dead. It was twice as big as the dead donkey that lay beside it. It measured nine feet eight inches from its nose to the tip of its tail. Eight men were needed to carry its corpse to the camp. Patterson was lifted high on the coolies' shoulders and carried around while they sang victorious songs.

The next morning, telegrams arrived from Mombasa to congratulate Patterson. Visitors came from every point of the railhead to view the skin and pat Patterson on the back. Patterson did not feel like a hero at that moment because the second lion was still out there. The dead lion had taken him eight months to kill; the second one might take even longer and that worried him.

Sir Guilford Molesworth, former consulting engineer to the Indian State Railway, came to inspect the Uganda railway being

The Man-Eaters of Tsavo National Park

constructed on behalf of the railway committee. He congratulated Patterson on his success in killing the man-eater.

Not much later, the second lion attacked a railway inspector's bungalow. Although the attack failed, the lion boldly paced the veranda for nearly ten minutes as it growled and made other frightful noises. At night, attempts were made to bait it with three goats tied to a 250-pound half-length rail. The lion picked up the smallest goat and carried it off in its jaws, dragging the other two goats behind it. Patterson rushed after it into the night with his rifle blasting, hitting the lion, but he lost the blood trail in the heavy bushes and savannah.

For nearly a week there was no sign of this lion. Patterson thought it must have been hit and was staying away to nurse its wounds. Then, it reappeared. On a day that can never be forgotten, the 27th December 1898, the coolies were besieged all night. The following night, Patterson decided to hoist himself into one of the trees that had been occupied by the coolies while they were under siege.

The night was cloudless and a full moon provided perfect light to see, especially around that particular tree and the nearby bushes. The night watch was shared between Patterson and his Swahili gun bearer, Mahina. When sleep was badly needed at two o'clock, Mahina was at watch. Patterson, though drowsy, suddenly became fully awake with a frightened feeling. His hair was standing on end. His sixth sense told him something was very wrong. Mahina agreed that he could see shadows moving at the edge of the thorn bushes. The lion was stalking them.

Though in danger, Patterson watched, fascinated by the great animal stealing round them and taking advantage of the cover of the bushes as he came nearer. The lion had to find a good place to spring on them. Because of the full moon it was a perfect target but this time Patterson took his time and let the predator come much

41

Chapter Two

nearer until only sixty feet separated him and the lion. He fired his rifle. The bullet slammed home but the lion did not fall and kept on approaching even faster. Patterson shot three more times before the lion leapt into the bushes.

The rest of that night, Patterson waited up in the tree. Wounded lions are very dangerous to tackle in the dark. In the morning, they found the lion's trail clearly marked by large bloodstains. After a quarter of a mile's walk, the two men came upon the man-eater in a thicket of thorn bushes. It was badly wounded and twice as dangerous.

Patterson fired at once and shot the lion but still it charged. The next shot missed. The .303 rifle was empty and Patterson reached for the carbine. He assumed Mahina was nearby and would hand it to him but, to his dismay, Mahina wasn't there. The terror of the sudden charge had frightened him. Patterson ran to Mahina's tree and climbed it. Lucky for Patterson, the lion's hind leg had been badly smashed by a bullet. Mahina, knowing he was not a good shot, quickly handed the carbine to Patterson who aimed at the lion, shot it and brought it down. Rather foolishly, Patterson leapt to the ground, only to face the dying lion's final charge. A fifth and a sixth shot ended the duel. The man-eater dropped dead, just five yards away from Patterson.

When he examined the corpse at his feet, Patterson found a seventh slug that he had fired ten days earlier.

Reactions from the coolies were very mixed. Some were jubilant, others furious, and they swarmed around the dead lion and Patterson. Some wanted to tear the dead lion to shreds. Patterson stopped them and then had eight men carry the big cat to his campsite. This lion was two inches shorter than its companion. The two big cats had killed thirty-eight Indian workers. That is the recorded number but it does not account for killings on other parts of the railway.

The hides of both dead lions had been ravaged by years in the

The Man-Eaters of Tsavo National Park

thick thorn bushes beyond any taxidermist's skills but they were still given a place in the Chicago Field Museum in the United States. Before they were put there on display, there was a brief moment of immortality in the House of Lords when Lord Salisbury paid them a back-handed and not altogether accurate tribute.

'The whole of the work at Tsavo,' he said, 'was put to a stop for weeks because a party of man-eating lions conceived a most unfortunate taste for our porters. At last the labourers entirely declined to go on working unless they were guarded by iron entrenchment. Of course it is difficult to work on a railway under these conditions and, until an enthusiastic sportsman was found to get rid of these lions, the enterprise was seriously hindered.' This showed the reluctance to reveal the identity of Patterson as the person who killed the lions.

The numbers of Indian labourers killed by the man-eaters was documented as thirty-eight but this was inaccurate as no account was made of the African victims. A conservative estimate would probably be well over one hundred, considering the attacks were not only on Tsavo but went beyond the rail line, rail post and nearby villages. The work at Tsavo continued until it was completed on the 7th of February 1899, and opened to traffic. Patterson must have taken a great pride in the bridge.

During the trip from Nairobi to Tsavo, at midnight, Mother and I sneaked out onto the open part of the train to see the beauty of Tsavo Bridge. Not many people or ordinary travellers knew exactly what had happened there, or about the stress, danger and troubles. Most would just think 'this is just a place over a bridge'.

Chapter Three

Experience of Coastal Life – Different Culture

THE TRAIN MOVED smoothly up and down some sharp but small hills; here the faintest drizzle transforms the dust on the track into fine mud which deprives the locomotive's wheels of all traction, so the journey was very slow as we approached the Taru Desert – a flat expanse of land, more like a dense forest of wire. During the time of the railway construction, it must have been a difficult spot for the coolies and the engineers. Bush clearing was hard, as jagged stumps cut and bruised the coolie workers who had no shoes or strong sandals. Heat exhaustion and thirst must have slowed down work, too. Vast clouds of thick red dust vied with quivering heat waves to parch the throat and make the brain idle. Sun rays came down on men's backs like a rain of lava and ricocheted in their faces from the baking earth; even after sunset temperatures seldom fell below 100 degrees. The once-daily water train saved their day; this came all the way from Maji ya Chunvi.

There was no game in Taru, meaning there was nothing to hunt for food. The midday sun heated up the steel, making the work slow and hard. One can imagine the difficulties these coolies met in 1896, when this railway was first constructed.

Coolies arrived from India looking for work in East Africa.

Experience of Coastal Life – Different Culture

Some undertook dangerous voyages by sea. There were stonemasons, smiths, carpenters, surveyors and clerks. These men required clean water for drinking, as Mombasa's ancient wells were not sufficient to meet their needs.

Materials were needed for construction of this railway if it was to reach Lake Victoria 600 miles away. Heavy bulky rails, sleepers, fish plates, fish bolts and steel keys were required, as well as locomotives, brake vans, goods wagons and passengers' carriages. Such bulky items could not be brought ashore in Mombasa by dhow since it was a cramped old harbour, so they had to move to adjoining Kilindini. This place had no existing facilities and was made into a modern port. Warehouses, shops, repair sheds and living accommodations for coolies, engineers and administrative staff sprung up in no time along the 370 acres of shore front. The virgin track to the terminus-cum-reception point, the 1,700 foot-Salisbury Bridge (later named Makupa Causeway) was crossed.

Passing over such a bridge must have bewildered Mother as she was not used to modern structures or heights. Some three miles before the airstrip, she could see mud houses, banana plantations, coconut and palm trees and goats.

After the cool, dry climate all the way from Nairobi, the heat and humidity came as a surprise. Tropical breezes stirred the coconut palms; beyond the line of white buildings and the waters of Kilindini and Mombasa Harbour was the Indian Ocean. Tiredness vanished at the sight of the palm-thatched roofing of the better hotels. The steady breeze from the Indian Ocean cooled Mother's face. Fireflies performed their dance among the bougainvillea and the air was sweet with frangipani, which bloomed in the early morning when it was still slightly dark.

The calls of muezzins echoed from the minarets, as they have for centuries ever since the first Arab traders came to seek profit and settle among a new culture, the Swahili, with a new lingua

Chapter Three

franca, Kiswahili.

The train made its way to the Mombasa terminus called Uganda Railway. It pulled into the crowded station and we alighted. The crowd confused my mother who was not used to such busy places with many Arabs, Indians and Somalis in brilliantly hued wrap-around cloaks, plodding along the streets. Swahili women were swathed in enormous robes of cotton in all manner of gaily printed patterns. The Bachun women (coastal tribe) who glided by in the grim black *buibuis* of purdah, looked as if they were carrying out exotically sinister errands. Indian women wore saris, glittering in many colours. Most had tiny gold jewellery flashing from their nostrils, ankles and necks.

Most men were bald headed; everyone seemed to have shaved, for cleanliness and coolness, and their heads reflected the intense glare of the sun. Most people on the streets, especially the men, were eating betel-nut sandwiches; the nut was encased in a green leaf and the chewers spat big gouts of scarlet juice into the street. Disgusting stains from the spitting were everywhere and there were beggars on almost every corner.

My mother was glad to see my father's friend among these crowds and he knew his way around. He took us to a nearby coffee place for Arabs and Asians. Outside hawkers sold more black coffee; one could hear the tinkle of the coffee sellers' cups.

We were left for a long while as my father's friend went to get a taxi. Then my father arrived, driving a government Land Rover. He drove us to a hotel near the beach. It was decent but not to my father's standard. Later on, Father told Mother he had lots of government meetings to attend and we had to stay for some days alone in this hotel until his work was done. It was as though we had arrived a week earlier than expected.

Lamu was home and Mother was looking forward to settling in. The coast is a coral strand that stretches 480 kilometres (300

Experience of Coastal Life – Different Culture

miles) from Tanzania in the south to Somalia in the north, broken at intervals by ancient river mouths, now tidal creeks, and the deltas of Kenya's two biggest rivers – the Sabaki and the Tana. For us this was lush in contrast to the deserts, plateau and mountains upcountry. It was a world away from the primordial wildlife that roamed the diminishing wilderness inland. The history of the coast is fascinating, mainly because it is so confusing.

One afternoon, before the week was over, my father drove to our hotel and picked me up to take me for a picnic at Fort Jesus. My mother objected, saying I was too young to be taken around a big town like Mombasa, but eventually Father took me. I was old enough to understand his Kiswahili. He pointed out places but I did not grasp their history until much later when I grew up.

Fort Jesus is a terracotta fortress, fifteen metres in height and two and half metres thick, with a nine-foot battlement tower overlooking the old town's alleys. Constructed by the Portuguese in the sixteenth century, Fort Jesus was designed by an old Italian as a huge pentagon, a style common in European forts of that era, to ensure assailants were met by crossfire from all its walls. It is surrounded by a twelve-metre-deep moat and guarded at each corner by four towers. Fort Jesus proved useful as a status symbol then as an instrument of security. During a seventy-year struggle, Fort Jesus changed hands like a baton in a relay race.

We picnicked with other loungers, sitting on the old cannons that decorated the seashore in front of the fort. Some of them were made in England at the end of the eighteenth century, during the era when Great Britain ruled.

Great Britain was foremost among all the nations of the world in both manufacturing and commerce. The British flag was seen in every port on the globe, and the British became the ocean-carriers of the world.

The cannons' production provided the clue to where they were

Chapter Three

tested, the height of the ball they threw and the charge of the gunpowder required to send the ball 300 yards at point-blank range. Most of them are eighteen pounders, although one or two are twenty-four pounders. These could, with a charge of six pounds of gunpowder, send a twenty-four pound ball 2,500 yards when fired at a ten-degree elevation.

On January 17th 1875, forty-nine of them were used as a coastal battery against the British warships, *HMS Riflemen* and *HMS Nassau*. These ships were anchored at the mouth of old Mombasa Harbour and called upon the rebel, Akida to surrender. Akida was the Sultan of Zanzibar's military commandant of Mombasa. He had taken possession of the fort. After a half hour's shelling by the men-of-war, including the six-and-a-half ton *HMS Riflemen*, Akida surrendered. That was the last time the old cannons were ever used. Now they rested and rusted, the only job left to them to act as seats for ruminators like my father and me.

British rockets at this time were iron-cased, projected from tubes and propelled by means of escaping gas from the after-vents. The weapons were dangerous in those days; they did considerable damage and were greatly dreaded by the Arabs. A lot was heard in those days about these new rocket guns. The Germans even proclaimed the rocket gun a 'secret weapon', though there was nothing secret or new about it.

Next to Fort Jesus is a monument that honours Muslims. Major Wavell commanded the Arab Rifles in World War I. The massive ramparts of this bastion slope gently down and are very scary and slippery in some parts because of moisture and dampness. We went down carefully to the old slave harbour where spies and slaves were brought. Here slaves were imprisoned in a cave with freshwater wells. This place has been left to decay and is only infrequently used by a few dhows that continue to trade with the Gulf and Asia.

Slaves were captured, mistreated and walked long distances

Experience of Coastal Life – Different Culture

through the jungle, chained together; they were frequently in the last stages of starvation when they arrived at these forts after a long journey in the Arab caravans. Some dropped dead before they were taken to the slave markets; others received a little humane treatment, since it was necessary to pretty them up for customers. Although the men were given no more than a brisk rubdown with oil, designed to make them appear fit, special care was lavished on the women. They were draped with cotton robes and decorated with bangles, earrings, bracelets; generous layers of henna and kohl were smeared on their faces, hair and eyelids. It was a spectacle combining honky-tonk and Grand Guignol.

The slaves were arranged in a line according to size, starting with the youngest. When anyone caught a spectator's fancy, they were examined in a manner unequalled in any cattle market in Europe. The purchaser ascertained that there was no defect in speech or hearing, and that there was no disease present; mouth and teeth were inspected, as well as every part of the body, including the breasts. The girls were handled indecently in public by the slave dealers. From the age of twelve they were exposed to examination by throngs of Arabs and subjected to inexpressible indignities by the brutal dealers.

Another common sight was the little boys dying slowly as they stumbled in pain through the streets, intestines dangling from jagged holes in their crotches. These were the results of the botched Arab attempts to produce eunuchs. It was believed that no more than one in twenty survived the gelding.

My father and I stepped out of the bastion into the cool breeze of Mombasa. Monsoon winds cool the whole of the coast, giving conditions that were key to the foreign exploration of East Africa. These seasonal winds breathe back and forth across the Indian Ocean with the regularity of a metronome. Local sailors know the monsoon by its Swahili names. Between October and April, this

Chapter Three

wind blows down from the north and is called the Kazi. When it rears on a 180-degree angle and retraces its path for the next six months, it becomes the Kusi. Although brisk, and at times vigorous, neither the Kazi nor the Kusi can be called tempestuous. Both drive as steadily as well-tended dynamos.

One can think of the monsoon as a sort of meteorological paving machine that converted the Indian Ocean into a boulevard for whatever maritime nations chose to ply it in their pursuit of commercial or imperial expansion on the East African Coast.

Four thousand years before the birth of Jesus Christ, merchant sailors from India, the Persian Gulf and the Eastern Mediterranean utilised the monsoon to carry out a spirited commerce with East Africa's coastal inhabitants. Very attractive business existed involving elephant tusks. Just behind the Benadir Coast, present-day Somalia was an inexhaustible wealth of cinnamon, frankincense and myrrh. There was a legendary mine at Ophir in the interior; it is believed that Ophir was the ancient and mysterious city of Zimbabwe, whose ruins still baffle archaeologists. But gold was mined there and it was one of the earliest industries.

Perhaps the most familiar reference to the trade is found in the Book of Kings: 'And Hiram sent in the navy with the servants of Solomon, once in three years came the navy of Tharshish, bringing gold, silver, ivory and apes and peacocks.' By way of payment, the foreign merchants brought in cotton cloth, axes, spearheads, knives, fruits, glass, ghee, wheat, rice, sesame oils, wines and other goods. To the people on the coast, these were valuable goods and the Kazi and Kusi wafted them with the sweet smell of success.

Europeans had no knowledge of these trade winds for nearly five thousand years; they were a secret except for Alexandrine, the Greek sailor who took long voyages down the coast and noticed the flourishing East African commerce. No Europeans sailed down, as the Dark Ages were overtaking the West. When Arabia went into

Experience of Coastal Life – Different Culture

economic depression, East Africa, as a member of Indian Ocean community, fell into a coma that lasted more than five hundred years.

The coast awakened from this slumber when Prophet Mohammed died in 632 AD and clashes among Islamic groups broke out over the succession to Mohammed's spiritual stewardship. Persia and Arabia represented the Shias and Sunnis; they suffered bitter conflicts resulting in a wave of Sunni migration to East Africa. They eventually became the foreign-ruled dominion in East Africa known as a Zinj – a Persian word meaning black people.

This is how old city states scattered along two thousand miles. They seldom, if ever, pledged allegiance to a single ruler. At first these people were Persian in culture, but they gradually took on an Arab personality. With the steady influx of immigrants from sheikhdoms along the Red Sea, the Hadramaunt and Oman, Persian and Arabs gave the coast a remarkable facelift. Zinj cultivated the land and harvested the sea. They took on the commerce in gold, ivory and spices that had attracted their forefathers. They were more shrewd business people than the African merchants. Dhows brought in carpets, silk, cut gems, bracelets, necklaces, gold and silver ornaments from India.

Mombasa, Kilwa, Pemba, Lamu became rich city empires. Zinj may have thrived on armed conflict, but they fought only among themselves and had little desire for territorial aggrandisement. If one town forced another into subjection for a few years, the second community would follow its own course. One could say that these city-states saw their struggle as a sort of diversion in which few innocent bystanders came to harm. It was all in the family.

Chapter Four

Competition for the Coast

VASCO DA GAMA was the reason for the decline of the Zinj as he made a claim for Portugal; this was a result of the first two centuries of European imperialism. The coast was used by the Portuguese to provide provisions for its ships bound for India; they ended up dominating Tanzania and Kenya's coastline and built forts within a decade of their arrival. They sacked, looted, burned, tortured and beheaded some leaders. Before long, submission to the Portuguese gave way to open revolt.

In 1586, a Turkish admiral named Ali Bey sailed to Mombasa with a heavily armed fleet of Xebecs, galleys and dhows. He told the local Zinj that he had been sent by the Sultan of Turkey to deliver the coastal people from the infidel but he had actually come of his own accord, and was a notorious corsair. The Zinj received him at the coast with joy and voluntarily teamed up with him to overthrow the Portuguese. Ali Bey was popular and went back to Turkey with the loot.

The Portuguese sent messages to India and help came to deal with the coastal cities that gave aid and comfort to the Turks. Three years later, Ali returned with the intention of driving the Portuguese from the Eastern Coast for good. The Viceroy of India, on learning this news, swiftly ordered twenty warships and blockaded

Competition for the Coast

the harbour. Ali Bey was held under siege until more troops came.

Zimba were Bantu tribes that were dreaded by the coastal people; they were well known for their cannibalism. The coastal people called them Cafres. The coastal people got help from the Zimba, though were careful not to be eaten themselves. City gates were opened for them and the Zimba devoured everything in their path. Ali Bey managed to survive, only to be put in chains and sent to Lisbon. The Zimba were wiped out shortly afterwards by sophisticated weapons.

The Portuguese rule did not last for long. Zinj and its sympathetic Mushrix neighbours continued to revolt against the Portuguese oppression. At this time both Britain and Holland had begun to extend their mercantile trade eastwards, and there was competition to control Indian trade.

In 1635, the Portuguese empire came to an end. Yusuf Bin Hassan gathered hundreds of Arabs and Swahili soldiers, massacred every Portuguese in the city and took possession of Fort Jesus. Other Portuguese bastions also crumbled and the strategic points of the coast slipped from the conqueror's grasp. People of the African east coast made an alliance with Oman, something they would later regret, and the Portuguese were finally driven away from the east coast. Oman began to regard the East African coast as theirs by right. Since they had helped the Zinj drive the Portuguese away, they slowly gained power by appointing imams from Oman, who collected taxes on their behalf. They had a religious and cultural bond with the Zinj. The Oman Arabs were still considered foreigners by the Zinj along the coast, and the Zinj resented being subjugated by the Omani overlords.

This is how Mombasa got its name Mvita, because the island was always at war. Oman appointed a ferocious aristocratic family named the Mazrui as administrators. This later proved to be a wrong move by Oman as the Mazrui governed the place and

Chapter Four

ignored the Omani who had placed them in power. Taxes were not handed to the imam and soon there was a tug of war. The Mazrui rulers became powerful on the coast and held the upper hand for a long time.

A century went by and Oman found it very difficult to control its colonies along the East African coastline. This was a time when two imperial powers, France and Britain, were in conflict. France wanted to control the waters of the Suez and to invade India; to do this France needed both the reigning imam of Muscat and Tippoo Sahib of India on their side. Letters were sent to them but were intercepted by British agents and forwarded to the Marquis of Wellesley, Governor General of India, who acted very quickly to incorporate Mysore into the empire. Tippoo Sahib was involved in the process.

Meanwhile, Seyyid Sultan found himself undergoing gentler treatment with the state visit of high-ranking Indian government officials. Diplomacy was necessary and was more useful than military force. Since a keystone of British Indian policy was to cultivate friendship wherever possible with countries lying on the exposed eastern sea routes, treaties were concluded. Seyyid Sultan played to British interests in India, and French ships were forbidden to enter or trade on the waters. The British East Africa Indian Company deployed a large sepoy garrison and built a port at Bandar Abba on the Persian Gulf. To bind this treaty in 1800, Seyyid Sultan agreed to post a respectable Englishman to be the full-time British agent in Muscat.

Oman became a client state to England so the British had a firm foothold in East Africa, in Mombasa and other smaller islands. This tenuous extension of influence eventually expanded into an empire so all the parties seemed to achieve their goals. Both the Foreign Office and the East India Company saw this treaty as an assurance that Oman was not dealing with Napoleon. As for Seyyid

Competition for the Coast

Sultan, he accepted the alliance as his long-awaited chance to drive out the Mazrui family in East Africa.

Things started to take shape in a peculiar manner. England seemed to establish her first East African colony without knowing she had done so, all because of the so-called 'Owen Protectorate', which started when Fitzwilliam Wentworth Owen was in command of two British ships charting the East African coast for the Admiralty. On December 4th 1823, Owens' junior vessel, *HMS Barraconta*, docked in Mombasa for supplies. The port was being blockaded by an Omani fleet preparing for yet another siege on Mombasa. The Muscat did not attack *Barraconta's* entry as the warship representing Oman. The Mazrui found a way to take advantage and persuade the British to protect them against the Oman delegation of Mazrui sheikhs and begged the *Barraconta's* commander for British protection against Oman. In return Said, the senior sheikh, allowed Mombasa to be ceded to England. The appeal was enticing but altogether out of the question; Britain remained bound by treaty to Oman. Owen, as a lower-ranking officer, could not tamper with an instrument that touched on the security of India. He could only sympathise with Mombasa's hard-pressed defenders, give an excuse and remove himself to his ship. A meeting took place in a small room in Fort Jesus. The Mazrui still pleaded and asked for permission to put up the British flag; when they were refused, tempers flared up and the lieutenant just managed to get away.

The only remaining option for the Mazrui was to run up the British flag, regardless of the consequences. Soon after, it was flying over Fort Jesus. The sight of this flag made the Omani blockade commander believe that the British had double-crossed them.

Captain Owen had just sailed to Oman and his ship *HMS Leven* was anchored in Muscat Harbour on a courtesy call, but also to strike a blow in Britain's recently declared war against slavery. It was time to make things clear to Seyyid Said that he must outlaw

Chapter Four

the trade in his domain within three months; he was told to read the Bible, which had been translated into Arabic. This way, the Mazrui also got their independence as a free state.

Owen was shocked when he arrived in Mombasa to see the British flag flying over Fort Jesus. He was received by the rebel leaders, who admitted having raised the flag without permission, and they repeated their request for British protection. The captain took this opportunity to loosen the stronghold of the slave trade on the coast and said that they would get his government's protection. He welcomed Mombasa into the British Empire – providing slavery was abolished completely. Mazrui accepted the terms and a new British flag replaced the fake one, not only in Mombasa but in some two hundred miles of coastline.

Owen had committed a breath-taking act of insubordination. He had openly defied the imam, the governor general of India, the directors of the East India Company, the lords of the Admiralty and the Foreign Office. This disobedience did not disturb him because he thought it was the best solution to the matter.

Owen left behind his third lieutenant, John James Reitz, as the first governor of British East Africa. The Mazrui honoured their agreement but only temporarily, and secretly went back to slavery. The economies of the East Africa coast and Persian Gulf states were geared almost entirely to slave labour for most of the nineteenth century and there was simply nothing to replace it.

Chapter Five

Adventure along the Coast

MANY ON THE coast still tell tales of the dark days of slavery; they have probably been passed down from generation to generation. An elderly lady who helped clean our rooms told my mother old tales of the coast, speaking quickly in Mombasa Kiswahili and I heard them all. The lady was not pure African but was of Arab descent.

These were horrific stories. The Arab slave traders had created passages inland. The vultures and hyenas shredded the slaves' bodies and left bones from an endless line of putrefying cadavers. Women were the most mistreated; they were tied to trees by their necks and left to die. Others were stabbed, shot or died of starvation. Food rations were low. These caravan headmen in charge of the transportation of slaves were brutal and ruthless.

Each morning, Mother was told a tale of the old days before the white men came along to save the situation. If the slaves were unfit to carry the loads allocated to them, their food ration was reduced and finally they would collapse – then they were shot and left behind. They were made an example of to stop other slaves pretending to be sick so as to avoid carrying their loads. If a mother was carrying a baby and a load and she became weak and unable to carry both, the child was killed. For every five slaves, only one

Chapter Five

made it to the coast.

Africa was depopulated in a demographic catastrophe that went nearly unnoticed. Dhows stood at the anchor, waiting to transport the slaves to their destinations. Normally these slaves were crammed below deck, partly kneeling or squatting in a most uncomfortable position. Meals were poor, there was no sanitation and there was the most intolerable stench from so many people packed together. Small children suffered smallpox and other diseases; the dead or half-dead were thrown overboard as fish food.

Blacks were captured because the Koran ruled out enslavement of fellow Muslims. Mother was very shocked by these stories; she must have asked herself what would have happened if the Arab slave traders had penetrated the Pokot and the Nandi people.

Thank God, Mother thought, that the British put an end to the slave trade, although their action met with great resistance by those who resented the British intrusion. There was a protest in the British Parliament against the spending of public funds on the Uganda railway. Thank God, the British had no option but to build the railway to stop the French or Germans interfering and making a mess of the empire.

Lieutenant Reitz, a twenty-two-year-old officer, became the first British commandant but his term was short. On May 4th, he crossed Makupa Creek and vanished into the dangerous mangroves to inspect the interior because word had come that the Mazruis had resumed slavery. On the 29th he returned, dying of malaria and in an awful state of delirium. Today, one of Mombasa's larger inner harbours is named Port Reitz in his memory. Most British settlers used to tip their hats to the place where Lieutenant Reitz is resting.

An exciting week passed very quickly, and soon Father, Mother and I were on our way to Lamu, travelling in one of the agricultural Land Rovers. After several hours we passed a place called Kilifi, then passed Watamu and finally drove through Malindi, a busy

Adventure along the Coast

trading and commercial centre that had made a great contribution to literature, arts and craft. Crude rag-and-coral homes gradually gave way to architecturally glorious tall residences with elegantly curved balconies that provided shade in the narrow busy streets below. The same building style could be found in all the coastal city towns. As we drove past Vasco da Gama Crossing, my father pointed out some land he had bought for development.

Malindi was popular with Kenya's big game hunters; settlers seemed to love this place and it had grown quickly. Deep-sea sports were popular here. Father owned several small motor boats as he was trying to start a business for tourists visiting Malindi. However, during the season when tourist numbers were low, he resented paying taxes as well as an extra person to manage the business in his absence. Keeping them anchored on shore meant regular maintenance so father finally sold them.

The town stands on the panoramic sweep of a wide bay where the Indian Ocean swells over broken reef and this makes surfing possible all year round. Water sports were undoubtedly the prime tourist attraction. This busy old town had a market place where buses arrived. We drove through the old town, including Juma'a mosque which stands where slaves used to be auctioned off each week until 1873. We drove through interesting Swahili residences, pre-war European retirees' houses and village quarters where the Pokomo people lived, still dressed in their native gear. The road to Lamu was remote, a journey through still unspoiled forests and sleepy coastal villages.

It was a very long drive to Lamu, and then we drove down a narrow causeway that ended on the south bank of the Tana River. Here a ferry waited to transport cars and people; it was very unpredictable and travellers could be stranded for days. During the dry season the river was easy to cross but the rainy season was worse; the Tana River often spilled over in floods for more than ten kilo-

Chapter Five

metres outwards. The road would be washed away or become a sea of glutinous mud; the current would be too strong to risk the perilous passage and at such times the ferry came to a standstill. The Pokomo used their boats or canoes to ferry waiting people across and a bus on the other side ferried people to Makowe, then on motor boats to the Lamu Islands.

Luckily for Father this was the dry season and the ferry took the Land Rover across. We drove to Makowe, where Father was given a motor boat that was used to ferry the agricultural staff across to the other side of Lamu.

A government Land Rover was waiting to drive us to our home, the only motor car belonging to the district officer. The main method of transportation here, apart from walking, was donkeys or dhows. Lamu was only nineteen kilometres by eight kilometres wide. The island consists mainly of high sand dunes and waving palm trees. Lamu Town and Shela are separated by more than two kilometres of beach.

Lamu Town looks across the channel to Manda Island. The seaboard is partially obscured by mangrove swamps. The Lamu people are unique; they have a slightly different character from the rest of the coastal people and their culture is very old and of mixed origin. They are staunch Muslims and they still have the Zinj characteristics in them.

We drove slowly through this elegant country. There were old houses, their courtyards filled with flowers and fountains, which one would imagine plumbing and simple air conditioning existed from centuries back. The Swahili, who are mainly Bajun by tribe, wore *kikois* (a night shirt), while the Arabs wore *kanzus* (white long robes). The Swahili women wore black *buibui* robes that denoted the modesty of their faith, with only their eyes revealed to the public gaze. Lamu must have been at one time prosperous and politically powerful and little has changed in this strictly Islamic enclave.

Adventure along the Coast

The place looked like it was rapidly decaying, the town a living monument to the past.

We drove past a government warehouse and a government office. Father popped in to make a quick written report, came out after twenty minutes and we proceeded home.

Our home was a one-storey house, which had high windows that were barred with shutters. The doors were made of *mvule*, a rare, rock-like indigenous timber that only grows along the coast. Our veranda extended outwards on pillars made out of thick *mvule* wood and the veranda was a great relief as it offered shade. Our house was built on a high point that captured the natural ventilation of monsoon winds blowing steadily across two thousand miles of the Arabian Sea and Indian Ocean. The harsh equatorial sun was not so hot and the steady blow of the wind, which seemed to encircle our house, cooled us down. Palms, mango and mangrove trees gave the place enough shade. The house was built in the European style, as were other government houses, and surrounded by bougainvillea, oleander, frangipani, jacaranda and one or two Nandi flame trees.

A week after our arrival, Father took me around the island on the back of a donkey. We sat on one donkey with my father supporting me as I was very small and unused to riding. We went to see the fourteenth century pillar tomb behind Riyadha Mosque, a national monument on the town's upper slopes. This mosque must have been built between 1900 and 1901. It was huge and popular and accommodated all Muslims, men, women and children, for Friday prayer. This mosque and all the other mosques on the island are involved in a famous Maulidi celebration, a major festival in the Islamic calendar. Maulidi is the Prophet Mohammed's birthday, marked by one week of religious festivities. Feasting and dancing attract other Muslim pilgrims from East Africa. One could imagine one was living in the time of the Arabian Nights.

Chapter Five

We had to take a short break at noon, after which we continued the trek to Shela Beach that took about one hour. This landmark cannot be missed. Fifty-eight steps take people up to the top and, once there, there is a marvellous panorama of the Shela sand dunes, which are said to cover Hadibu, the island's first seventh-century Arab settlement and the scene of the eighteenth-century massacre.

Shela's waterfront is spectacular and the beach beyond is unprotected by reef; it is the only place where anyone can surf, if they really want to. Beaches on Manda, opposite Shela, are enhanced by mysterious cannons that are scattered around.

The day came to an end but there was still much to see. Hopefully another day I would get a chance to see more of the historic sites.

Mother was superstitious and told Father that the island was full of *Jini* and *Shetani* (the devil); taking me around would make these mysterious beings follow us back home. According to Mother, *Shetani* appear in the local mangrove thickets looking like ordinary men, clothed in the *kikois* and many gourds are tied around their necks.

My mother talked too much about magic at the coast. She had been listening to a Bajun native man (from one of the coastal tribes) who owned a shop and sold groceries and vegetables to people in the area. One particular night I overheard her talking about the mystery of the coastal people, the Wadigo. They have lived for many years along the coastal strip and they are called *Watu wa Fisi* (the hyena men); at night they are believed to change into hyenas and walk in packs. The coastal people have their own version of the legend, which they still believe today. Father called it rubbish, a figment of overactive imaginations, and said they did not really exist.

Mother sounded very persuasive when she talked about life after death. This idea was very popular with the Pokot people. They believe implicitly in dead spirits. When a man dies he automatical-

Adventure along the Coast

ly becomes a spirit and is given malignant powers. The spirit can bring sickness and disease to the living but the living can appease the spirit by visiting a tiny hut in the middle of a native *shamba*. 'If you look inside,' Mother was told, 'there are pots containing fruits and a few coins on a rag near the centre of a hut. These small offerings are enough to ward off the spirits.'

My mother was friendly with a Bajun native man who owned a shop nearby. He said that the island was full of *ma-jini* (black magic cats), which changed into beautiful women at night; they went to the night clubs all dressed up with jewellery to lure men to bed. During the day they went back to being black cats. Mother became afraid of all black cats and always reminded Father to come back home before dark.

I went with my mother to a wedding *ngoma*. The natives were arrayed in their feathers and danced to the traditional drumbeat. The house roof was made out of *makuti* leaves. We were given sweet tea and *mahamri*, triangular wheaten cakes. There were delicacies provided for guests; the tables were laden with food. Females were never allowed to mix with the males and we had to sit on soft carpets while eating. Everybody shared in the happiness, *karibu, karibu* –invited to join in the celebration.

I saw that the people looked prosperous and clean. The men were in suits worn only for this celebration. The ladies wore their *buibui* in public but in the room occupied by women and children, these were put aside. I imagined what it would be like during the holy month of Ramadhan when they would feast every night from seven o'clock.

We walked back home a few miles along the beach accompanied by some young Muslim lads. Father seemed happy that we had had a lovely evening out. I was getting into bed when my mother saw a large *dudu* (insect) on my sheet. She rushed to my father's dressing table, picked up his tweezers, removed it and placed it in

Chapter Five

a bottle. The next day, we had a good look at the insect and found it was a healthy-looking scorpion. Never had Mother and I been so frantic. Every night she went round the house, under beds, tables, covers, corners, just in case there was another scorpion.

In September, my father had to go to a place called Hindi for two days. My mother was not happy to be left alone. The night he went away, after the cook left for his quarters, was beautiful and moonlit and perfect for a midnight walk. Then it happened: a strong whirlwind came from the mainland. It caught part of the oceanfront and came back – and this time our house was right in its path.

The noise was terrific. Mosquito nets lifted up, bedsheets disappeared and everything loose in the room rattled and fell.

Mother was frightened to death and I was screaming and trying to find somewhere to hide. These peculiar winds moved so fast and hit the rooftops with a terrific blast. Sheets of corrugated iron were carried off rooftops. Luckily, the wind only lasted for a minute or two, otherwise it would have done great damage, but it left us awake, wet, cold and miserable and surrounded by debris.

When Father came back from Hindi, he was shocked to find our place in a total mess. The cook had to go to the market to get fresh groceries, as the ones we had were scattered and most were now rotting.

My father's friend, who lived in Mombasa, came to stay with us for a few days. Having him around was exciting. I remember a fishing trip. I was scared of water and the sea creatures but my fear left me because Father was next to me.

The fishing trip started about seven o'clock in the evening. At midnight there was no experience more beautiful than being on a sailing boat on a moonlit night. The anchor ropes went down; they were made from common sisal rope, but once down on the seabed they looked like bars of gold. All the lines were exactly the same;

Adventure along the Coast

they fell through the water like thin gold wires and the darker the night, the brighter these lines appeared. We had to sail further off to catch kingfish; we caught a lot as they take the bait so easily. It was very tiring for my father pulling them up all the time, and on the deck they jumped and flopped around. After the sun came up, we made our way back home.

Chapter Six

Lamu in the Year 1962

ALL BRITISH OFFICERS used boats to go across to Pate Island. Normally it took two hours to get there, a slow process, and the tides would interfere with the return journey if it was not planned properly. The danger was not over when they landed at Mtangawanda; there was still the journey to Siyu village, walking along footpaths.

At Siyu, the inhabitants have great skills; they are very artistic and nearly everybody here is religious. There is a port right at the end of this island that was built early in the nineteenth century. It has lots of rusting cannons and looks very mysterious; its past is reflected in the still waters of the mangroves and the creeks.

Faza settlement was not too far away; we had to pass it going through mango and coconut plantations and dense bushes as we continued to Pate. Finally, we arrived at our destination, which is rich in walls, tombs, mosques and mysterious edifices. Pate has a lot of historical sites on the south-eastern shores of the island. The 1,200-year-old city state of Shanga is nearby; we paused briefly, saw its ruins. This place must have been a busy trading centre during the eighteenth century but today it is completely ruined, all its beauty vanished with its past civilization.

During the 1950s, a man named James Kirkman stumbled upon these ancient ruins. It was overgrown with creepers; baobab trees intertwined with bushes and weeds. Rich merchants must have

Lamu in the Year 1962

once lived here in splendour with their families. Only twenty acres of ruins remained to tell the tale of its existence.

One particular day, my father was driving to work with me to his agricultural projects along Lamu road near Fundi Issa, some twenty-one miles from Malindi. The main project was building up sand trails to link the mainland to the island. This island was named Robinson Island after my father. I remember as a child being carried across at low tide from the mainland to this desert island in ankle-deep water. Many years after independence, the European settlers turned the place into a desert-island resort for holidaymakers and it still carries the name Robinson Island.

My mother's behaviour, which involved constant drinking, was not a surprise to my father's friends, most of whom had worked as officers since before 1950. Father took no notice but stayed out of her way. The Europeans had experienced such behaviour in the natives, who remained in a mysterious state of non-development. They seemed to have no ambition and liked to live in villages; they didn't want to break out of the cycle they were chained to, and were steeped in the endless life circle where customs and traditions were important to them. They were not naturally a curious race; they had nothing to explore or look forward to, no desire for change or improvement except owning cattle and having many wives and children. Their ancestors lived in the same way and they continued to accept things as they were. The people from my mother's side had not handed down their country to my father's people as a magnificent gesture; the white men took the country to protect it from the slave traders, who were mostly Arabs and Somali. They wanted to bring law and order, education and the so-called modern religion of Christianity. As things improved, more settlers left their countries to farm the rich Kenyan agricultural land in the highlands.

Some years back, my mother's people must have owned their

Chapter Six

land. Kenya was a kaleidoscope of people and culture; local boundaries existed in accordance with the traditional balance of power. Kenyans were tribal; their strength was that of warriors whose history of battles dates back one thousand years or more. Their characteristics set Kenyans apart from the rest of Africa.

One morning, Father surprised my mother by saying that he had to go to Malindi, a town along the coast, where there was a property for sale. We were slow in packing a bag and getting on our way. By the time we arrived at Makowe, on the way to Malindi, it was late afternoon. I knew we would have to spend a night or two before we came back.

It was very late by the time we got to the place. Luckily, there was a small house that was used for holidaymakers and a cook was available for us. The grey-stone house was weathered and around it were a few mango trees. The scenery was divine; it was clean and the blue Indian Ocean lay before us, the deep creek and long unbroken coastline of pale grey and yellow coral as far as the eye could see when the tide was out. I would walk out from the house, accompanied by the house help, to pick strange shells and starfish.

The following morning, Swahili fishermen came to our house in loincloths with red or blue turbans round their heads to sell us their fish. My mother loved fish; it was one of her favourite meals apart from the local foods that she and I were used to.

The house was built high on the cliffs. I walked down to the deep caves below where I sheltered from the sun when the tide was out. When the tide came in, it filled the caves to the level of the ground on which the house stood. And always the sea sang and sighed in the strangest way in the porous coral rock as the long waves came running in. That night, there was a full moon and it was beautiful. We slept with our door open to the silver sea, the warm breeze whispering as it swept in a little loose sand on the stone floors from outside.

Lamu in the Year 1962

My mother refused Father's offer to buy the place; she would not have it, probably because she was not used to being far away from her people. As for Father, he could not live alone there and the cost of making the place comfortable to suit a white person and travelling back and forth would have been too much for him.

My mother began to get seriously sick. At first we thought she had bad malaria but later we discovered that it was due to pregnancy as she was expecting another baby. My father paid for her ticket back to Kitale.

Later on, I was big enough to understand why Mother and Father were constantly quarrelling: it was over another woman. She was to come and take Mother's place in our Lamu home. This was very confusing at the time, as I did not understand the friendship that existed between our father and this particular woman.

The tiny white community stationed at Lamu lived a miserable life. The Europeans were forever quarrelling among themselves. All was wearisome monotony; there was no excitement. Sport did not exist because the place had a treacherous climate, and the few white people there soon lost the habit of walking along the beach. The island's drinking water was not fresh and in some places dangerous to drink. Venereal disease was endemic, everyone was in constant danger of contracting cholera and malaria, and doctors were unknown. In consequence, very few white women lived on the coastal stretch; the women were mostly Abyssinian or Somali. One required either great fatalism, a great love of money, power or adventure, or a sense of duty to live willingly in this beautiful and exotic place. Father must have also, like the rest of the white population there, been lonely at some point.

The journey back was not as exciting as the one to Mombasa. Mother was very ill and depressed and I did not get the attention I normally received.

We arrived at Kitale railway station after three days' and three

Chapter Six

nights' journey from Mombasa. We were very tired. Father's manager from Longleat picked us up and took us to our father's farm, which was eight kilometres from the Kitale town towards the Cherangani Hills. These hills stretch as far the eye can see and are crowned with Elgon teak, cedars and rosewood. Here everything looks green and untouched.

Our father's farm had three partners, including Father. His partners were white settlers; because Father was always away on duty working as an agricultural officer in Lamu, these two partners were left to run the farm and make a profit. The white partners lived in the main house while my father had to have the farm's guest house, which was situated at the far end of the farm near a farm office where all the accounts were kept. This farm was 1,200 acres; it grew seed maize, and cattle were kept for beef. My mother was not allowed to use this house in my father's absence so we were given two tiny rooms among the farm labourers. We gladly took these as this was better than going all the way to the Pokot up in the mountains in Lomut.

Kitale was a small colonial town. There were some good buildings and the streets were clean and tidy. Flowers grew on the sides of the paths. There were hospitals, courts, a police station, post office, departments for veterinary and agriculture, and the District Commissioner's office. As well as the main street, there were two other streets large enough for cars to drive down and parking areas. Shops were built along the sides of driveways; they were owned by Indians. There was a roundabout in the centre of this pretty town where a beautiful jacaranda tree grew, which had yellow flowers. It was unique; no one had seen such a tree give out yellow flowers before. It gave shade to the people who sat on a bench beneath it. Nearby there was a big hotel called the Kitale Hotel, for white settlers only. On the outskirts of this town were shanty *dukas* (shops) for Asians only.

Lamu in the Year 1962

Kitale was where all the government and central offices were located; from here the law was maintained. A town always plays an important part in people's lives; it does not make much difference whether you have bad or good things to say about it, it will still draw the mind to it by mental law of gravity.

The luminous haze of the sky above the town at night could be seen from a distance. Here everyone bought food, heard news, danced at the Kitale club where the upper class were members. They had a fine ballroom and pretty garden, and played golf and polo.

During this time, the workers' houses were very different to the Europeans' – they were dirty. There was a slum that attracted all job seekers. This place was mostly built out of old iron sheets that had begun to rust. It became a place for squatters and it did not have a good name, but it was lively and gaudy. Any number of things went on.

The Indians of Kitale dominated business. The merchants had their little villas just outside town. They gave tea parties in their gardens with Indian pastries. They were very polite and clever with figures and they kept to themselves. Their jobs all seemed to be the same and they all dressed the same; you would never know who was the boss or the lowest paid among them.

The road back to Kitale Farm was stony and dusty and it was a tiring journey to our two-room house. We passed through small maize fields and a banana plantation. I could see blue smoke from huts of the people who lived on the squatters' edge of the farm.

Chapter Seven

Mother Returns

SUNDAYS WERE DIFFERENT, sometimes exciting, and I held the day as special. On the farm everything seemed quiet; it seemed to close the whole place in. The farm labourers were happy as it was their day off. A few labourers went to the Catholic mission five miles away on the opposite side of the main dusty road. Missionaries built the Catholic mission church with assistance from the native congregation; it was beautifully built with fine building materials and a bell tower. You could hear the chiming of the mission bell a long way off in the clear mornings. The sun was up and the air was getting warm but the labourers who came to mass wore lots of old sweaters to keep them warm. The nuns from the convent school were there and all the people were lively.

The church was laid out on four acres of land. There was a nursery and primary school run by nuns from the nearby convent; this was essential, as the locals had to be encouraged to attend primary school. The education was run on religious lines; not many books were translated into Kiswahili except the Bible and the hymn books.

The Catholic missionaries owned three hundred acres of land and kept dairy cows on it. Most of the milk was sold to the Kenya Creameries Dairy Board in Kitale town, where the government had built the factory. Some milk was given to the children at the

Mother Returns

convent school. The Catholic fathers and nuns were very friendly. The convent had a doctor, who was assisted by several nuns, and a very basic hospital. All serious cases were transferred to Kitale Hospital in Kitale town.

My sister Safia was born on the farm but not in my father's house. The labourers' wives helped as midwives. That night was one of the longest that I had ever experienced. It was very noisy as the women rushed up and down doing their midwifery duties. I was not allowed to stay next to Mother but slept on the floor in the other room on an old mattress. Early next morning our father's friend Mr Bertie Hunt, one of my father's partners on the Longleat estate farm, came riding up on horseback. He galloped a few metres past our house then came back, tied his horse to the tree outside our house and knocked on the door. He stood at the doorway of the small living room. This living room was used as a cooking place and a *jiko* (charcoal burner) was on, so there was smoke everywhere.

Mr Hunt stood at the doorway and demanded to see the new baby, wanting to know what colour skin she had. Mother's sister carried Safia to him as he stepped outside where the morning sun was rising so that he could see the child clearly. The baby was screaming; my father's friend took one look at her then turned round, walked to his horse and galloped away. The inside of our house had basic furniture: one old sofa set, which was untidy and torn in some parts, three wooden stools and a small table. This was not much of a place for Father's friend to sit or have tea.

After two weeks, my mother was ordered to leave this small scruffy house and move to my father's big house. From then on, she was taken care of like a proper housewife and given support and care. We children were looked after properly. Our father's cook cooked all our meals and we started to eat proper English food. At first we were not used to it but gradually we enjoyed the meals,

Chapter Seven

though Mother sometimes had to have her native foods. Father came to see us; I always remember him being very happy to have his two daughters with him but there was always a worried look on his face and an expression of regret because these were hard times for mixed couples. Blacks and whites were not allowed to marry.

I liked to walk to the labourers' quarters for company and play with children of my own age. Although my mother had asked her sister to look after me, I managed to sneak away. As I walked along the narrow paths towards the huts, I glimpsed the older women preparing or weeding their little *shambas* (land) that had been allocated to them by the farm manager.

This Sunday was different. I wandered farther than I should have. I saw these beautiful big butterflies with yellow and orange colours on their wings and I wanted so badly to catch one of them. Every time I came close, they flew away and I kept on following them, running along a little path into the woods. This led into a huge forest full of native trees.

I must have been gone for a good while, still chasing my butterflies, not knowing I was getting deeper into the woods until I looked up and everywhere was full of grey and black monkeys. I stood still then I quietly walked through the forest. I was a little afraid and aware of them staring at me. The smell of them lingered in the air, a dry and stale mousy smell, then I would suddenly hear the rush and whizz over my head as the colony moved. I kept still and caught a glimpse of one or two of the monkeys sitting immobile in a tree. After a while, I discovered that they had not gone but that the whole forest round me was still full of them. Some were dark, others grey, and their tails hung down behind them.

There were so many that they frightened me. I made a sudden move to run away and they all disappeared into the dark parts of the woods. Still afraid, I started to find my way back out of the thick forest. I knew that this forest had leopards because we had

Mother Returns

been told not to wander far from the main house, especially when it was dark.

I tried not to panic; I concentrated on staying calm, controlled my breathing, and pushed away the first symptoms of panic. As soon as I felt a little more relaxed, an inner sense guided me out of the forest to safety. Soon I was drawn to one side of the clearing where I found the faint trace of the path that I must have followed coming in. I walked back along it and soon I saw the labourers' huts far off, with smoke coming through their thatched roof. I ran quickly towards them. When I got to my mother's house, she was furious and gave me a beating. She told me never to wander away into the forest alone again.

Father and his two partners would have visitors on their farm and at night they would dine, talk and laugh until midnight. The big house would be lit up; the labourers could see the big house from their huts and it looked like a star in the night. Father's friends drove expensive cars, smoked the finest cigars and drank the most exquisite wine. The wine was very tempting for Mother and she would get drunk and make a fool of herself.

Father had a library full of books, mostly about history, Latin and Greek and agriculture. These books became part of his life and he was grateful to have them in Kenya. The characters in the books, especially the colonial history books, influenced his personality. As he walked through the fields or rode on horseback, his mind was on the books; they found a special place in our home. No one was allowed to touch them except the housekeeper who had to dust and polish the shelves once a week.

Father had a beautiful gramophone that he played most afternoons until evening. It was Second World War music, which sounded very sad. We could hear it round the lily pond outside the driveway. The melody streamed towards us as it played and brought with it the clear cool air of the evening. The workers liked

Chapter Seven

to listen to it, especially the younger herdsmen; they had a habit of bringing their goats or cows to graze, wandering about in our courtyard. Our father's gardener would not let them come too near to the house but sometimes we saw them swarm through the bushes beyond. Later on, Father bought a piano and he played Christmas carols on it.

The surrounding area was full of Nandi and Pokot tribes. They had intermarried. These tribes share the same customs and their languages are similar. They have great respect for the virginity of their daughters; they exchange their daughters for many cows as a bride price.

My father had to get a letter from the District Commissioner giving them permission to brew the *tembu* (local beer). This was a drink made from fermented maize mixed with sorghum. After fermenting it was mixed with honey or sugar and distilled to make a deadly drink called *chang'aa* (local beer with high alcoholic content).

The native festival dances are called *ngomas*. There were special *ngomas* for circumcisions. These alternated; one year would be for females and the next year for males. The older men would sit on three-legged stools with their snuff, drinking the *tembu*. Patches of earth mixed with cow dung were glued onto their heads with ostrich feathers stuck in the middle; it made them look like crane birds.

These dances normally took place after the young circumcised girls were discharged from their huts after a period of a month. They were kept there to heal. Now dressed traditionally, they waited to meet their future husbands. A girl's good reputation was very important both to herself and her parents, and they had to be virgins to get husbands. The young men who had been pledged a wife had to pay the bride price and settle his payment of cows before taking his wife home.

The *ngomas* normally started in daytime and went into the night, usually when the moon was bright. Negotiations and celebrations would go on for a week. Crowds of onlookers followed these festivals and some would participate in the dancing. The young girls wore traditional clothing of greased leather shirts and mantles. They normally sat close to their mothers, being still under their protection.

The young men smeared themselves with a particular kind of pale red chalk, which gave them a weird look, like fossilised statues cut in the rock. The girls wore embroidered tanned leather garments, covered themselves with red soil and wore beads round their necks and ankles.

The *ngomas* were always noisy. Jumping, dancing, flutes and drums filled the air, and the music and drumming were often drowned out by the clamour from the audience. The middle-aged women who participated in the dance made strange, loud, shrill sounds whenever one of the male dancers jumped high or swung his spear over his head in an exceptionally fine manner.

Here and there, ancient Pokot women caroused with a calabash between them, all absorbed in gay conversation as it reminded them of the old days when they were young and took part in such dances, their faces radiant with happiness as the sun went down on the horizon.

The supply of *tembu* and *chang'aa* continued to be handed down to the older people. These festivals are precious and sacred to them. The dances and ceremonies are many years old, kept up from generation to generation. During colonial times they were considered immoral and the authorities tried to abolish them by law, but they were done secretly.

Elders/chiefs formed tribal councils, which were low-level administrative courts. Their knowledge of the psychology of their tribesmen gave the elders an enormous advantage that could never

Chapter Seven

be acquired by any European. Other tribes proved equally receptive to the innovation, and the eventual result was formal recognition of the tribal councils as a quasi-official arm of the protectorate government. These bodies were empowered to make and enforce many of their own laws, provided that such native laws and customs were not repugnant to morality. Cases of intra-clan stock theft, assault, magic, disputed bride-price agreements and other matters of traditional law were adjudicated by the tribal councils. The headman system and the tribal councils represented the first halting steps towards Kenya's management of its own destiny.

Most tribal councils did not get permits for the circumcision of young girls; rather they applied for permits for other types of festival and incorporated the circumcision. All this was done in secrecy within the community. Most times on our Longleat farm, Father and his partners had difficulty getting straight answers from the Pokot natives because they did not know how to answer a question directly or tell the truth. They gave elusive replies. Some elders would come and ask for a permit for festivals but they always hid the fact that they brewed *pombe* or *tembu* (the Swahili word for local wine). If they were asked to explain their behaviour they pretended not to hear and looked at you as if they were seeing you for the first time in their lives.

There seemed to be a great distance between the whites and locals but if the Pokot got to know you, they spoke in a friendly and open way. If my father was asked to attend their *baraza* (public gathering), it showed that they really liked him and looked to him for leadership.

So, on those noisy nights, Mother would go to the *ngoma* festivals as they reminded her of her youth, and she would always take me along. After dark, fires were lit around the *manyattas* (huts). Fire was very important to create an effect; it made the dancing place into a stage and showed all the colours and movements. The Afri-

Mother Returns

can moonlight is marvellously clear and gives the place glamour. Younger boys and girls made sure the fire stayed alight. The place was arranged so it looked spacious and big, and the smoke was kept down to avoid choking or to stop it getting into people's eyes.

Small parties of people arrived from distant villages. The young men jumped very high as they swung their spears to show how good they were in using them. Their singing was more a rhythmical recitation than a song; everyone around them joined in the chorus. This went on all night: the drumming continued; the jumping went on for hours; one group of men started, then the next group took their place. Their faces took on expressions of ecstasy, as if they were really ready to die for one another, then suddenly a cry pierced the dark night. The mood changed and became warlike; the air was filled with the changes in their movements and voices, as if they were reminded of the many years of massacre and looting caused by cattle rustling or stealing. Such *ngoma* could make a white man's blood run cold.

It was soon time for my mother to take me back to my father's house. She asked for young men to escort us. We hoped all would end well and they would not challenge one another to a fight or quarrel over their wives.

Next morning, some wounded men came to the house to be taken to the mission hospital by my father but most natives walked to their villages and were treated with herbal medicine.

Father's favourite place to camp out in the Pokot area was Chepareria. It was a long drive down a narrow, dusty, country road and we had to start very early in the morning. The previous night Kazungu, our Giriama cook who was originally from Lamu, had put provisions aside for the camp: hurricane lamps; tents; utensils and tinned foods. My mother never went on these safaris. She preferred to stay at home to look after my sister Safia, but we knew she would be busy drinking the illegal *tembu* or *chang'aa*. The govern-

Chapter Seven

ment stopped the natives brewing this drink as the labourers drank too much and became lazy, and then they would fight and quarrel.

Father carried his double-barrelled twelve-bore shotgun. Before sunrise, we started on the journey with my father driving his Land Rover. As we drove high up towards Kapenguria then up round the Kamatira hill, there was a tangible coldness and freshness in the air. As it flowed against our faces, it made it difficult to see clearly. After twenty minutes, we arrived in the valley. The road was very bad and there were stones everywhere. By sunset, we arrived at our destination near a small river. The air was very cool.

The land was open and undulating with no fences, no ditches or roads. There was no human habitation except the native Pokot villages, and those were deserted half the year when the Pokot went off to look for other places for pastures for their herds of animals. There were some thorn trees on the plain and clear paths here and there. This place had green grass near the river at this time of the year and various types of gazelles came here to graze. Far off we saw a herd of elands, their long horns streaming backwards over their raised necks, the large loose flaps of breast skin that make them look square, swaying as they jogged. We could see giraffe far off. I had never been out on a shooting safari before. Very soon it would be dark and it was open ground so a circular fence of thorn trees was built round our campsite. The Land Rover was parked close to one tree and a tent built for sleeping. Our supper was baked beans with sausages, which my father's cook Kazungu prepared on the open fire.

Father took the first watch and, after midnight, two Pokots took over the night watch as this was lion and leopard territory.

The vault of the sky swung back over our heads and, as we sat looking upwards, new constellations of stars came up from the east. The smoke from the fire in the cold air carried the sparks away and the fresh firewood smelt sour. From time to time I got scared and

Mother Returns

snuggled close to my father. I could see Kazungu standing on the back of the Land Rover. Lamp held high, he swung it about to see beyond the blazing bonfire that was kept going most of the night. I saw that the two Pokots kept their spears within reach and cast anxious glances into the inky darkness beyond the circle of the firelight. We all seemed afraid. The next morning we had a very basic breakfast, only bread and butter with tea and boiled eggs. In the morning we heard birds singing musical songs.

African antelopes are not much bigger than fallow deer. They are called bushbuck and are very shy and furtive. The males have delicately turned horns. The Pokot area is full of them. Near our camp, before we went hunting or at sunset, we saw them come out of the bush into the glades. As the rays of the sun fell upon them, their coats shone like copper.

Before we set off hunting, the sun was already out and it was starting to get hot. It was decided that I would remain behind with Kazungu, our cook, and not go out to the hunting grounds as they planned to go trekking into the thick forest some three kilometres away from our campsite. I hoped that Father would make a kill of two or three deer, or of the much bigger animals, for food. I did not like the idea of too many nights sleeping out because, when sound travelled far in the quiet stillness of the dark African nights, I could hear the roars and snarls of the lions. The sound of the lions was a dreadful purring that filled the air and rang in my ears for days afterwards.

Still, we were out again for one more night. The Pokot reserve was beautiful at sunset. The river and the plains with their thorn trees were beautiful. The air was clear and we saw a single star in the sky to the west, which grew big and radiant like a silver point in the sky. The air was cold, the grass wet and the shrubs gave out a spiced, astringent scent. Everything seemed wonderful until after ten o'clock when the fires were lit to scare away the wild animals.

Chapter Seven

The next morning, they went out hunting again and managed to kill three antelopes. The government only permitted settlers to shoot four antelopes per month for meat; that was the law in those days. My father was distressed and very quiet; later on I learnt that, while out hunting, they had come across a dead body, which must have been left in the bush three days earlier. The smell of the dead man was so strong that the hunting group could not miss it. Pokot natives are afraid to touch bodies and, when this particular dead man was found in the bushes, vultures had not eaten him. The Pokot hunters would not help to bury him as they were too terrified to touch a corpse. They dug the grave a few metres away but my father rolled the body into the grave and covered it with soil himself.

The Pokot do not bury their dead but leave them above ground for the hyenas and vultures to deal with them. That was their way of making the body return to nature and become part of the landscape. They believe the spirit of the dead person is released into the spirit world quicker this way. Although the government tried to make the Pokot natives change their ways, and they were taught to lay their dead in the ground, it will take a long time for their culture to change. Driving home afterwards, everyone sat silently. I was very tired and I fell asleep behind the back seat of the Land Rover.

My father still had influence as the agricultural officer and was called to settle the quarrels that took place among the native tribes, especially the Pokots. They seemed to be the ones that were considered the troublemakers as they held a strange position among the surrounding tribes. There was always tension among the Mount Elgon Sabaot, the Karamajong of Uganda, the Turkana, the Marakwet and Tugen tribes. My father was brought into their quarrels, especially when it came to cattle stealing. He could be called to settle such cases, and he was always present at the *baraza* (meeting of native courts) with the elders and chiefs.

The chiefs of each tribe looked bulky and immovable as they sat in a semi-circle alongside my father, with burning attentive eyes. All agreements were put down on paper and certified. The elders sat at Father's wooden table, made out of a stump of an old tree trunk. They dipped their thumbs in blue ink and pressed them down upon the agreement. Most tribal leaders did it reluctantly and whimpered a little when they touched the paper as if it would burn them.

The crowd was noisy and the chiefs would turn around and talk to the screaming mob. Witnesses came forward to put their mark on the paper and then the chiefs and Father's signatures finalised the agreement.

The natives had their own laws but when the colonials arrived they brought in new laws, which became the laws of the land. The tribes practised their native laws secretly. For instance, if a murder was committed or cows stolen, this was dealt with by replacement. There was no looking deeply into the motives for the crimes. Losses were addressed and action was taken to replace the lost or stolen items. For murder, there was a big fine; one human life would be replaced by one hundred cows. If the culprit ran away, the clan or family would make the payment. The chief and elders were always in the baraza to weigh the charges and fix the penance. Sometimes matters were brought to the District Commissioner but the native courts secretly tried most cases of murder. Hanging was never their way of justice.

Chapter Eight

South Nyanza – Homa Bay

We had to make a journey to Homa Bay in South Nyanza, near the big town on Lake Victoria (named after HM Queen Victoria of Great Britain). My father had the experience of living in harsh hot climates. In the 1940s, my father had managed a big farm in South Sudan at a place called Barakat. Mother had to accompany him to Homa Bay, which had a similar climate to Barakat South Sudan, as he would be there for a short time.

As we drove into Kisumu, the air was humid and soon we were surrounded by palm trees and emerald-green mangoes. Finally, the lake came into view. Since our house was very near the shore, we could hear a continual cracking noise, especially where the papyrus grew. It was the slapping of the waves on the reeds and the whirring of countless fireflies and crickets. It was very beautiful and yet there was a mysterious and disturbing atmosphere. One could feel primitive Africa.

At dusk everything became sombre and silent; there was a heavy nothingness in the humid air. It conjured up noxious undercurrents of magic, superstition, plotting and ambushes. It was made worse because there was nothing definite to fear. These natives, the Kavirondos (people who lived on the lake Basin region), were mighty drinkers of *pombe* (alcohol) and much worse than the Pokot. When they had drunk away their depression, boredom and idleness, they

South Nyanza – Homa Bay

gave way to infantile outbursts of passion and hysteria. Then they got out their drums and beat them. They gathered around and started dancing; the quality of these dances was savage and sometimes menacing.

The locals were making only marginal use of their fertile soil and this brought in very little income. Poverty was common. The only way to make these people work was for the government to impose on them their quarter allotment; if they did not meet it, they would be penalised or fined.

Kisumu was vulnerable to malaria, dysentery, black water fever and a range of tropical scourges. Most of the officers posted to Kisumu in the early 1930s to the late 1950s developed what was termed 'fear complex' because of the climate. Most government posts had nothing to offer but unhygienic surroundings and a hot climate, and duties were rarely performed well. Since my father's stay would be short, we were given a small furnished house not too far from the other officers' houses.

Kisumu has a hot climate. The natives started their day-to-day work at around ten o'clock. My mother slept all the time; at one time we thought she had caught sleeping sickness. My father's cook accompanied us, so we had someone to take care of the house and cook our meals.

Our house was close to a wet swampy area; not far away was a small stream that drained into Lake Victoria. I liked to play in these swampy places and I had a habit of taking off my shoes. Nearby there was stagnant water and I could see children on the other side playing and bathing in this dirty water.

After three weeks, we had to come back to Kitale. Father had to report at his post in Lamu District. A couple of weeks later, before my father left for Lamu, I started to complain of pain in my lower belly and between my legs. Every time I urinated it was very painful and my mother noticed that I had drops of blood in my urine. I

Chapter Eight

started to have a fever and to itch all over.

I was immediately driven to Kitale to see a doctor. My father's doctor was Dr Litch; she told my father that I had blood flukes (schistosomiasis – bilharzia). This is an infection caused by a worm that gets into the bloodstream and was common in the Kisumu area. I was lucky that we noticed it in time; these worms can only be seen under a microscope and, if treatment is delayed, it can cause kidney damage, swelling of the feet and then death.

My father was furious at my mother for being careless and lazy and not taking care of me while we were at Kisumu. He explained to her that blood flukes are not spread directly from person to person. Mother argued; she did not understand how I had been infected during such a short stay at Kisumu. One reason might have been that I was in the dirty, swampy water without shoes and the worms' eggs got into my feet through wounds or cuts. The Kisumu people were very unhygienic; they urinated and defecated directly into the stream and the children swam and bathed in the same water. There was no safe drinking water.

Lamu was far away but my father had to go. I was very sad but he reassured me that soon we would join him. I thought I had lost him for good and it grieved me to see him go.

We lived on the farm, waiting for Father's return, and no word came of his whereabouts, except one letter that told us he had arrived in Lamu and was well. I later learnt that this silence was because he had to go to the UK to be treated for a bad disease that he had contracted from one of the women who lived with him in Lamu during my mother's absence. The woman was well known to my mother; she had a home in Kitale and lived in town. After treatment, Father had to stay in the UK for a month to recover.

While he was abroad, he was homesick and very lonely. He went to visit his old friends from Oxford University who lived in Kent. He had not missed the green Kentish countryside. He talked with

South Nyanza – Homa Bay

his friends over dinner and a glass of wine and he drove his sister's old Morris car through the chestnut woods. As he drove through Tonbridge, he remembered a thousand and one memories of his boyhood and remembered friends he'd almost forgotten. The adventures of a young man thirty years ago occupied his mind and he thought about his Oxford days and the war. But sadly, things had changed.

It was raining steadily as he drove through the Kent countryside, row upon row of grim, dark looking houses and it was cold; there was a strangeness about his homecoming. He wished to be transported back to Kenya, to his farm at Longleat. Looking out of the car window, he saw meadows and woods and great arterial roads. Buildings had spread through the countryside; everything had changed. When he fell sick with flu, he became very miserable and lonely.

The trip back to Africa was one of the worst journeys he experienced. There were lots of delays. Arriving at Nairobi, he found a telegram at the Nairobi Club. It was bad news: I was very sick with whooping cough. All colour and life faded from my Father's world; the bleak and stifling Nairobi Club room that he occupied looked empty and desolate. Still, the mind has great power of self-renewal and during the night hope of all being well returned. He looked forward to being with his family again and seeing his old settler friends, retired officer acquaintances from Friday nights at the Kitale Club or the Kitale Hotel.

Whooping cough is a terrible illness. I had been exposed to other children who had the illness. It started like a cold, with fever and a runny nose. After two weeks, we thought it would go away but the cough got worse and I began to cough rapidly many times without taking a breath, and bring up plugs of sticky mucus. I felt the air rush back into my lungs with a loud whoop. Many times my lips and nails turned blue because of lack of air, especially at night.

Chapter Eight

I vomited a lot and did not get well; I kept on getting fits of whooping cough until my father arrived from Nairobi. Then I was taken to our family doctor, Irene Leach, at Kitale Hospital, a whites-only hospital for the settlers.

I got a serious fungal scalp infection that spread all over my head, forming large swollen patches with pus. My mother's hygiene levels were very low and she did not supervise our daily bathing. I must have got infected when I went out to play with the labourers' children who hardly ever bathed. My mother took me to the mission hospital across the road but the sores didn't improve because the swollen patches had to be treated with warm water twice daily. It was important to pull out all the hair that grew in the infected parts and use Griseofulvin on those areas.

I was a victim of roundworms, hookworms and tapeworms because of uncleanliness, especially when my father left us to go to Lamu for work. Mother went out drinking and stayed out late and Safia and I suffered lapses in our personal hygiene. The cook had left us because he had to cook for our father at Lamu.

My father loved books; he continued to read voraciously. He seemed lost in his books, probably because he lived for too long in the Sudan during the early 1940s to the 1950s. He belonged to that small group of Englishmen and women who were born with something lacking in their lives – a hunger and nostalgia that can be satisfied only in exotic places like Africa. Whatever the reason, whether it was a natural revulsion for the narrow horizons and the wet and cloudy climate of England, or the Victorian code of manners there, my father was more at peace in Africa. He returned to Kenya again and again like a migratory bird; he was never at peace when he was away, yet never able to stay for long without succumbing to an overwhelming restlessness.

My mother was given tickets to travel by train to Lamu to visit my father. Mother had done this journey before, so she knew ex-

South Nyanza – Homa Bay

actly what to take with her, but this time she had two children in her care. She decided to ask her brother, who could hardly speak Kiswahili, to accompany her as she knew she might have to stay for a long time in Lamu and she needed her relatives with her.

My mother's brother did not come by himself; he had to bring his wife, Chepsiror. He dressed up in Pokot gear, cow dung stuck on with an ostrich feather, which the Pokot put on their shaved heads, and he carried his stool and a spear. His wife borrowed a couple of dresses from my mother so she did not look too traditional. My mother travelled second class while her brother and his wife travelled third class, which was a most uncomfortable way to travel for two nights and two days. You had a seat but nowhere to sleep.

This time, when we arrived at Mombasa, Father was there to pick us up. He complained to my mother that she had brought her native relatives along with her and said that the Lamu climate would be too hot for them, but she said she would make use of her brother as a watchman.

We did not stay at Mombasa but drove to Malindi to stay with Father's friend, John Cullingford, who had a long beard like a Billy goat. He had a Nandi (one of the Kenyan tribes) wife and they could not have children. They tried to persuade Father to let them adopt me as their child. My mother never understood the word adoption; she always termed it as selling me. My father's friend was very well off and owned flats near Lawford's Hotel, which was established in 1934 by Leo Lawford, a retired district officer. Near here are mosques; the main one, Juma'a, is a mosque that stands where slaves were auctioned off each week until 1873.

It was the end of February when we arrived and the end of many classic international fishing contests. These were events where deep-sea sport anglers flew in to joust with the giants of the deep. Malindi was not crowded with tourists as it is normally from June through September, when the Indian Ocean swells over the

Chapter Eight

broken reef making good surfing possible. The seasonal monsoon sweeps in magnificent rollers.

The next day, John's wife took me out for a long walk on the sandy beach. She wore a swimsuit and a white cloth round her waist. I think she liked me very much. As we walked, the sun was getting high and the tide was out, so we could walk into the coral. By bad luck, I trod on a coral snake. It gave a convulsive wriggle and I jumped; the snake chirred off through the low water. Most of the legends I have heard about bites from these reptiles are greatly exaggerated but the bite is not pleasant and I felt shaken. These snakes are seen on the reef; their little heads look like mice peeping from holes in the coral.

The tide was still out when we walked seawards. I had put on rubber shoes for protection against sharp coral stones. I was picking up strange shells and starfish. We could see Swahili fishermen wandering along to sell their fish, wearing only loincloths round their waists and turbans round their heads. Some of their fish were tasty; Mother loved fish and she used lots of pilipili (red pepper). She got this habit from the Arab woman at Lamu.

Native legend has it that the following rite occurs every day in the Goan hotels and boarding homes. The first Goan arrives; he sticks his head into the kitchen and asks how many *pilipili* (red pepper) are in the soup.

'Ten,' says the cook.

'Put in ten more,' says the hungry Goan.

The next Goan arrives and repeats the performance by a further ten *pilipili* and it goes on until the soup nearly bursts into flames with its heat. And that is why *pilipili hoho* is the Swahili name for the Goan.

If Mother wanted to make the *mpishi* (cook) smile, she would ask him, '*Pilipili ngapi ndani ya supu*' (How many red pepper in the soup?).

South Nyanza – Homa Bay

His answer would be, '*Kumi tuu.*'('Ten only.')

The next day, while being driven by Father's friend, we saw lots of young Muslim boys all in white *kanzu* (Arab gowns). My father's friend had to drive very slowly to avoid the large crowd of boys. This was an interesting Mohammedan custom, which normally takes place at the coast, called Hitima ya Mji (the prayer for the sick). When there is sickness, the local inhabitants gather all the children at various burial places of good and famous men and they go in little bands, each one with a book of prayer from the Koran. The praying youngsters cross the town and in the afternoon the ceremony ends with feasts at their mosques. Men with baskets patrol the town all morning and the faithful contribute loaves, while the rich send along some cattle. Everything must be cooked that day and eaten at the feast. The old custom ends with prayers for the sick and the poor have a tuck in, free of charge.

The next afternoon we were taken by surprise by a warm wind that first waltzed with the Kusi (which blows from the south). From a point inland it began to move quickly and became very destructive. My mother and her relatives had never experienced this and it frightened them. Luckily for us, we lived a few blocks away from the ocean so we were not directly in its path.

It started with a few branches being broken off mango trees then its fury increased. The track of devastation was a hundred yards wide and coconut palms were laid flat as if by a steamroller. More than forty mango trees were destroyed. Above the pandemonium was a roar I can still hear but cannot describe. The sky seemed to be filled with debris. Later on, Father narrated the whole event; he and his friend were near the beach and witnessed the tornado strike the water. There was an outsize waterspout that reached 200 feet, before it broke and levelled out. Luckily there were no people out in canoes; they had all paddled furiously to safety. Despite considerable material damage, not a life was lost and there were no injuries.

Chapter Eight

After the storm, Father decided to travel to Lamu. Malindi was not an attractive place to stay since the damage of the tornado was devastating. Plants, trees and rooftops had been blown off. Most people were busy repairing their places and they looked very gloomy and sad.

The road was very bumpy. Lamu is close to the Somali border and it took us eight and a half hours to drive there. Father was driving at twenty to thirty kilometres an hour to avoid holes and stones in the road. We came to the Tana River; there was no bridge, only a large wooden raft attached to a rope strung across the river. We had to get out of the Land Rover and Father eased the vehicle onto the raft. Some natives were always there to help for a few shillings. Everybody piled on the raft. Positioned near the rope, the Land Rover lurched forward a foot or two and the natives hauled the rope hand over hand to get the raft across the river. By the time we arrived at Makowe, everyone was exhausted, boats were there to take us across, and vehicles were left behind.

At Lamu the donkeys were ready to take our luggage and any of us who were willing to ride them. My mother and her native relatives did not ride to our father's house. The donkey is the only means of transportation and there are many of them. Besides transporting food and building material, they act as ambulances to transport the sick to hospital and many times they are used for weddings.

As we went across, we saw a few villages dotted around Lamu nestled against high sand dunes. There were tracts of mangrove forest then we trotted along stretches of golden beach. In the narrow streets were men in *kikois* or simple *jelabeyas* (Arab dressing), and women in *buibui*. Although I had seen all this before, this time they looked different because I had grown up and understood the Muslim people and their culture better than before.

Here daily life is totally rooted in tradition. Islam is practiced

South Nyanza – Homa Bay

peacefully with the five calls of the *muezzin* to prayer. They are the basis of all the other sounds that form the music of the island, in harmony with the crashing waves and the wind rustling through palm trees, the occasional donkey braying, the sing-song birds and the melody of *jambo* and *salaams* sung out by human voices. At various festivals and holidays that mark the Lamu calendar, a different energy fills the streets as natives throw themselves wholeheartedly into cooking, singing, dancing, poetry recitals, dhow or donkey racing.

The next morning, my mother's brother, Yokunyan, was given a different house to occupy. It was two hundred metres from my father's house, so every morning his wife came to take her ration of food. Eventually my father gave Arap Yokunyan a job as a watchman.

After a month, his wife came to our house to complain that Yokunyan was missing most of the daytime and did not come to rest as he was on watch from six o'clock in the evening to six o'clock in the morning. After two months, Yokunyan was completely changed in his behaviour. His wife complained and threatened to go back to Kapenguria. Later we heard that he had become a Muslim and taken a new Swahili wife by the name Khadija. We tried to make him change his mind, told him that the wife he had was good enough, that he had two more wives back at home in Kapenguria and that he was too old to take another young wife. He came to my father and asked for money to pay Khadija's bride price. What good would come out of this marriage? My mother told him that he had lost his judgement; the new bride was from a poor family and her family did not demand a wedding feast. Giving away their daughter to get some money was good enough for them.

Khadija had no grace or gaiety in her like the other Swahili girls. Yokunyan's other wife remained in the background and sulked; she continued to complain and wanted a ticket to go back home, while

Chapter Eight

her husband Yokunyan's face was radiant with triumph and full of joy. My mother complained that the new marriage would not last.

One morning, my mother sent Arap Yogonyang to buy fish from the fisher boys who were normally on the beach. I accompanied him and we walked towards one fisher boy who had dived from his canoe and heaved up his basket. He pulled the fish from the trap and they spilled out into another of his baskets. Yogonyang bought a couple of fish at a good price and we walked back.

We came upon a sea anemone at the edge of the water. It looked like a flower of the sea. I was fascinated by it and I looked closer, bending over. In a fold of its flower, orange and turquoise fish darted to and fro. Yogonyang, finding the flower interesting, decided to run back some metres to fetch a spade and a big bucket. He came back and started to dig.

There was a little drizzle of rain and the flower closed up. It looked like a large crocus bulb, five inches across at the widest part. At the foot of the bulb were suckers. The little fish remained until the last moment and escaped just as we put the anemone into the large bucket.

Once ashore, we examined our find. Yogonyang fed it with some small fish. As soon as the fish touched the suckers, they were held fast. A mouth in the middle of the green 'flower' received the fish then inflated, drawing the fish in with the water. The water was then expelled.

We carried the bucket with the anemone inside it to show my father. As we arrived at the door of our house, Yogonyang became inquisitive and sniffed the anemone. As soon as his nose touched the suckers they held him. He drew his head back and the anemone came with it. With much huffing and puffing, the anemone released Yogonyang. He ran away and was not seen for the rest of the day.

Eventually I accompanied Father to take the anemone back to sea. The tide was still out, so we walked through the shallow water

South Nyanza – Homa Bay

and my father tipped over the bucket and the anemone slid back into the water. As soon as it touched the sea water, it propelled itself to the bottom.

My mother's brother, Yogonyangg, although he still had his native wife, Chepsiror, favoured Khadija, the Swahili wife. She was very clean and cooked delicious food. My mother complained to him that he should use his salary fairly and treat both women equally.

Before two months were over, Yogonyangg started behaving awkwardly. He asked my father for more money, saying it could be taken from his wages. He gave the money to an Arab man, who took him through a narrow alleyway late at night to a dark house. You could barely see the women inside this dark house.

There was a kerosene lamp in the middle of the room; Yogonyangg was told to select one lady. They all looked the same in their *buibuis*, with only a pair of eyes peering out of the black cloth. The *buibuis* had special lace and glittering beads, which covered the face. After Yogonyangg selected one lady, they were directed to a room next door. Yogonyangg was surprised when he entered and found carpets and hangings, brass and silver vessels, swords with ivory hilts and noble blades. This looked like a place for a wealthy person. The beds were hung with old glowing tapestries and embroideries.

The woman sat on the bed, dark-eyed, and looked straight into Yogonyangg's face. She did not speak a word. Yogonyangg stretched out his hands to feel her. At first, he thought he was imagining things so he asked the lady to undress in Kiswahili. There was no answer. Yogonyangg pulled her towards him and discovered that she was not a lady but a man! Yogonyangg quickly went back to get a refund of his money, but was told that was what he had paid for and women were not allowed in these quarters.

Chapter Nine

Longleat Farm

TICKETS WERE BOUGHT for Mother and her relatives to go back to West Pokot. Mother did not want to leave but it was necessary for her to escort her relatives. Yogonyang had created more problems than necessary. His Swahili wife Khadija was not allowed to accompany him; her parents objected, fearing Yogonyang would go back to his native religion and forget the Islamic faith. That would be against Islamic law and the marriage code. This did not go down well with Yogonyang and he nearly got into a fight with Khadija's parents. Eventually Father stepped in and calmed the situation; he persuaded Yogonyang that on his next visit, which would be soon, he would get back his wife and would be allowed to take her to West Pokot.

There was a small *duka* (shop) of corrugated iron near where we lived; this is where Mother bought the groceries and sometimes chatted to the old Arab owner. His name was Abdallah. I used to go to his little *duka* to buy sweets and fruits and *mahamri* (little sweet cakes). He was fond of me and my sister Safia. Abdallah objected to my mother and her relatives and me and Safia going to Mombasa by dhow, saying this was the season for the Kusi (the wind that blows from the south) and he was sure there would be a bad storm at sea. He asked my mother if he could have the tickets. Mother ran to the house, got the tickets and gave them to Abdallah. He hid

Longleat Farm

them and said no one was to board the *dhow* to Mombasa for it would sink at sea and everyone would perish.

Abdallah was very fond of Safia and me; he thought we were the loveliest children on the island. Father was furious to hear that Mother had lost the tickets; she invented the story of the tickets getting lost. That day, everybody was unhappy. Father called her all sorts of names, saying how useless she was.

The next day, which was the day we were to have sailed off in the dhow, a big wind hit the island. For two and half hours it roared in from the sea at gale force. The dense rain that accompanied it lashed through doors and windows and one could not see more than a couple of yards. Our dhow must have been caught in this storm beyond the reef. After a while the wind died a little; looking out to sea, the breakers were as big as my father had ever seen them, rolling and tumbling upon each other towards the shore and coming right inland.

The next day, news arrived that all who were on board the dhow to Mombasa had drowned when the dhow sank in the sea. The look on our father's and mother's faces was of horror and shock. Abdallah had saved our lives. When Father heard how Abdallah had kept the tickets, he was very grateful; he visited him and gave him a donkey-load of groceries to stock his little *duka* as a thank-you present.

We waited for one week for the Kusi wind, which is the south monsoon wind that brings the rain and takes the *dhows* back to the Persian Gulf, to calm down. The origin of the word Kusi dates back to ancient times when all lands south of Egypt were called 'Kush' or 'Kusu'. The Hebrews believed that descendants of Cush, the son of Ham, populated Ethiopia and beyond, so this old Biblical name is associated with the south wind of the East African coast. This time Father bought tickets for the bus that travelled to Malindi, then to Mombasa; Mother totally refused to board anoth-

Chapter Nine

er *dhow* to Mombasa.

We travelled by bus from Makowe and it was an hour's journey to Malindi. The journey was the worst nightmare come true; the bus was damp and old, the seats were uncomfortable. My mother, Safia and I got the worst seats, not by the window but the inner seats, so everything inside the bus smelled like rotten eggs. I threw up several times. I was given water to rinse my mouth but the vomit and spit were all over me. Looking back, I remember we were packed like sacks of maize and the bus was overloaded with other luggage as well.

In front of us, two seats ahead, there sat six Muslim women wrapped up in their *buibuis* so we could hardly see their faces, all chatting away in Kiswahili. When we reached a very muddy part, the bus swayed, slid and skidded from side to side. I heard shouts and the screeching of the brakes. There was a lot of rain; the bus driver complained about the wipers not working properly and his vision of the road being blurred.

We were en route to Kismayu – the border of Somali and Kenya near Garissa. The people who lived here were the Bajun and others who called themselves the Kapra people. The soil was red, and red soil turns into sticky mud during the rainy season. This was a very frightening journey and the Swahili women kept screaming whenever the bus went off balance. After half an hour of skidding and driving through deep puddles of water, the bus rolled over to one side in slow motion. It came to a standstill on its four wheels. Glass was everywhere as all the windows had smashed. People were hurt and most of them had cuts. My little sister's left hand was cut and bleeding badly at the wrist and her elbow was dislocated. Mother's left hand was cut by the window glass. Luckily, a doctor happened to be travelling with us and he started to bandage the wounded using every piece of clothing he could get. Everybody worked together.

Longleat Farm

My mother could not find me in the confusion and she shouted out my name loudly. I was nowhere in the bus. The bus conductor tried to step out of the bus but the door was badly damaged and jammed as the hinges could not rotate properly. Three men helped push the door outwards and it swung open. My mother, still holding Safia's hand, rushed out with the conductor still shouting my name. She was very afraid. Then suddenly she heard my voice from the other side of the bus calling her name loudly and crying. She ran towards me with a man and they picked me up. While the bus was skidding and turning from side to side, I had been thrown out of the open window from where I was sitting. Luckily the bus did not squash me and I had no cuts or bruises. My guardian angel must have looked after me.

It was getting dark and the driver told us that he did not know the extent of damage to his bus. This was especially true of the wiring, so he would not risk travelling in the dark without the bus headlights in case we came across a herd of elephants or buffalos or other animals. The women and children were ordered to stay in the bus while the men had to go out and gather wood from the thorn bushes to build a big fire to keep the wild animals away and to keep everyone warm till morning.

That night everyone was sad. One or two people tried to tell a tale of strange happenings in Somaliland or some made-up tale about the Arabian Nights. The stories were not pleasant to hear, especially this far from civilization; they were about the sea-faring nation of Somalia and how the Somalis were believed to have been great pirates of the Red Sea in the olden days. Someone in the dark shouted to the others to shut up as no one wanted to hear such stories.

When a full moon came up, everyone sat round the fire. The stars came up from the east and the smoke from the fire in the cold air carried long sparks with it; the fresh firewood smelled

Chapter Nine

sour. Some of us were hungry as we had only eaten snacks and drank some water on the journey. I was close to my mother and we squeezed together to keep warm.

Although hyenas are harmless when they are not grouped together, some came close to the camp. Then the fearsome howling began and we small children were very afraid. The hyenas stayed until three o'clock, and then moved off before sunrise.

We were all up and the fire was put out. After a quick inspection of the bus, we started our journey to Malindi. Just as we were pulling out, we saw a family of giraffes walking gracefully with their long-stemmed speckled necks slowly moving ahead. As the bus progressed we saw two rhinos in the distance on their morning promenade, sniffing and snorting in the cold dawn air. We had to pass them and were glad to put distance between them and us, as rhinos are very unpredictable animals and they could have charged at the bus.

I could hear the groans and moans of the passengers and children as some people, especially the children my age, complained about their wounds. They hoped to arrive at Malindi to be treated properly with painkillers and other medicine.

At one time we heard an aeroplane fly over at about twelve thousand feet, then it flew low over the bus in the opposite direction of our travel. In a little while it must have turned because it flew back over our heads; probably a telegram had reached Malindi from Lamu and our absence was noticed, so the aeroplane was scouting for us to make sure all was well.

The morning was bright and cloudless. The road improved as we neared Malindi. We arrived at around eleven o'clock, all very tired and some in terrible pain. Safia, my sister, kept crying all the way. Doctors were ready to receive us and treat the wounded. My mother and sister were treated and Safia had to stay in hospital for one week.

Longleat Farm

My father's friend, John Cullingford, and his wife were there to meet us and take us to their house until we were ready to continue our journey to Kitale. Safia's cut was very serious and she lost her appetite; her body hurt everywhere from fever. We hoped she had not got malaria.

My mother's brother, Yogonyang, and his wife never said a word all this time. They seemed to be in shock. After a week, we took another bus to Mombasa then travelled back to Kitale by train. The journey was miserable; I knew I would never go back to Lamu again. This was because there was great political change in Kenya and Father would soon come back to Kitale to live with us. He had to make up his mind if he was to leave Kenya or stay and take on a job in the new Republic of Kenya. He came after six months and he looked very depressed. I overheard him telling my mother that his partners in the Longleat farm were no longer interested in it. Word was going round that Kenya would not be under the protection of the colony protectorate and life could be very difficult for those who remained. The farm was not doing well and could not pay, so it had to be sold. Father did not want to give up his land but he did not have enough money to buy out his two partners. The other two partners left Father to deal with winding down the farm.

My father left Lamu to take charge. The truth dawned on us that the farm no longer belonged to our father. This was the place I had loved as a child; I hoped that things would change and we would get the land back if Father could buy out his two partners. That was wishful thinking. The truth was that the farm was no longer our father's and we would have to leave soon.

Every place on this farm where I had played, walked or danced, which had been part of me, changed. Everything disengaged itself from me; I stood back and saw it clearly and as a result I saw things differently.

The labourers were not friendly because they thought that my

Chapter Nine

father was the reason for them having to leave and find new settlements elsewhere. I felt their hostility towards us; their children would not play with me. They avoided me. Everybody was conscious of the situation and every morning a group of older people sat round my father's house from early morning till nightfall. Their village leader had a group following him around like a flock of sheep. They came every day until my mother talked to them in their Pokot language and explained that they must go back to the Pokot reserve. They needed to find some unoccupied land and take their families, cows, goats and sheep along with them, as there was no place for them here. These people had been on the farm for many years. Some had been born here and knew nowhere else; the idea of moving scared them as they were used to clinging together. Some decided to move back into the reserve area, back to their great-grandfather's homeland in the Cherangani Hills in West Pokot.

My father packed his books and gramophone, his furniture and all his silver utensils – knives and forks, spoons, kettle. They were part of his inheritance from his great-grandfather and his grandmother Sewell Robinson, which had been in the family for many years. His books were very special to him. Books in the colony play a different part in one's existence than they do in Europe; they become part of your life. Some of my father's books were written in Latin, Hebrew, Greek and Aramaic. He liked to read in these languages. Some books were about the Roman Empire, other books were on World War I, Winston Churchill and World War II. My father was grateful to have these books, more so than he would have been in a civilised country.

The English are very brave people and they came to Kenya to live and farm and make it their home. They took their place as one of the Crown's self-governing dominions beyond the seas. But at first the immigrants had to prove their worth as tillers of the soil.

Longleat Farm

Kenya was being occupied by landed gentry who would serve the Empire by serving the country.

The Empire started with difficulties; the settlers encountered problems as they did not make the profits they had expected. They used their imagination, cleared the bush, created wheat fields and bred cows and bulls. To live in Kenya and see the Rift Valley, the cloud shadows along that valley, the jagged white summit of Mount Kenya, the wind blowing through Leleshwa, gave them a feeling of liberty and their dream was to turn the virgin soil into their new home. Most liked the African experience better than home. Here they had a beautiful veranda and outside there was a guest house and a pit latrine built with seats to sit on.

My father was never happy about political change in Kenya and independence came much earlier than expected. He had not planned to stay and take a job after Kenya gained its independence. He realised that politics in Kenya had gradually changed and the native communities had come together strongly to make their demands. The British government supported the idea of handing back the land, as they thought the interests of the African tribes must be paramount. Kenya, after all, was in the African continent.

There was a rift between the Africans and the Europeans and it continued, especially after World War II. Veterans returning home had been exposed to new influences. Strikes started everywhere; the police tried to suppress them but things got out of hand. The Kikuyu formed secret societies and members were sworn in through ancient, traditional oath ceremonies; they were called the 'Mau Mau' (a war-like secret underground movement). They took to the forests to begin the war against the government and settlers.

Around 1949, warning letters circulated and settlers wrote to the governor of Kenya about the Mau Mau who wanted to frustrate the government. There were outbreaks of violence against the Europeans but no action was taken. Every day went on as usual,

Chapter Nine

despite families who lived far from the protection of the government being harassed.

Our father was very disturbed and he too wrote warning letters to point out that these secret societies had been left to continue, frustrating both government and settlers for too long, and would get out of hand. Mistreatment of black people happened on some farms but the whites were not anti-black, and these settlers did not dislike Africans. There was a fear that the natives could revolt against the government and settlers but the masters played their role of stern but benevolent way. There was a rigid code of justice in race relations between black and black, or white and black. Delamere, as one the first settlers, upheld the law strictly.

Delamere exercised great power but he also looked after his labourers and fed them well and gave them blankets. Other settlers did the same; wages were paid on time and advances were given before the end of the week. Medical care and homes were built. When the doctors were not available the *memsahib* (the white-settler's wife), most of whom had rapidly become skilled midwives by attending a multitude of African births, was available. Holidays were granted to the natives including at harvest time or for *ngoma* festivals, which occurred on a monthly basis. All this had taken place for seventy years and more in Kenya. This generated a robust climate of feudal good feeling which seemed to suit the natives as much as it did the Caucasians.

It was too early in history for most Africans to think of themselves as victims of discrimination. For instance, among my mother's native tribe, physical abuse existed in their societies, especially from the superiors of their race. Wealthier ones, who owned many cattle, many women and children, had not yet acquired Western education to know how to work the modern ploughs, or opened their eyes to a new set of values. The African farm workers were happy and had little cause for complaint.

Longleat Farm

Changes came about at the turn of the century. Things changed rapidly between the fifties and sixties but still a happy relationship existed between Father and his African workers. During visits to their settlement, my father would walk through a narrow entrance to the group around the huts, raise his hand and exclaim, '*Jambo!*'(Good morning).

The greeting was returned, '*Jambo, bwana.*' (Good morning, boss). A child would bring a stool to the centre of the clearing and invite my father to sit; all the children came out to see him, smiling and touching him, especially his hair and legs, to see if he was real.

The chief came to the circle of huts. Another man followed him carrying a newborn lamb, and they were followed by its bleating mother. The chief walked to where my father sat. Father stood up then stretched out his hand in a token of good fellowship, and greetings were exchanged. The chief sat on a chair which seemed to be placed there specially for him. A calabash of milk was brought out and was offered to all of us. I drank and Father drank some too, but sparingly.

When, after a long conversation, my father stood to leave, the chief would spit on his hand. Father spat on his hand too and they shook hands to show trust and respect for one another. My conclusion is that only very few whites bore grudges against Kenyan Africans.

On the other hand, the British colonists in East Africa had to cope with the Indian immigrants. They called themselves Ramji, Punjabs, Shah and Patels. They came out to Kenya in large numbers in search of work and a new life. Most settlers accepted the Indians and together they lived in harmony.

The Indians quickly started businesses to control the economy. A fairly large percentage of the Indians in Kenya, about seven thousand or more, had come in as coolies to build the railway and chosen to remain in the protectorate. They continued to work to

Chapter Nine

finish off the railway but others became clerks, masons, cabinet makers, cobblers, and tailors. A small group joined professions as physicians, lawyers and bankers. Others became what were called *duka wallahs,* operating tiny shops which sprang like mushrooms across the country. They sold every imaginable article of cheap merchandise, from blankets to cigarettes and matches.

Farming in East Africa was difficult for the early settlers. I crept down one night, hid behind the cupboard and overheard my father and two of his friends talking about the old times when the settlers first came to farm in Africa. It was very late at night and I could not sleep. I heard them very clearly and, although my spoken English was not too good, I understood what they were talking about. Early settlers had left their homeland and come out to lease land from the Crown. Recruitment of farm labourers was difficult, since the native men never worked and women were expected to cultivate the *shambas* (land) or do the housework around their *bomas*. The men did not value being paid but some came to work if they were offered goats, sheep or cows in exchange for labour. Other labourers agreed to rent land from Europeans and their rent was deducted from their wages. Most of these natives were unreliable; some just walked out on the jobs whenever they felt like it.

The yield of the farm produce depended very much on the country's perverse meteorology. The most worrisome time was in March, when the six-week rains never came on time or came late. There was either a meagre crop or, if the rains came too early, they washed away the investment.

There were innumerable parasites that waged relentless and deadly warfare against the farmers, like locusts that could erase a coffee plantation in a year. Potatoes were attacked by beetles and ended up with blight. Poultry died of diseases as vaccines had not yet been invented. Apart from other misfortunes, livestock died of east-coast fever and other diseases; the farms were fenced, but this

Longleat Farm

did not stop wild game coming in and contaminating them. Termites ate the posts, so fences would fall down, and there were regular night attacks on the livestock. The law was that a settler could shoot no more than four antelopes a month; lions were killed by sportsmen, not the farmers unless they were caught in a livestock *boma*. Local natives stole their boss's livestock and the native herdsmen and chiefs would not surrender the culprits.

The early pioneers encountered many problems; it's a wonder their farms did not revert to bush or their livestock did not vanish entirely. There was no market from which to sell their products, although some produce was brought down by railway to Mombasa to be exported to other marketplaces. Trains running back empty from Mombasa were uneconomical and the long waits meant that most vegetables went rotten. Only a few farmers got government food contracts. The land was one of the most productive in the world but having no market for what they grew was a problem. Most sold out; others kept their heads above water to pay back loans or persuaded the lender to extend the loans.

So the Mau Mau uprising was based on the mistaken idea that the settlers had stolen their land. The Mau Mau broke the law for no reason; they wanted to get rid of the settlers and take their hard work, knowledge and investment that the settlers had put into their farms.

During Mau Mau time, the Kikuyu (one of Kenyan tribes) defied the government in a manner uncongenial to peaceful negotiations. African policemen were murdered and their bodies mutilated and they challenged the administration to do something about it. Paths leading to the Mau Mau villages were riddled with hidden pitfalls where warriors placed sharp wooden stakes on which to impale unwary government police. Tribesmen ambushed an invading Askari (policeman) with the silent swiftness of a cobra striking, and they used spears and poisoned arrows. Camping out at night,

Chapter Nine

officers normally encircled the camp with thorn bushes or barbed wire but this sometimes proved useless. The Kikuyu warriors were able to advance under blizzards of rifle fire and dig on the perimeters of the camping places. This was done to break down government defence lines and to move the Mau Mau warriors forward.

A wounded government soldier, if not rescued by his comrades, would be speared or clubbed to death. The Mau Mau, who comprised of Kikuyu, treated their prisoners in a horrific way. If a settler was caught, they dragged them to their villages in the forest where they pegged them down and wedged their mouths open, then the whole village – men, women and children included – would urinate into their mouths until the settler drowned. This often happened far from the nearest police post, so rescue was not prompt.

On the other hand, the Nandi also stole livestock and used poisoned arrows. They took every opportunity to express their contempt for local officialdom and its laws. It was not surprising to hear stories that some Nandi had chopped off the government clerks' heads when they approached villages to ask for what was then called the 'hut tax'. They returned sacks with the clerks' heads inside as a message that this was the tax that was being returned. The Nandi grew more daring as the years went by. Murder and cattle raiding were reported in every part of their territory.

The Kikuyu hid in the forest to train in guerrilla warfare. The government called the elders to *baraza* (big meetings) but the elders complained that they could not hold back the younger hotheads in their tribes who were clamouring for war. The *laibon* (chief medicine man) preached war against the white government. Exchanges of rifle fire and poisoned arrows became commonplace but the people that suffered most were the settlers. The warriors laid ambush to their farms and homes and hails of poisoned arrows killed many settlers and their families as they tried to escape. Poisoned arrows are very deadly; if they pierce the flesh, it takes ten minutes for

Longleat Farm

the body to turn blue. If the poison is not sucked out one can die.

The Kenyans started to call the settlers land-grabbers; they thought that they had been betrayed but they forgot that the Maasai chiefs had welcomed the colonial government to protect them against slave caravans. This was a trade that used to thrive along the East African Coast. Now, some years later, some Kenyans were educated to govern their country. They could have waited for the settlers' leases to expire and taken back their land. They did not recognise that the settlers had been encouraged to come and farm in the first place. The Government taxed their farms and got revenue to govern and run the country.

In the beginning very few settlers moved to East Africa, particularly the Kenyan highlands, due to the climate. Although it was obvious that wheat, corn and barley grew well in the highlands, the European capacity for survival in an equatorial region was limited because of disease and the climate. Also, when products were ready to be shipped to Europe, freight charges were high; that was another problem faced by livestock breeders. So, these settlers must have taken great risks to migrate to East Africa. The settlers encountered problems and in the first few years made no profit because of crop failure, drought, locusts and pests. A few farming materials were shipped in but these had to be taken by rail to Nairobi and finally taken by oxen to the farms.

As time went by, farming improved and exports from the highlands helped bolster the British free-trade policies and reinforced the empire's position in the world produce market.

From 1914 to 1931, one of the country's larger coffee estates was run by the Danish baroness, Karen Blixen, better known by her pen name Isaak Dinesen. She wrote the book *Out of Africa*. The collapse of the coffee market forced her to sell her farm and move back to her home in Denmark in 1931.

Lord Delamere was successful after many failures in farming

Chapter Nine

and in cattle breeding and he sowed the seed for Kenya's farm industry. Other settlers came from humble beginnings and they were soon accepted as equals among the farming elite; taming the wilderness left little time for snobbery. The settlers were big men physically and they had enough training with guns and tools and how to handle animals, but not many were intellectuals. However, they managed more than five thousand acres of land. When Kenya attained independence, an epoch in the history of the colony came to an end. Some settlers stayed behind to continue farming their land; others left. As years went by, this was seen as a turning point. Kenya had been a great hunting ground and everything changed as a lot of settlers moved out of the country. Some standards were lowered – including the standard of gallantry.

Chapter Ten

Siyoi Farm in West Pokot District

My mother soon got tired of living on my father's thirty acres on the outskirts of Kitale town. My father had made the place very comfortable for us. Our house was built out of corrugated iron sheets and painted red; it looked like an English country house with red-brick walls. It was well-plastered inside, with huge glass windows overlooking a terraced lawn and a formal garden. Inside was a room where my father kept his piano. There were oil paintings, leopard hides and zebra skins on the walls. We had Persian carpets and the place was very beautiful. Father told me that from 1900 to the 1940s, rifles were hung on the walls opposite the fireplace but the laws kept changing and rifles were now kept in store rooms under lock and key.

We had fifteen milking cows and the milk was taken to Kenya Co-operative Creameries Kitale Depot using a cart with two mules. There were two acres with trees and a beautiful spring that fed into the stream that flowed to a swamp at the bottom of our land. There was thick vegetation and the swamp was at times very muddy and marshy. This was a refuge for animals – the eland antelope, sitatunga, crayfish, tortoises, tadpoles, birds of all species, reptiles and fish. Herons, cranes and guinea fowl used the marsh as a feeding place and sometimes to breed.

Mother was not happy here but I was very happy. Mother prob-

Chapter Ten

ably missed her people and their customs, especially the *ngoma* (native festivals for circumcision) and the Pokot tribal ritual of dancing before a wedding takes place. She missed being with other women of her age to see the Pokot girls and boys dancing together during the initiation ceremony when more than a hundred girls passed into womanhood.

Eventually Father got so tired of Mother's complaints that he bought her 116 acres of land at Kapenguria–Siyoi district. It had pyrethrum and coffee trees growing on it, planted by the previous owner. Father built a small house for her, and bought seven milk cows to start her in dairy production. The farm was high up on the slopes of Cherangani Hills. Father was keen at first to concentrate on growing more coffee trees and expanding on what he found there, but coffee is a long-term project; it takes five years to bear fruit and needs a lot of investment.

Father decided that coffee did well here, and about fifty acres of land was prepared for young coffee plants which were bought from the agricultural centre at Kapenguria. My father hired an old tractor that had a trailer and could carry many of the young coffee plants right up to the farm. It took several days to haul them up before the rainy season. He placed them under a temporary shade that he had built. Holes were dug and farm labourers carried the young coffee plants to set them in regular rows in the wet ground where they were to grow. They were shaded against the sun using branches from the bushes.

Luckily for us Siyoi West Pokot never gets drought, but there is disease and the bold native weeds can grow and choke the coffee trees. Between the trees two oxen dragged the cultivators up and down the fields to keep down the weeds. Each year these coffee trees grow higher. After four or five years, the fields look beautiful as these coffee trees flower at the start of the rains. It is a beautiful sight, like snow in the mist. Then, after months in the drizzling

Siyoi Farm in West Pokot District

rain, the coffee berries ripen as they turn red. Children, women and older men pick the coffee. We used carts pulled by donkeys to take the coffee beans to the store near the house where women and children graded them. Sacks were sewn up with a saddler's needle, and a day or two later the coffee was taken on carts pulled by several donkeys to Kapenguria coffee-processing factory where it was weighed and sold.

When pyrethrum is ready, the flowers look like a common daisy; they were harvested, taken to the factory in Kapenguria and processed to produce pyrethrum extract. When Father had to go to Nairobi to extend his visa or get a work permit, he didn't want to worry about the farm – but in his absence everything went wrong. The cows got east-coast fever; luckily there was a veterinary officer who was my father's friend. He checked on our cows to see if they were in good health and made sure my mother's head workman dipped the cows regularly once a week.

My mother started to go to the Makutano Bar, not far from Kapenguria, and some nights she did not come home. Life became hard, especially when Father had to go on weekdays to teach at Ole Kajiado, a secondary school. When he came back, we were lonely and underfed. One time, he told me he would spend more time with us as it was the school holidays. I was happy to have him at the farm for a month.

Mother stopped drinking and she also stayed to look after us. Our half-brother, Rotich, came to live with us; he was a very dirty, rude boy and would not go to school despite warnings from my father. Father tried to get him in a primary school but Rotich never went. He used to go into the coffee plantation and not return until evening; he was out with much older boys and they had a habit of meeting at the big river down the valley where the forest was. We were warned not to go to this river because all sorts of snakes had been seen there. Mother's brother, Yogonyang, once visited our

Chapter Ten

farm and, while bathing naked at the river, came across a giant python. Luckily, he ran back home to report it and told my mother not to let us children go down to this particular river, which curved round the bottom of our farm.

One morning, Rotich went bathing with some boys to this river without informing anyone of his whereabouts. The water was deep in some places and the heavy March rains had transformed it into torrents. In a hunt for food, a python followed the swollen tributary of black mud on either side of the riverbank. It glided to a spot where its massive body was barely visible in the murky shallows. It slowly lifted its large head so its eyes and nostrils just broke the surface of the water, and waited.

It had rained very heavily for three days and most people had stayed indoors; the sun had finally broken through and the air was hot and muggy. Rotich decided to get the other boys to go for a swim in the river. He ran shirtless and barefoot through the fields with our two dogs, Scooby and Simba. Unfortunately, he only found one of his friends, Thomas; he was eleven years old while Rotich was ten years old.

Rotich and Thomas ran along a narrow path to the river. Rotich was far ahead of his friend down the muddy trail leading to the spot where they loved to swim. Scooby was at his heels. Both Rotich and Scooby loved to play; their favourite game was diving for rocks. This particular day I also came running down to see them swim. I never liked the river water. Sometimes, after the rainy season, the flow was too rough and I was scared that I would be carried away and drown.

I watched from a distance. Scooby and Simba sat beside me and I stroked their fur. Rotich seemed to be racing in and out of the river. He saw what looked like a log floating a couple of metres away. He did not see the glistening eyes that locked on him. The python patiently tracked Rotich's movement. Its flickering tongue picked up his scent – a prelude to its strike.

Thomas stopped running and walked slowly, still at a distance. This python was very large and it had a huge appetite. Pythons devour what they can swallow – sheep, dogs, small antelopes.

Slowly, the snake cocked its neck into an S-shape and, with blinding speed, shot its head out of the water. Rotich reflexively dodged the long dark shape that was coming at him. The snake's mouth glanced off his right shoulder but, as Rotich tried to run, the python reared back and struck again. Its jaws were wide open and it sank its teeth into Rotich's right side. Pythons are not venomous but they have needle-sharp teeth that curve backwards to hold their struggling victims.

The snake slid its powerful body out of the water and in seconds wrapped its muscular coils around Rotich, from his toes to his head. At that moment I arrived at the ridge overlooking the river. I saw the last few seconds of the attack and ran back uphill screaming, Thomas ran behind me and the dogs barked furiously.

By the time I got to the house, I was breathless. Father heard me shout that a snake had got Rotich. Immediately he grabbed a knife from the kitchen and ran downhill. We were all scared the python would swallow Rotich.

Arriving at the edge of the big river, we saw a huge knot of a green-and-black speckled snake writhing and squirming around its victim. Father grabbed the wet, shiny coils and frantically pulled. He could see the top of Rotich's head, then his head as it popped up, then his eyes filled with terror. And then something horrible happened: Rotich's face turned very dark. The snake's tail was jammed in Rotich's mouth and he started to suffocate.

The snake's powerful body knocked Father into a half-sitting position with his arms pressed to his sides. Father managed to yank the python's tail and Rotich was able to breathe. He gasped and I cried out that he was dying.

Chapter Ten

Father had to act very fast. The deadly python could kill by squeezing tight to stop Rotich breathing, or it could drag him under water to drown him. Death can come in minutes. Father fought the twisting, muscular serpent and pulled the snake from the boy's shoulders. What he saw gave him his next shock; clamped to Rotich's side, just below his armpit, was the python's head and it seemed to be glaring right into my father's eyes.

Father grabbed the snake just below its head and it snapped open its mouth. Father picked up some stones, shoved them down the snake's throat and it swallowed them. Father gripped the two halves of the python's jaws and pulled them apart but still the snake would not let go. Its lower jaw dug deeper into Rotich's side.

My mother and Uncle Yogonyang had run down the hill towards the river. Mother had a big knife, which looked more like a machete, and was screaming at Father to save Rotich. Father picked up a rock twice the size of his fist and, using all his strength, brought it down on the snake's head, hoping to loosen the snake's grip.

Rotich screamed, '*Na kufa!*' ('I am dying'). My mother's machete was from my father's toolbox; it was a small *panga* (machete) that was used to prune the flowers and fences around the house. The wooden handle was broken and the blade was blunt and rusty.

Father wrestled with the python. As soon as he pulled it partly away from Rotich, the snake bent into a muscular knot and tried to twist out of his hand. It was as flexible as a rope and it was fighting to keep its prey.

Father had pulled one and a half metres of the snake off Rotich when he realised it was trying to wind itself around *him*. He grabbed the snake's body and sat on it as the struggle continued, but the fight was taking all his strength and the snake was still wrapped around Rotich from his waist to his feet with its jaws clamped fast to his side.

Siyoi Farm in West Pokot District

Father shouted at Yogonyang to help and sit on the part of the snake that had come away from Rotich's body but Africans are scared of snakes. Mother handed a machete knife to Father as he must have dropped the kitchen knife in the fight. She was still panting from the run downhill to the river. Father grabbed the knife and swung it at the python but the heavy blade bounced off harmlessly. He kept hitting it again and again, until the loose nails in the knife's handle tore open his right hand – but he was able to make a cut through the snake's body.

For a moment, the snake relaxed its grip and then it tightened it again. Two more cuts seemed to have no effect. My father grabbed the snake's head in his left hand and, using the knife, smacked its skull between its nose and its eyes. He hacked away in a frenzy and cut into his own hands. The blows shattered the snake's upper jaw and it went slack. The suffocation and compression eased. Rotich pushed the coils of the snake off his body, crawled up the steep slopes of the riverbank and stumbled towards the hillside with blood streaming out of his right side.

Although he was frightened to death, Yogonyang was a great help to Father who was still locked in a deadly dance with the angry snake. Holding the snake's head at arm's length with his left hand, he pounded the snake with his right hand using the knife. The huge serpent was furiously whipping and twisting its powerful tail, trying to ensnare my father. Yogonyang finally sat on the python's tail while Father went on hacking until he felt the python go slack in his hands. Relieved, he dropped the mortally wounded snake to the ground on the muddy bank of the river. The struggle had lasted thirty-five minutes.

My father walked uphill very wearily, Yogonyang at his heels, to find out if Rotich was okay. Mother had washed Rotich's wounds and Father had to take him to the hospital. It was a long drive; Kitale was far away and the road was rough. Thank God Rotich

Chapter Ten

only needed a few stitches to close the puncture wound and he only had marks on his neck and arms.

The trauma was too much for Rotich and he never seemed to recover from the shock. The story went round to watch out for pythons on riverbanks and no one went swimming in that part of the river again. Even the cows hardly ever went there to drink. Father bought a Lister engine and water pump and built cattle troughs to water the cows. There was no bathing in the river again and no butterfly adventures for me again; the forest was out of bounds for children of my age.

I was fascinated with nature and I had endless sources of distraction. I had my small collection of seashells and fossils that I kept in a small box. I had brought these little treasures from Lamu. I liked to go out each morning bird watching; I did not go deep into our forest down by the river, just on the outskirts, and I discovered a startling variety of butterflies. I started to collect them. My father noticed my interest so he bought me small glass-topped bottles. I ended up with several trays of glorious specimens, carefully labelled and mounted. They came in all sizes and hues, from deepest blues to brilliant yellow, scarlet and shimmering emerald green.

It is not easy to catch butterflies. There was one particularly big butterfly that I wanted to catch. Each morning I raced down the valley with my butterfly net. This big butterfly was orange and had white tips; its wings were huge and I was determined to have it. For a whole week I ran after it but it was clever and flew up beyond my reach. These pretty insects went deep in the forest and I could only go to the edge and watch them float gracefully above the trees. I tried to climb up to reach them, encumbered by my net and collection jars, but they were always beyond my reach like white and yellow confetti on the treetops.

Each morning I looked for my butterfly. One day, I wandered through the bushes and hedges, keeping a wary eye for my elusive beauty. In the midday heat, I saw green lizards dancing on the footpath in the burning sun. I came across butterflies of all types floating in the air above the wild flowers but, as usual, the great orange one remained high above the others. I walked back home but, as I rounded the corner near a hedge, I caught a flash of brilliant white out of the corner of my eye. I looked up and there it was, about a metre away, settled on a big scarlet flower. As it fed on the nectar, its wings moved. I froze in my tracks, transfixed. After a while, I raised my net little by little, my heart pounding, the sweat trickling down my brow.

Suddenly the big butterfly moved to another flower and I swung my net and caught it. It started to flap its wings furiously, trapped inside the fine mesh. I could scarcely believe my eyes – at long last I had it. Gently I reached in and took it by the thorax, with every intention of putting it into my jar.

Father had put just enough formaldehyde in the jar to kill the butterfly but my hand froze and I simply gazed, astonished, at what was in my hand. There was the brilliant, iridescent bloom of orange on the tip of its glowing white wings. I could feel the creature's fear between my fingers as its little legs scrambled frantically in my palm. And then, on impulse, I tossed the butterfly away into the clear bright air and watched it float away; flapping its beautiful wings like a perfect living organism. It sailed high above a nearby treetop, then disappeared from sight.

Chapter Eleven

The Turkana Adventure

Paul Kelly was one of my father's great friends; he had worked for the British colony as provincial commissioner of Kenya's Northern Frontier Province between 1936 and 1963. His province covered about half of Kenya; it was largely arid and sparsely populated by nomadic tribes. This area was very wild then. The Turkana natives were almost naked, wearing very little to cover their bodies, just small cowry shells which had been made into pretty necklaces. Some of them had necklaces made out of beads that they wore around their necks, waists or wrists. They wore a cow hide around their lower parts and cow-hide sandals. These Turkana lived in small round huts called *manyatta* clustered around their temporary homesteads. The *manyatta* were made out of dry sticks and mud or cow dung. The Turkana were always on the move, looking for grazing fields or water for their livestock.

Paul Kelly made visits to this district. Sometimes he flew in in a small aircraft or rode on horseback or just walked. He must have appeared odd to the Turkana because he always wore a huge pith helmet; he reminded me of a giant mushroom.

Sometimes my father took me to Lodwar to see his friend. We had to use two vehicles, which had double spare wheels; we had a local guide as well as enough water and fuel to get back to Kapenguria. My mother did not accompany us; she did not trust the

The Turkana Adventure

Turkana, as there were tribal wars between them and her Pokot relatives. They were always stealing cattle from one another, quarrelling over grazing areas, water points and bore holes.

My father took my half-brother, Rotich, and me. Our cook came along and we carried camping gear as it was a three-day journey because of the rough roads. Very few lorries travelled up north with food and fuel supplies. The journey was very tiring; we had to go through Turkwell Pass then Marich Pass, down to the South Turkana plains and we skirted places, finding any elephants and *kudus* (antelope).

There were remnants of forest on the summit of two small mountain slopes; this is where the elephants survived. Some places were arid and there were thorn bushes everywhere. There is a gorge in this place that is joined by two tributaries – the Suam and Morun River.

During the day the heat was stupefying; the drives were long, with nothing to do but to stare morosely at the shrubs and thorn bushes and bare desert as they whisked by.

At the night we camped and slept under the stars. The air cooled, the moon hovered and the Milky Way was luminous. The sky was inky black and the moon cast a metallic light on the ground. One night, the place, which was partly desert, looked particularly radiant; I was overjoyed to be alone for once and tempted to move away from the camp.

After about an hour, I got tired of my own company and turned back towards where I thought the camp was. It was not until then that it dawned on me how far I had gone and I had no idea where I was. I used the moonlight to look for footpaths but I saw none, as the place was hard-baked earth. With horror I realised there were no landmarks and I had left no trails.

I started to panic and looked up at the sky as I imagined what one is supposed to do in such situations but I was utterly clueless

Chapter Eleven

about celestial navigation. I stumbled onwards. I was lost with no water, no food, and no warmth. I was still a child and I felt like crying. There was no sound as the tears dropped down my cheeks.

The cold descended and I was shaking. I lurched over the featureless land; if only I could see the light from our campsite at least I could try to walk towards it. I hoped I would not meet any wild animals.

I searched for what seemed like hours and could not see even a glow in the distance. Then I came upon huge rocks clustered everywhere. I stumbled over the smaller ones, nearly tripping. I hoped snakes or scorpions were not hiding underneath them. My only plan was to find a place with many rocks and sit between them as protection against the cold. Luckily I was wearing a sweater and I curled up. It took me a long time to fall asleep as I imagined all sorts of frightening animals ready to come and eat me for their dinner.

I was awoken by noise; at first I did not know who was speaking to me. When I looked up, I saw that it was my father. It was very early in the morning. He told me they had searched for me as soon as they had noticed I was not at the campsite. After four hours, exhausted and worried, they decided to wait till early morning. Luckily these huge rocks drew their attention and they decided to look at them. Father had been restless the whole night and had not slept a wink till daybreak. Fortunately this part of the country was not lion or leopard infested.

After a quick breakfast we had to hurry before noon, when the sun would be scorching hot. Passing through Turkana territory reminded me of the Pokot people. They are similar in culture and tradition. Cattle, goats and camels are the only wealth a man owns. The men herd and water the cattle and sing and dance to them at seven o'clock in the evening when they bring them back to the *manyattas* (mud huts with thorn enclosures). There the men oil the animals' horns as a blessing so they will acquire many cattle in the

The Turkana Adventure

future. Small girls and boys herd the sheep and goats; these are killed for their guests at minor celebrations.

The climate became hot and very windy, with fierce and frequent gales. Some parts of the road could not be seen and we had to drive very slowly with all our windows closed. The constant wind whipped the dust around so it swirled everywhere. We did not see any elephants, but lots of *kudus* and other animals. Father pointed out snakes crossing in front of us; he was careful not to drive over them. After three days of hard driving we were exhausted and glad to arrive in Lodwar town.

Lodwar is a major crossroad for the region. In the west there is a road that leads to Lorukum on the rift's escarpment, which forms the border with Uganda. The main road continues north to Lokichogio and the Sudanese border, and another road leads east to Ferguson's Gulf and the Jade Sea (Lake Turkana). There are mission buildings and a small hospital, a police post and an administrative post, and a post office not far away.

Paul Kelly met us here. He had a small house made out of bricks with a corrugated roof. Half a kilometre away was the Turkwell River which made the place cool. Lodwar town had one main street with Somali shanty shops, a ramshackle beer shop and small rooms for accommodation. At night the place was lit up by a huge generator. It was here at Lodwar that Jomo Kenyatta, the 'first president of Kenya', was held under informal house arrest before being moved to Maralal, and then released from prison at distant Lokitaung.

Paul Kelly was very happy to have visitors and Father had brought him a food supply. We stayed for two days at his humble home before we went to Lake Rudolf (now Lake Turkana) Fishing Lodge. The lodge catered for white settlers who came out to go fishing. It was well kept and organised and owned by retired white British administrators. There was a campsite, lodge, bar, restaurant

Chapter Eleven

and a fresh water supply.

My father and Paul Kelly stayed at this lodge for two weeks for a modest sum. One day, Father hired a fishing boat and some fishing rods. The lodge cook would cook the fish for us. The first fishing expedition went well and we caught a fair good number of fish, which lasted us the whole week. Then my father and Paul Kelly decided to take two boats and visit an island nine miles away from the lodge.

The Central Island in Lake Rudolf has a rare, fragile ecosystem. Its indigenous bushes and wild fruits form a critical link in the migration chain of birds en route from Europe to South Africa. The island's three crater lakes have for ages been the breeding ground for Turkana's population of Nile crocodiles and have the largest concentration of them in the world. They are believed to be the survivors of an epoch long before mankind appeared on Turkana's eastern shores and live in perfect harmony with their environment. They feed off the prolific fish.

Father had his gun with him in case he needed it for protection. We carried a good supply of soda, fruit and cooked fish in plastic containers. Paul Kelly took some beer and we all looked forward to an enjoyable day out.

Father knew that we would be coming back when it was dark, so we took torches and some life-saving equipment with us. Four natives came with us, two in each boat. My half-brother Rotich was not supposed to come but he managed to sneak on board. My father was unaware he was with the group until we arrived at the island. Father warned him not to get up to mischief or wander away.

He warned us that the island was full of crocodiles and everyone had to stay close together. The crocodiles are cold blooded; they depend entirely on external temperatures and they regulate their body heat according to the time of the day. They leave the water early in the morning to warm up, return to the water to escape the excessive heat of high noon and bask in the cooler part of the day until around sundown when they return to the water for the night. They stay submerged for up to an hour.

Nothing bad happened and we all got into the boats to come back. We had caught plenty of fish. It was getting dark as we paddled back and it took a lot of energy for the four natives and my father to get the two boats moving before it got pitch black.

One moment Rotich was at my side, the next he was gone! Confused, I rushed to Father's side and told him that Rotich had fallen overboard into the water. It took a while for the men to paddle and turn the boat round. I took a small torch and switched it on to focus on the bay, which was very dark. The beam from my torch was no match for the cloudy dark night and I switched it off. Then Father shouted at me to switch it back on as he had seen something moving in the water close by. When the light came on, I pointed it at the figure. It was Rotich! He was panicking; one minute he was under water, the next his head was above it. Father dived into the water and swam to the side of the boat with him. Paul Kelly's boat was close by and he immediately started mouth-to-mouth resuscitation and pumped water out of Rotich.

Chapter Twelve

Lake Turkana Tour

EVERY MORNING I walked the shores of Lake Turkana. The water swelled up to the lodge steps; this was the rainy season and the rains fell heavily. In most desert places, the rainwater drained into seasonal rivers which eventually drained into the lake.

I did not know how to swim, so most days I stayed indoors as the heat was unbearable. My half-brother was never allowed to step out of his room. He liked to play with the El-Molo natives' young boys and was very friendly with them. My father got scared that he might be persuaded to visit their *manyatta* dwellings and be persuaded to go fishing out on the island with the older boys. My father and Paul Kelly went out fishing most of the time for the fun of it and to catch fish for our supper.

This season the lodge was empty except for us; visitors only came during the other seasons. One day, when the water did not come right up to the lodge, I was tempted to sneak out to the lake shore at around four o'clock in the afternoon. I took my father's binoculars with me so I could watch birds with them.

Very quietly I took a position in a thick clump of papyrus with a good view over a stretch of clear water. The place was dry and I settled down comfortably and watched the beautiful, very colourful birds: barbets – black, yellow and pink, as they flew down in big flocks. Some other water birds zoomed, spiralled and turned wing-

Lake Turkana Tour

tip to wing-tip. As each flock passed, the noise was like surf in a gale-force wind.

I watched them drink. Each flock swooped in turn down to the surface of the water, flattening out as it did so for a fraction of a second. There was a flutter on the surface and up they shot again, leaving the surface of the water quivering. In that fraction of a second every bird drank; it was a beautiful, swift and delicate operation.

As I was watching these birds, I heard a swish of wings and a great African fish eagle alighted not far from me. He saw me and flew away; I could only see his enormous wings in the distance.

I sat for a while in the silence. Then I saw a boy, thirteen years or so, quietly swim into the deep waters until the water was up to his cheeks. He was motionless among the reeds watching what I thought was a crocodile, which lay with its cavernous jaws wide open, motionless on the far side of the lake.

A small green frog floated above the flat lily leaves on the water; an elegant little lily-trotter was busy running to and fro, its slender legs twinkling as its elongated feet carried it lightly over the leaves. There was a gleam beneath the surface and suddenly the little bird disappeared under the water; it had probably been grabbed by a tiger fish or some other animal. I thought that was the last of it, then the little bird reappeared on top of the water having escaped. Instantly, he ran at full speed straight into the open mouth of the crocodile, chattering fiercely as his unseen enemy pulled him down.

Soon I got tired of watching. The El-Molo (Turkana tribe) young boy would probably fetch his father to catch the crocodile, as this is what they ate as well as fish and hippopotamus meat. I did not feel scared for the boy; I knew this happened all the time and it was their way of hunting food for survival.

The two-week vacation ended and Father and Paul Kelly put all our gear in our two vehicles ready for the long journey home. We

Chapter Twelve

had enough supplies. This time we started the journey very early, at about four o'clock in the morning, when the Turkana district was cool and the midday sun was many hours away.

Soon we were driving away. My father let me use his binoculars and I sat on the front seat. As we drove along, I saw endless plain and horizons with shrubs and bushes. We arrived at Lodwar and did not stop for long, only to get fresh water and some beer for my father and Paul Kelly.

That night we camped out in the open but I was put in the tent to make sure I did not wander away. The campfire burnt straight and friendly in the evening air. The moon was up and we had some buck meat roasting on the slow-burning fire. The tea kettle purred like a satisfied cat. We were all happy and the Turkana natives who escorted us were bedded down a distance away from us. They too were roasting buck meat. Father had shot a buck on our way out to Lodwar.

Early next morning, coffee was ready and we ate last night's leftovers hurriedly. We wanted to cover some miles before the sun got too hot.

Our next spot to camp was on the border of the Turkana and Pokot people at the end of Marich Pass, near the big river where trees grow along the rivers and give out shade to keep the place cool.

Father and Paul Kelly decided to go out for a morning hunt. Paul Kelly knew this place well; as a district officer he had walked for a long distance or rode on donkeys several times in the past, and the natives knew him very well. It was only dangerous when the two tribes started to steal cattle from one another and there was the risk of dying in the crossfire.

I did not go out with Father and Paul Kelly. I stayed behind, looked after by the Turkanas. Father took his rifle and Paul must have taken his too. The bucks and *dik-dik* are usually scattered and lethargic at this time before the sun warms the ground. The first sight of them would be one or two or three phantom shapes suspended against an invisible background.

From far off we heard the crack of a shot in the morning silence, then another and another and that was the end of the hunt. Those early rifle shots would have sent all the other bucks, *dik-dik* and antelopes far away over the horizon. Father and Paul Kelly returned and the native escort carried the three bucks to the vehicles.

The queen ant is the most important and every small anthill has a queen living there. If the queen is killed or hurt, all the ants stop work and hurry back to the nest. It certainly looks as if they are responsive to the sudden stopping of something at the centre of the organism. 'Organism' is the right word; all these highly differentiated types are like organs of the single body. They have been conditioned for millions of years to the state in which each group of workers performs its own function, completely subordinate to the central will. It is a perfect democracy of the new model, where the state is all and the individual is nothing. These creatures work in unity and we are told they have their usefulness in the African soil.

We went on towards Kapenguria, but first we had to pass through the dangerous territory famously known as 'no man's land'. This was the meeting point for the Pokots and the Turkana to fight and raid cows from each other. The sun was up in its full glory and its heat penetrated our skin; sweat dripped down our faces but the movement of the vehicle brought enough wind through the window to cool us.

Most of Turkana and Pokot areas have termites; sometimes they are called white ants and they are everywhere. They are a great nuisance; they invade the dwellings in millions, run tunnels up the walls and eat anything that is made of wood. Driving through Pokot land, you see these huge anthills, some twice the size of a lorry. No wonder no one builds anything out here.

Chapter Twelve

Several times we arrived at huge seasonal rivers and waited for hours for the water to go down. My father dare not drive through if the water was coming fast, carrying huge tree trunks, logs and branches. One could easily get drowned or carried away in these torrents. At one point when there were many vehicles on either side waiting to cross, a vehicle drove too close to the riverbank, slipped and disappeared into the water. The car was carried away several metres but the people inside managed to get out with the help of those on the riverbank.

The Pokot and Turkana still hunt and fight over this territory. The hunting instinct is in the entire human race; in the Pokot and the Turkana people it is older than agriculture or herding their flocks of animals. The wars between the Pokots and Turkana start mainly because of rivalry over hunting grounds; the hunters do not want power or to change the culture, they just want to protect their hunting territory. Pokot *moran* (young men of an age to marry) raid the Turkana to get cattle to pay for a wife's dowry.

Crossing the border of two fierce tribes is very scary, especially in times of food shortages, and the government was unable to deal with such challenges. As we came close to the river that divides the two tribes, Father sensed danger. The place looked deserted; not even the animals were moving.

As we drove to the wooden bridge, we saw dead bodies everywhere. It looked like this had happened a day ago and already the corpses were starting to decompose. Father and his friend had their guns ready in case someone rushed at us from the bushes near the river. We drove quietly past the bodies. There was blood everywhere. There were no weapons lying around; it seemed as though the winning party had taken the weapons and anything of value. What a terrifying sight! My father ordered me to sit on the floor of the Land Rover, covered up beneath the seat so I could not see the bodies.

Lake Turkana Tour

We drove fast, putting distance between ourselves and the bodies, until the car started to climb up the hillside and down into the valleys and we knew we had passed the Marich Pass. We were driving in Pokot territory past the junction which branches off to Lomut. We met some army lorries driving towards the direction of the Pokot/Turkana tribal war zone and knew the government was taking control of the situation.

Chapter Thirteen

Family Separation – Siyoi Farm Taken

We felt safe in Pokot territory and the climate was much cooler. The hills extended for miles and we drove round them, up and down the valleys, until we got to Kapenguria and finally to our Siyoi farm. At our farm entrance, we had an ordinary tubular paddock gate. These were popular in Kenya with the settlers. It swung on iron hinges on a stout upright post on the right; on its left stretched out barbed-wire fence round the farm which was padlocked into sections for rotational grazing.

Our gate was wide open. That seemed odd because it was always shut. We drove to our house. As soon as our father got out of the Land Rover, he heard that my mother was in labour and was about to be taken to Kapenguria District Hospital to give birth. Hurriedly Father put our mother in Paul Kelly's Land Rover; it was decided that Mother should be driven to Kitale District Hospital, which was well equipped and had better facilities. She was made to sit on a mattress behind the driver's seat.

We did not see our parents for one week. I was left behind with my sister, Safia, and half-brother, Rotich. Our house was a mess and our cook had left his job. There was no one to clean, cook and take care of us except my mother's sister; she was no use as most of the time she went off to drink native beer and came home late.

As the older sibling, I decided to take charge. One evening, I

Family Separation – Siyoi Farm Taken

went to cook some meat and sweet potatoes in hot wood ash in the open air. A log fire burned in the centre of the compound in front of the thatched hut belonging to our native workmen. My left foot slipped into the hot ash and I burnt the side of my foot. With no one around except Rotich, I put my foot in a cold bucket of water and cried loudly for a long time.

Rotich ran to my mother's brother who lived some distance away. He came immediately and carried me on his back all the way to Kapenguria District Hospital. There was an English doctor there by the name of Mr A.J. Cox. He and his wife had come out to West Pokot as missionaries. He was a doctor and his wife worked under the Christian Mission of the Anglican Church, which introduced primary schools in West Pokot. Mr Cox took care of my burnt foot and then he noticed I had a high temperature. After a few tests he found that I had bad malaria and I was kept at the mission for treatment until my father came back to take me home. Then I met my little sister, a tiny baby named Selina. Safia always stayed next to Mother. She was afraid of cows and dogs. She never played with me as I was the adventurous one.

My father still taught at Ole Kajiado Secondary School and at weekends he came to see us and buy us enough food to last a week or two. My mother could not be trusted with the housekeeping money; she would leave us with the family who lived next to our farm to go drinking at Makutano Bar. She had become more sophisticated and did not drink the local native beer but drank modern beer. My father did not take too much notice of this as he had other worries.

One day, while Father was having his evening walk round the farm, he came across a baby cheetah. He told us that its mother might have abandoned it and it was all alone. Father brought this baby cheetah to our house. My mother was very afraid of it and would not touch it. We never put him in a cage or tied him up but

Chapter Thirteen

let him walk around the house. He never went far; he was scared of humans because they threw sticks and stones at him. He was friendly and lovely to look at but never tame.

I liked to walk him around the farm; he would sometimes disappear into the woods then re-appear and run alongside me, though at times he speeded ahead of me. Some evenings he sat next to me on the edge of the veranda, upright in the fashion of cheetahs, gazing straight in front. Every now and then he growled deep in his throat; it was nothing in the foreground that interested him, he was watching movements a mile away. He sometimes spent the whole day in the bottom of the valley. Everyone on the farm got to know him eventually. When he went near the cows, they got really frightened and jumped about in circles.

When cheetah was happy, he rolled on the grass and purred with a noise like a motorcycle's exhaust. When visitors came we had to tell them immediately about cheetah or he would frighten them to death.

Eventually he disappeared for a week. I was worried but Father reassured me that the cheetah was okay and had gone back into the wild. One evening I saw him. He ran towards me and I ran towards him. He knocked me over but I was happy to see him. He purred and let me pull his ears and fondle him. I saw he had changed and he was restless. Then, just as I was calling him to follow me to the house, he refused and faced the forest. He ran off and I stood for a long time until he disappeared totally. That was the last I ever saw of him. He had gone back to his own kind, to his mate, and that was his way of saying goodbye.

My mother and half-brother were glad he had gone. They never understood the relationship I had with him; they worried that he would attack our cattle, sheep or chickens. Our neighbours were also happy to get rid of him. Others started to blame him for attacking their sheep down the valley but I never believed them.

Family Separation – Siyoi Farm Taken

One weekend, Father took me with him to live on the Kitale farm, which we finally named Small Farm. We had a new cook, Kazungu, whom Father had known when he was in Lamu district. Kazungu was a good cook and had a great memory for recipes. He did not know how to read; he must have cooked for the British government officials in the 1950s and stored everything he had learnt in his clever head. Father had a little bell that he rang for the cook to come and take away the plates and bring in the next course.

One day, just before lunch, we were honoured to have one of my father's best friends, Alistair Burn, for lunch. Kazungu did a great job cooking lunch. It was a long time since Alistair Burn had last visited us. He owned five thousand acres of land near Kwanza district beyond Endebess at the base of Mount Elgon. He said he would be glad if our family would visit him, especially my father whom he had known from colonial times. My father and Alistair planned to go out on safari to the east of the Pokot area where there were plenty of giraffes, buffalos, impalas, elands, lions, bush buck and antelopes. Everyone looked forward to a hunting adventure.

They called it hunting but it was more of a sport or safety valve. Hunting becomes a sort of game; sometimes it's a game where the hunter turns out to be the hunted. Father and his friend did it for fun. They had this passion to get into the wild whenever they could and live like their ancestors. The pursuit of game was not the chief attraction; there was more to it than that. They liked to be away from a civilised existence where they were no longer driven by schedules and were away from books and newspapers and social life.

Their physical senses became sharp again; they heard more and could see much further. They could track footprints in the dust and were aware of movements far away; at night they were out in the open with the stars above them. Out there, there is an attraction of its own; the colours are more exotic. Nature has a hostility about it;

Chapter Thirteen

whether you are in the hot, arid country or the fiercely lush tropical valley, it is not friendly.

There is something ominous about Africa at times. When you are out there in the wild, the threats or challenges are all part of its magic. There is an atmosphere due to the mist and shadow which are only known in Africa in the fleeting moment just after dawn.

In countries where the sun never seems to rise fully, you get depth, mystery and enchantment in the landscape but you can only appreciate this when you have spent time in the sunshine. The overhead sun of the tropics eliminates shadows, except in the forest. The landscapes are often dark and uncompromising. The atmosphere is entirely different to that in Europe.

Bertie Hunt was another of my father's very good friends; he came from the same place in England, Tonbridge in Kent, and they never lost touch. Another of his friends was Mr Williamson, who married a pretty Turkana girl and had three children who moved to the UK in the 1970s. He sold their farm and left Africa for good. His wife never changed her Turkana ways and it took her a while to adapt to England. While in Kenya, she dressed in Turkana style with her hair in dreadlocks and shaved on both sides. She looked very exotic, with beads round her neck, lots of African earrings, and cow hide for a skirt. Beads made into jewellery indicate a woman's wealth and marital status.

Before he left for England, Mr Williamson moved to Kitale in the late 1960s. I went to the Jack and Jill Nursery school with his two daughters. They were my age and Father maintained the friendship with his family for a very long time. It was sad for my father when Mr Williamson left for England for good. I heard that in the UK, Mr Williamson's son had built a small Turkana round hut and refused to live in the big family house – although probably during winter he lived in the big house and during the summer in his Turkana round hut.

Family Separation – Siyoi Farm Taken

Very soon I had to go to stay at Siyoi Farm with my mother because Father had to go back to teach at Ole Kajiado. Things did not get any better on our farm. Mother bought herself a second-hand car – a Ford Anglia – and employed a driver. We were told she had borrowed a lot of money from a relative of hers by the name Rotino Moiben. They used to go drinking every night when Father was not around, at a bar called Taifa Bar in Makutano town centre. I remained alone with my two sisters and we were hardly fed. My mother's sister did not take care of us and Selina and Safia became ill. The cows on the farm started to die of east-coast fever.

Father only made it to Siyoi at weekends. This went on for nearly six weeks. My mother was never cut out to be a farmer and left everything to her farm manager. She blamed the decline of the farm on pests and diseases, the labourers not being efficient, lack of machinery and the unpredictable rains but deep down I knew she had no love for her land. If only my mother had understood that the land and its production are the most important things in the world – they underpin everything. Without them, civilisation will collapse. The lesson is being learned today to make sure that food supply is always top priority.

The farm salaries and expenses had not been paid for a while and the workers did not turn up. The coffee plantation was full of weeds and the coffee berries were not picked on time. There was growing sluggishness about everything and things went wrong. Our cattle fell sick.

My recollection of those days is still fresh. As a child, I felt these were the worst days of my life. Seeing the once good world round me dying and knowing I could do nothing about it was sad. Our farm became a heavy burden on our father. He loved his job as headmaster at Ole Kajiado and did not want to lose it, but at the same time he struggled to keep the farm going by driving back each weekend to save the coffee, the pyrethrum and the few cattle that

Chapter Thirteen

were still alive.

Father was also worried about our welfare. When he returned to Ole Kajiado to teach and we were left in our mother's care, Father warned her to be more responsible about the farm and the children. My little sister Selina got very sick with malaria and Mother had to take her to Dr Cox at Kapenguria Hospital. She did not return that night, so we were left under the care of Mother's sister, as usual.

Very early in the morning we were awakened and told that a new owner had taken our farm from us. We were not allowed to take any belongings with us; we were driven out of the farm gate and told to go away. This very cruel-looking man, Rotino Moiben, the man who used to take my mother out to the bars, had spent many nights at our farm when Father was not around. First he came as a visitor, then he started coming every week; he bossed our labourers and behaved as if the farm belonged to him.

So, we were told to leave. We could only carry a few belongings. Yogonyang, my mother's brother, carried Safia on his back and me and Rotich walked down the hill to Makutano in search of our mother. We did not find her and we ended up with another relative by the name Lorkan for a few days.

Father had been away for a while and hadn't come to visit us because he was busy buying a new car – a Morris Minor saloon. The Land Rover was old and had started to break down. Our father found us at the home of the lady who owned Taifa Bar. He picked up Safia and took me by my arms and took us to his car. Selina was very small and he could not cope with a child that still suckled.

Father drove back to his Siyoi farm. Luckily we found our gate wide open, so we drove to the house. Father got out of his car and was confronted by Rotino Moiben who had just come out of our living room. A lot of words were exchanged and Rotino started to threaten my father. He told him the colonial era was over and white

Family Separation – Siyoi Farm Taken

people should have left; he said he would bring young *morans* (warriors) from the village with poisoned arrows to kill him.

Rotino was a native warlord. My father had no alternative but to drive out of the compound and go to the local police, who did not help him recover his land or most of his equipment. Somehow he got some of his books back because they were of no value to the Pokots.

We drove back to Kitale in total silence. Father looked very worried and sad. He had endured a great loss – and what would become of our sister Selina? It would be a nightmare for her to live with Mother's relatives and have a native upbringing. Safia and I wept in one another's arms; we had lost our land and lost our family except for Father. Every now and then I looked up at my father's face; he seemed to be strong in the midst of woe. He absorbed all the misery and could still be gallant.

When we arrived at the small farm in Kitale, the place looked different. Kazungu, my father's cook, said hello to us in Kiswahili language and took us to our tiny bedroom right at the end of the house. This was to be our home for a very long time. First we had to clean up and sit at the table with our father for meals; we had not done this for many months and we enjoyed it.

Things changed greatly. I never heard any news of my mother, my sister Selina or half-brother Rotich. Father never talked about them or the Siyoi farm; all I knew was that he went back once to ask for his books. He was only given back his personal belongings: the books, silver ornaments and copper trays. Everything else was taken away from him. The government did not help him recover his wealth, which he had invested in his farm. Father never stepped onto the Siyoi farm again as he was afraid to go near it. He let everything slip away and it became a memory.

Safia was the most affected and she could not stop wetting the bed at night. Our father employed a lady to help look after us. She

Chapter Thirteen

lived with her family at the bottom of the farm in a round grass-thatched hut, so it was convenient for her to come up each morning to care for us. Father still taught at Ole Kajiado and every weekend he spent time with us.

Kazungu became our permanent cook and Father had to employ another for himself for his Ole Kajiado home. I was warned not to wander too far from the house. My father told us that at the bottom of the farm near the spring there was a great snake population; while walking round the fields we were to be particularly careful and search the ground. The surrounding grass and bushes were cleared and our gardener killed dozens and dozens of snakes, mostly cobras, puff adders and the deadliest snake in Africa – the black mamba.

As the days went by, Father wondered if it would be a good idea to take me and Safia to get a better education in England. He could probably move to the UK to settle with his two daughters but he still needed someone to look after us. His parents were old and needed care. Our auntie was living with them. Grandfather had lost most of his fortune; he had been a solicitor in London. They'd had to sell their big house and Bourne Farm at Tonbridge and move to the countryside where it was cheaper. My grandmother was not used to working, since ladies of her generation did not work but ran their husband's houses and supervised the servants. They moved to Edenbridge, where Grandfather later died. Auntie and Granny continued to live in Edenbridge, Kent, in a cottage with a fairly large amount of land around it to grow vegetables and fruit.

My grandmother originally came from South Africa, the Cape Colony. Before the Boer War, her parents had come from Great Britain and settled in Kimberley. After the Boer War, in which the British were defeated, the Boers and Britons lived together amicably; only by their names would one know who was British or Dutch

Family Separation – Siyoi Farm Taken

by descent.

Gradually, after many years, it was possible to adapt to the Dutch South African way of thinking as they were the majority. My auntie, living with her mother, was advised by her to let my father sort out his problems himself and not to take us in, as she had a lot to cope up with. My auntie still lives in her cottage in Eden Bridge and is a happy, old retired woman.

Chapter Fourteen

A New Lady Taprandich (Stepmother)

FATHER TOOK ME to Thika and enrolled me in a school run by nuns but after one term he realised that it was impossible to separate me from Safia. I came home but after two months events began to change. Father brought home this tall native woman of Maasai and Tugen descent. They had known each other during the colonial period; she had worked as a kitchen helper for my father's cook while he was at Chepareria West Pokot during 1958–1959, and they had kept in touch in their own mysterious way. Father had helped her to get a big piece of land, close to three hundred acres, in Chepareria West Pokot where I heard she kept native cows, sheep and goats. All her relatives lived on it as a big clan.

She was brought in to care for us temporarily. Her ears had been cut and she had a hole in the middle of both lobes so as to wear lots of Maasai beads and copper-wire jewellery. Her skin was smooth; she had lived on a diet of milk and blood. She had elegant high cheekbones; her teeth were white and shining as she smiled then laughed at a joke. Her eyes never left my father and she was always near him, as if to get special favours and attention.

At first she was charming and we liked her and thought what a wonderful woman she was. Two months went by; she became a bit bossy and arrogant, as if she was a white settler. Once or twice Father and Taprandich drove off to Kitale Hotel and ended up in

A New Lady Taprandich (Stepmother)

the Blue Room Club for their evening drinks. They came home late and behaved as if they were a married couple. I asked myself over and over again: had Father forgotten about my mother and my little sister?

Taprandich moved into our home. She kept it to a high standard, cleaned everything and took care of Safia and me. Sometimes in the evening, when we were supposed to be tucked in bed, I tiptoed to the living room to see what she was up to. Father would be sitting in his armchair facing the fire and she would be seated on the carpet beside him, with a glass of wine; they spoke in Swahili and laughed together. I thought Father looked happy around her.

I was not happy and knew something was going on and this was no ordinary house help; they were too intimate. I noticed that our cook Kazungu did not get along with her. She tried to take over the cooking as if she was trained to do so but she only knew basic cooking. I was told she had cooked for her previous boss who was a white settler.

She was taking over our house and behaving as if she was the mistress. Every now and then I heard my father call her Taprandich. One evening our father told us that we had to go to Malindi by train to see his old friend, John Gullingford, and his Nandi wife. I did not like the idea of Malindi; all I wanted was to see my mother and my little sister Selina. I missed them so much but, being a child, I had no choice but to go to Malindi with my father and Taprandich. My father and she seemed to be getting very close and I wondered if she had come to replace my mother.

The safari to Malindi was boring. We travelled by train and this time we all travelled first class. Father and Taprandich travelled as a couple. Taprandich held Safia close to her; she was very fond of her. She did not like me much and kept on shouting at me over small mistakes: 'Get away from the window, Susan, the wind is too much for you.'

Chapter Fifteen

Malindi

AFTER WHAT SEEMED like a very long journey, we finally arrived at Mombasa. John Gullingford and his wife were there to pick us up in his brand-new saloon car and we drove to his residence at Malindi. That night, although we were very tired from the journey, all four grown-ups did not go to bed but stayed in the sitting room that had a veranda overlooking the sea.

I crept up very quietly and hid behind the open door. They had a bottle of champagne open and all four chatted away. I was not happy; something was going on and I could not figure it out.

Gullingford talked more than anyone else, mostly to my father, as if his soul was starving to be heard and he could 'stand it no longer', he kept saying. He went on till after midnight. He had a pipe and the tobacco he used was the local one, which smelled horrible. He would not let anyone talk; if Father tried to get a word in, Gullingford would shriek, glowing with the fire within him. He had a lot to get rid of and talked about the Kenyan government and slow development. He talked about the colonial days and how the white population of Kenya was selling up their property or pulling out. Politics had not favoured them; nothing was to be gained and much was to be lost. In most parts of Kenya, the living standards were miserably poor by European standards. What was needed was higher revenue, which could only come from higher taxable capac-

Malindi

ity and that meant capital and industries.

Back in the 1940s, the British Parliament had passed the Colonial Development and Welfare Act, which provided millions of pounds annually for development, particularly for social services, in all the countries of the empire. The Act embodied a welcome new principle, but it was absurd to believe that it was sufficient. Something had to be done to improve the educational standard and health of the Kenyan population and to force it gradually to stand on its own feet.

There was one difficulty: when most Kenyans get rich, especially in the cities, their priority is leisure and this leads to them not working hard, while others in the village have the native culture for their way of life. Suddenly you have two groups: one very rich and developed and the other poor and uneducated. One group takes advantage of the other and the poor group ends up being disadvantaged.

After some hours, John had no more to say. He sat peacefully for a while, a humble look on his face. My father told him to go to bed as he'd had too much to drink.

Next morning, John Gullingford and Father drove to Malindi Town to see his plot near the fish market. Taprandich dressed me in a swimming suit and we left Safia at the flat with John's wife. These flats were high up and we were staying on the third floor. We walked down to the sea; it was a paradise, palm-fringed beach, caster-sugar sands and translucent, cornflower-blue sea. The offshore reef that stretches the length of the South Coast is some few minutes swim away; even at low tide, the water was deep enough for a swim.

Taprandich did not know how to swim and I did not dare go out to sea on my own, so we picked some shells and walked back to John's place. As we approached the front steps leading to the stairs, we heard loud cries. We looked up to where the noise had come

Chapter Fifteen

from, only to see John Cullingford's wife dangling Safia in mid-air over the balcony three floors up. Taprandich quickly ran up the stairs to the house and I was right at her heels. Opening the door, Taprandich ran to Safia and pulled her out of John's wife's grip, back to safety. She slapped the woman's face twice and took Safia into our father's bedroom.

John's wife spoke in Swahili as she followed Taprandich to the bedroom. She said loudly that she was not interested in adopting Safia; her interest was in me. I was very shocked to hear this and to learn that this long journey to Malindi was about Father giving us away to this couple, who seemed incapable of looking after children.

Everything was revealed to me. It would be tragic to leave Safia and me under the care of John's wife. What was Father thinking? Why did he want to get rid of us? After a long discussion, it was decided that Father would take us back with him to reconsider giving us to John and his wife. Taprandich stood her ground and would not let us stay behind. Soon we found ourselves on the long journey back to Kitale.

Before we got to Kitale, we stopped at Nairobi. Father had to see a good friend of his, Travers Garland. They had worked together for the Crown during colonial times and kept in touch. Father needed advice and Travers was waiting for us and collected us from the train station.

Travers was a successful businessman who had bought several companies. After the colonial era, he worked as a manager for several big factories and eventually bought a factory that manufactured Wisdom toothbrushes and imported spare parts for injector pumps. He went into partnership with two other Englishmen constructing wooden houses, which became very fashionable in the seventies and eighties.

Travers Garland was a member of the Muthaiga County Golf

Malindi

Club, the Karen County Club and the Nairobi Club. He lived in Karen area, where he had built a beautiful English-style house. As we drove towards his house, we could see the suburb beneath us. It was here that Karen Blixen settled in 1914 with her husband, Baron Bror Blixen, to establish a coffee farm.

We had to drive through the Karen County Club. I learnt that it was founded in 1937 and was one of the oldest golf clubs in Kenya. A large part of its eighteen-hole golf course was built on Karen Blixen's former coffee estate. The view of the Ngong Hills was the backdrop. Looking out through the car window, I saw indigenous trees, flowering shrubs, fauna, wetlands and lots of birds in many colours. *dik-diks* darted across the road and some grazed alongside the road at the edge of the vegetation.

We arrived at the drive on Travers' land. There was a neat fence and roses grew everywhere. The car stopped at the front porch. The house was huge and looked rather square. There were pillars at the porch that made a beautiful formal entrance. The door was mahogany. The house was European style, very colonial.

Travers' English wife came out to meet us. She did not stay for long; she announced that she had to go to the Jockey Club racecourse, which was not very far along Ngong Road. She was dressed in her riding breeches.

Taprandich was lodged with the servants while my sister Safia and I were given a room upstairs. Taprandich was not allowed to eat at the table but had to have her meals with the servants. The short time we were at Travers' house, I noticed that his English wife would not sit at the table with us during meals and eventually a table was laid out for Safia and me in a separate room. I started to wonder if this was what they called the colour bar, then later I realised it was their way of keeping to themselves.

Another afternoon, Father insisted that Travers take him to Muthaiga Golf Club. My father was never a golfer but loved to

Chapter Fifteen

read. The library at Muthaiga Club had about twenty thousand books or more, all from the colonial era. Some were donated by the early settlers.

Travers and Father dressed up in suits and ties, which were compulsory for men after 7.30 pm. No woman was allowed in the member bar, no flip-flops, no T-shirts, no hats. Those were the rules and they were kept strictly. The club held championship tournaments and was limited to members only.

Another club was formed in 1901 by Boustead and Ridley, who were businessmen in Zanzibar and moved to Nairobi. They started the Nairobi Club; after two years of trying to run it, they relieved themselves of it because it did not bring in enough income to sustain itself. It started small and grew. It is in the heart of Nairobi City, is the second oldest club in Kenya and very popular. Lawn bowling and croquet are still played and it holds bowling competitions.

Neither Travers nor Father took part in these games; they only went there for conversation and to meet other settlers who had decided to remain in Kenya to farm or do business. The Nairobi Club has a beautiful library and my father borrowed books and returned them via Travers.

We came back to Kitale thinking what a waste of time and energy the Malindi trip had been. Father looked settled and he became very close to Taprandich. I gathered that an agreement had been reached between them that she would move permanently to our small farm to take care of Safia and me. She persuaded Father she would be a mother to both of us, especially when he went off to teach at Ole Kajiado secondary school.

My father got involved in a relationship – with a woman in Kitale by the name of Chepatali. They went out for evening drinks to the Kitale Hotel; behind it was a bar where white men would bring in their African girlfriends to socialise and have drinks. This

Malindi

bar was called the Blue Room and was for mixed-race couples. Father's girlfriend spoke fluent English. She had a bad habit of talking intimately with white men and that upset my father so he finally split up with her. In later years she settled down with a white Englishman; they got married and became farmers at a place called Endebess, towards Mount Elgon.

One afternoon, as we were all sitting under the avocado tree playing, I saw my mother's car being driven onto our farm by a driver, Hassan Ndamwe. It stopped some metres away. Mother got out of her car, walked towards Safia and grabbed her to take her to her car. Naturally I ran towards the house. Father and Taprandich were drinking beer and relaxing in our living room. Mother was just behind me and she charged into the living room, demanding to see Father. In her rush, she tripped over a Kisii stool, which was made out of *mvuli* wood, which is as hard as a rock. She fell over it, broke four of her upper front teeth and started to bleed very badly.

My mother accused Taprandich of tripping her up. I was not watching so I did not see everything that took place. All I saw was her run out of the house to go to the police station. Father drove after her and persuaded her not to go to the police, that it was an accident. After my father parted with some money, my mother let things go and did not come to the small farm for a very long time. She went for treatment but she lost her looks; even today her front upper teeth are missing. My father never bothered to take her to the dentist to get artificial ones.

Kazungu, our cook, was not happy with what happened. Safia cried for weeks and wanted to go with Mother. As for me, I had mixed feelings. I liked Father though I missed Mother a lot. Taprandich had turned into an unpleasant woman and I distrusted her. It was easy for her to pick up and carry Safia around and pretend that she really cared for her. I was not easily persuaded by her motives and felt she had come to stay permanently and ruin our lives.

Chapter Fifteen

When Father had to work at Ole Kajiado, she was left in charge of us. We had started school at the Jack and Jill Nursery School. The school was only for white children but my father, being a white man, had managed to get us a place. Safia was in the beginners' class, the baby class, and I was put in a pre-unit class before I joined Class One. We encountered a colour bar in this white settler's nursery school; we were classed with the Asians because we did not look white or African. At this time there were no Africans in this school. We did not feel out of place but still I felt the discrimination.

This colour bar was there in Kenya at this period; it had not totally disappeared. It's not something that can be removed; it will only fade away with time. We were caught up with this colour-bar issue, which people pretended did not exist, but which we could feel. This started when the settlers were not feeling safe; some were selling up to move back to the UK, some were going to South Africa, while others remained to make money. They had to live together to protect themselves as a community of a different culture and race. I have heard that the settlers complained that it was difficult to have a dozen different African tribes on their farm and depend on them to work. Most of these labourers at times could be stubborn, irresponsible, infuriating. One tribe would not get along with the other tribe, as they had many differences in culture and spoke different languages.

At this time, the Africans had this idea that these whites were bullying exploiters. In actual fact, the whites had to be careful when dealing with these labourers. In many ways, the Africans had the power for they could easily leave their jobs and survive without the white settlers – but the settlers could not live without them and the Africans knew it. If an African thought the work was harsh, and conditions and pay were not satisfactory, they left and went back to their villages. A contract with them in those days was meaningless. On the other hand, educated Africans were ready to take up low-

Malindi

paid jobs and replace the white settlers. Some educated Africans began to acquire land. The white population kept to themselves and seldom mixed with the few up and coming African businessmen or well-paid African government officials.

My father was a good example. When colonial rule ended, he either had to leave Kenya and look for another job in the UK or take a job as a head teacher in a secondary school. Because of us he sacrificed his English life, which would have been better for him, and stayed in Kenya to take care of us. I owe everything to my English father. He took a job as a teacher at Manor House School, teaching English, Latin and Greek, but as the settlers were leaving, the job came to an end.

At school, it was not easy for us. We had a tough life, especially when Father was away teaching at Ole Kajiado. He did not leave Kazungu to cook or care for us; Kazungu went wherever father went. Taprandich stayed behind to take care of us but she never did a good job of it.

We had to walk to school every morning. The school was two kilometres away and the bottom of our farm was full of indigenous trees and had a swamp that attracted all sorts of animals. We would wake up very early and, after a simple breakfast of tea and toasted bread, we used a short cut next to this swamp. Snakes crossed our path and it's a miracle we were never bitten by one.

Crossing through the labourers' camp was always frightening. The children ran out of their thatched huts and lined up to stare at us and call us *watoto wa Mzungu* (white man's children). We soon got used to it because it happened all the time.

My sister Safia was a bed wetter. Each morning, I did most of the work to help her change her smelly clothes and put on a clean uniform and reminded her to put on her knickers, which she always forgot. Safia's life was traumatic and full of fear: fear of people down at the bottom of the farm, animals, snakes and the big forest.

Chapter Fifteen

She even became afraid of Taprandich, who had started to shout and bully us when our father was not around.

Safia was afraid of everything: lizards, frogs, colobus monkeys, water bucks, *dik-diks*, spiders, guinea fowls, eagles, crane birds. We encountered these animals while using the short cut to school each morning. During the rainy season, the path could be very slippery. We were happy to have Father for the weekends – and happier still to hear that Taprandich had to go see her family at Chepareria in West Pokot district.

Word had come that the Pokot natives had raided all her cows again and she had to go there. She would be gone for a very long time to settle this matter of cattle theft; it was a brave thing to do, especially for a woman.

Luckily the school holiday was just a week away, so Father and Kazungu once again took care of Safia and me; everything returned to normal with no more Taprandich around to bully and boss me. We spent more time with our father and he took us to stay with him for a while at Ole Kajiado Secondary School. Travelling by car to Ole Kajiado was fun, although it took two days to get there. Kazungu made sure we had enough sandwiches and tea or coffee in the thermos flask, as we had no time to stop to eat at hotels or restaurants on our way there. I sat on the front seat when Taprandich was not around, with Safia and Kazungu seated in the back.

On our way, before reaching the small town of Soy between Kitale and Eldoret, Father loved to stop at a spot by a small stream which ran parallel to the road for four kilometres. There were several varieties of fig trees and these attracted fruit-eating birds, baboons and monkeys. It was always cool to walk to the stream and use the shade from the trees to sit down to watch the birds eat the fruits while watching my father stretching his legs as he took a walk.

After driving on for a while, the scene changed and we came to an open area. We stopped to see the giraffes as they browsed the trees. Some were crossing the road; we stopped to watch and a baby giraffe came running alongside its mother.

We arrived in Eldoret town and Father bought some cakes from the bakery. Soon we drove the long distance to Nakuru through Gilgil. Before Naivasha, there were a lot of zebras and more giraffes, eland antelopes, bushpigs, all grazing. It was beautiful seeing all these animals at peace and undisturbed.

After Naivasha, we started to climb up the Rift escarpment road. This road was built in the early 1940s by Italian prisoners of war. At the foot of the escarpment, just before it levels out on the valley floor, there is a thanksgiving building. It was consecrated on Christmas Day in 1943. Driving up to the Chapel of St Mary of the Angels, we arrived at the escarpment. It gets very cold and foggy; the fog is cloying and makes it difficult to see the car in front of you. Accidents often occur here.

Father had made arrangements with his friend Travers Garland for us to use his home for the night and the next day we were on our way along the Kajiado road. Driving past Nairobi towards the Tanzanian border, we drove through grasslands where we occasionally saw zebras, wildebeest and giraffe. Parts of these places have Maasai *manyatta* (round huts.)

We arrived early at Kajiado, a small administrative headquarters. It had a small police post and shopping centre built out of iron sheets. The centre was full of Maasai who were dressed in traditional attire made of animal hides. A few men were wearing very bright multi-coloured *shukas* (traditional blanket used by the Maasai) and beaded jewellery around their necks and arms. Some wore simple sandals made out of animal hide while others were barefoot. The women shaved their hair and removed the middle teeth on the lower jaw for oral delivery of traditional medicine.

Driving slowly through this small centre was fascinating. Father

Chapter Fifteen

stopped to talk to some Maasai elders under a tree. He seemed well acquainted with them. The Maasai cows were everywhere.

We drove through the town's cemetery; Father had to show me the place because he loved to teach me history. The cemetery contained the graves of twenty-four casualties of World War I, killed when General Paul Von Lettow-Vorbeck's German Army defeated a British force in a battle at the base of 8,625 foot Longido, just across the border from Namanga in Tanzania.

We had to go some six kilometres straight along Arusha Road before we took a left turn to my father's school. At a junction, Father drove down the left-hand road that led to his house. This was just an ordinary square house, made out of stone, and had one kitchen, a living room that also served as a dining room, two bedrooms and a toilet and bathroom outside. There was a long-drop toilet for when water was scarce. My father's cook had his house in the servants' quarters at the far end of the school compound.

Chapter Sixteen

Ole Kajiado and Amboseli Game Park Tour

Our stay at Ole Kajiado Secondary School was one of the happiest times in our lives. Our cook Kazungu cooked all our meals and we ate at the table with our father. A lady came in three times a week to help with the house cleaning and other chores.

A telegram arrived from Nakuru from Father's friend, Bertie Hunt. He and his family were coming to stay for a week and we all looked forward to being with them. Safia and I would have a chance to play with his two daughters who were our age. Two days after their arrival, a camping trip was organised to Amboseli National Park. We all fitted into the Land Rover; this would be a three-day sightseeing vacation and a drive through a proper national park. All sorts of animals were out there grazing or looking for water and hunting for food.

Large herbivores together with smaller species: wildebeest, gazelle, zebra, buffalo, impala, topi, hartebeest, giraffe, eland, elephant, antelope, rhino, warthog, bushpig, and giant forest hog; and the predators: lion, leopards, cheetah, hyena, wild dog, jackal and many small mammals, birds, reptiles, amphibians and insects crowd in the Amboseli National Park. During the dry season, they migrate further away to look for water and greener pasture.

As we drove through Amboseli National Park, it appeared un-

Chapter Sixteen

attractive with the dust blowing but its magic and charm grew by the second. Sitting in our Land Rover, looking through binoculars, there was a lot to see. Sometimes we drove very close to a herd of elephants, male, female, juveniles and the very young. Although I was afraid, I found them interesting animals to watch. We drove very close to Tanzania's border beneath the north-west face of Kilimanjaro.

We could see Kilimanjaro, the highest free-standing mountain in Africa, at close quarters ringed by a halo of cumulus clouds, its wedding-cake peak floating magically in the incredible blue of the African sky. At sunset, we drove towards the self-help *bandas* at Ol Tukai guest accommodation and retired for the night. That evening at seven o'clock, the owners of the guest house arranged for Maasai warriors to entertain us. We were eating at the table when the Maasai started to display their jumps. A small booklet was handed round about the Maasai culture and way of life. To be a Maasai is to be born one of the world's last great warriors. When the warriors jump, it is part of a dance to find a mate. The one who jumps highest gets the girl. Besides these jumps they have other rituals, including circumcision.

Circumcision is a ceremony to show that a *moran* (young man) is ready to hunt, go out and look for cattle and is at an age to join this jumping dance to attract girls. The next level of elevation is *eunoto*, when the *moran* graduates to become warriors. Now the young men can own cattle, start a family and be elected as elders. The last state is the *olng'eshare* ceremony, which happens only if a man reaches middle age; he becomes a senior and has more responsibilities in the society and is respected.

The Maasai have a deep, almost sacred, relationship with their cattle. They believe that God created cattle especially for them and that they are the sole custodians of all the cattle on earth. This bond has led them into a nomadic way of life, following rainfall

Ole Kajiado and Amboseli Game Park Tour

over big areas of land in search of food and water for their large herds of cattle. Animals are a sign of wealth and are used to pay their dowry.

All the Maasai women build homes, collect firewood, cook and do other domestic work. They build their homes in a Kraal out of mud, grass, wood, cow dung; the houses are semi-permanent, small and circular. The Kraal acts like a big fence to provide security for the cattle and families. The Maasai men are polygamous and as a whole the Maasai are monotheistic, believing in a single deity, Enkai. This god has a dual nature – Enkai Narok (black god) who is charitable and Enkai Nanyokie (red god) who is unforgiving.

My father and his friend enjoyed the evening and we retired to our *bandas*. I could not sleep as the animals were out roaming; although our campsite was securely fenced, I felt afraid knowing the animals were not far away from our camp. I heard lions roar and it made me shudder but eventually the noise moved further away, then finally it was no more.

The next day, we drove to the Tanzanian border beneath the north-west face of Kilimanjaro. Most of the park is taken up by a seasonal lake. The dry soda bed of the lake gives it its name, Amboseli, which derives from the *maa* for salt dust. During the dry season the heat creates a series of shimmering mirages over the lake basin. Most of the park is hot and dry, covered with patches of semi-arid acacias and fragile savannah. This is where animals come for salt. At the south-eastern end there are three large swamps fed by underground springs from the melting waters of Kilimanjaro, which filter through its volcanic strata to appear pure and crystal clear. These springs, with their papyrus edges, are the only sources of permanent water and the major points for the wildlife.

We drove to a lookout post on a hill, one the highest points of the park. It gives a panoramic view of the whole place, the Enkongo Narok (black river) and the Engone Naibor and Longinye

Chapter Sixteen

Swamps, which stand out a brilliant emerald green. Elephants, hippos, giraffes and buffalos are found more around the southern edge of Longinye Swamp.

By afternoon we were exhausted as the heat had got to us. Driving through some grassland alternating with thickets of bush and forest, we saw a herd of grazing buffalo. There was one very old, big black bull in the herd, some younger bulls and a number of calves. Hearing the Land Rover some distance away, the old bull started to walk out in front of the herd. He raised his horns, ready to run, but then suddenly he began to trot away. After a moment he broke into a canter and the whole herd followed him, stampeding away and plunging into the bushes. Dust rose up behind them. You could see them far off as they stopped.

Driving back to Ol Tukai guest house, we noticed the pools that were left during the dry season far from the underground springs from the melting waters of Mount Kilimanjaro. This stretch has rippling sand and a collection of shallow pits three or four feet deep with water oozing through at the bottom. These are made by elephants, partly to save themselves the trouble of a long-distance walk to drink at the springs and partly because they are wise creatures that have learnt to suspect the hidden dangers of an obvious water hole. My father was careful to drive round these water holes to avoid the Land Rover getting stuck in them.

We drove for miles through the rough roads to get to Ol Tukai guest house. Here and there, owing to the rains, the roads petered out and trying to figure out the next section was very tricky. We reached a swampy patch and Father's friend had to get out and walk through to see how deep the mud was. It seemed we had gotten lost and had been driving in circles, but finally we saw our guest house from a distance and drove in that direction. Because we got lost, we were late and arrived when dinner had been served and the Maasai dance performance was over. We were glad to be back, safe

Ole Kajiado and Amboseli Game Park Tour

and sound.

Next morning, the guesthouse was awoken by lots of yells, shouting and confusion. We dressed quickly to go out to see what was happening. Our father took hold of us children and told us to go back into our rooms. I was the oldest and I was not going to be left out of the fun, so I disobeyed his orders and went out. A twelve-foot rock python had appeared near one of the guest rooms. Luckily it did not get inside but had entered a hole and they were trying to smoke it out. After about an hour or so, the rock python reared with the speed of lightning. People ran in different directions away from it. The Maasai men near by took spears and threw them at the python. Two of them missed the reptile's head by an inch or two. Then a third Maasai man threw his spear; it caught the snake in the middle and pinned it to the ground.

The snake managed to wriggle free and charged at the crowd again. Other Maasai men hurled huge stones at its head then it went still. Everyone was twenty feet away from it and no one dared go near it. I was right behind my father and I looked at where the rock python lay. Its body was thick and covered with coloured, broad, irregular stripes. The body marking was brown-yellow and the head was triangular. It had a dark brown mark on top shaped like a spearhead; its teeth looked sharp and yellow and curved backward. These rock python are non-venomous and kill by constriction. After gripping their prey, they coil around it and tighten the coil every time the victim tries to breathe out. Death can be caused by cardiac arrest rather than by asphyxiation or crushing.

These pythons, when they are fourteen feet long, can swallow a twelve-year-old child. The guest-house owners were worried in case it attacked or swallowed one of the guests' children. There was a big hunt to smoke them out in case there were more in other holes about the place and in the nearby bushes and rocky areas. This was my second encounter with a python and both incidences

Chapter Sixteen

were very scary.

Half a kilometre away from our guest house there was a water hole, where the wild animals came for a midday drink or just to walk around in the cool of the evening. We watched them from our veranda using binoculars while having late afternoon tea.

We saw more wild animals. We drove to a bluff, one of the finest observation points imaginable. This particular day we were very lucky; the sun was high and down the bluff was a small river. We all sat quietly in the Land Rover then we heard familiar metallic chuckle of a troop of guinea fowls.

Bertie Hunt, who had got out of the Land Rover to walk, was at the river's edge. He turned to look upstream then he whistled a signal. Father got out of the Land Rover and ran to join Bertie with his binoculars still in his hand. We sat in the Land Rover and watched both Bertie and Father; they were watching something some yards away. I took the spare binoculars, which were on the dashboard, and looked through them. There, walking quietly across the dry sand about three hundred yards away from Father and Bertie Hunt, were three lions. The two in the lead were male and behind them was a lioness.

These lions walked upright and proud, as lions do when they are neither hunting nor suspicious. Behind the lioness was a flock of thirty or so guinea fowls, necks craned and they were scolding vigorously. The lioness was paying no attention to them. As I watched, the two leading lions disappeared into the dense bushes by the riverside. The lioness stopped, turned her head in the direction of Bertie Hunt and Father and yawned. She made not a sound. The guinea fowl behind her stopped, as if frozen stiff. Then this great beast walked on in a leisurely fashion and behind her followed the squawking guinea fowl and they all disappeared into the bushes.

It was the most unusual and exciting experience to see them at close quarters. When Father and Bertie Hunt got back to the Land

Ole Kajiado and Amboseli Game Park Tour

Rover, I saw they were happy to have seen the three lions at a close range. We were lucky to see more animals as we were returning to our guest house and crossing a small stream. We were driving slowly and watching through binoculars. Our Land Rover was just about to cross a small bridge when the engine was switched off just as we saw a male kudu close to the river edge. He was a magnificent specimen with his great spiral horns, a good sixty inches long. Behind him were three more bulls, two with average-sized horns, and one young animal whose horns showed just a single twist – probably a three year old. Seen in the open like that in bright sunlight, kudu bulls must be among the most magnificent animals.

Kudu bulls have different behavioural patterns. They don't fall behind the others, as some antelopes do. They are beautifully proportioned, a perfect combination of strength and grace. This big bull was five feet at the shoulder and a blue-grey colour – and he was a bully, too. He stood there challenging the younger ones to take him on. As one of the younger ones took a step towards him, the bully bull made an intimidating sweep with his horns first to one side then to the other side. It was obvious he had the others completely cowed. After a minute or so, standing there to make sure all knew he was the boss, he turned to the river and drank. The others stepped forward to drink alongside him but not all at the same time, for there was always at least one on watch.

Suddenly one of them noticed us and registered alarm. All four heads were up in a flash and off they went to the far bank of the river in a sinuous leaping movement. The next moment the place was totally empty.

Very soon we were driving through open grassland and bush with big anthills and tall trees evenly spaced for many miles on all sides. We found the road to our guest house. We were exhausted and knew that tomorrow we would have to get back to Ole Kajiado and start the long journey back to Kitale and school.

Chapter Seventeen

Safari back to Kitale Farm

We arrived at Ole Kajiado and spent two nights. Bertie Hunt and his family returned to their home in Kitale before us. Father had to remain behind to hand over school duties to his deputy.

We were soon on our way to Kitale, a long and tiring journey. Safia slept most of the way. Imagine getting back home to our farm at Kitale to find Taprandich there! We were told she arrived one day after we left. She looked very comfortable and had taken control of our home as if she was our father's wife. She had come with her three children: Chepkering, who would later be known as Florence; Kimeli, who we would later call Jimmy, and Kipchumba, whose other name was Stephen.

Stephen was very light in complexion. He was four months younger than me but we were the same height. Our bedroom was occupied by them and already looked a mess. Our books, toys and some belongings were missing. I later discovered that Stephen wore my nightclothes when he went to bed.

I did not like what was happening; things were changing fast. We hardly knew this new so-called family and yet they had taken over our home. That night, Safia and I were made to sleep on the floor on mattresses, while Florence occupied Safia's bed and Jimmy and Stephen occupied my bed.

Next morning Safia and I had a difficult time looking for our

Safari back to Kitale Farm

school uniform and shoes. Breakfast was tea and bread; we ate sitting on the kitchen floor. As I passed the dining room, I saw my father and Taprandich sitting on the chairs by the dining table and having what I thought was a serious talk. Father did not notice me, so I left to go to school using the short cut down by the swamp and river. Safia cried all the way to school.

At school we were very hungry. No one had bothered to pack food for us. Kazungu, our cook, was very confused and unhappy that Taprandich was back and he hardly spoke a word. At school break time, we sat on the benches under the shade while other children ate apples, cakes, biscuits, chocolates and drank juice. We had come empty handed.

Safia was not feeling too well so we left school a little earlier than normal. I held her hand to comfort her as I led the way back home through the eucalyptus forest, the swampy path and the grass-thatched huts of the labourers. I did not notice the labourer's children chant out to us, '*Watoto wa mzungu, watoto wa mzungu*' ('White man's children, white man's children').

When we got home, we found Kazungu had packed his belongings and was going to take the bus to Ole Kajiado to my father's house at the secondary school. Taprandich was to be our new cook and in charge of our father's house. She had prepared some food for us, which we hurriedly ate seated on the kitchen floor.

That night sleep did not come easily for me. I tossed and turned, restless, hot and then cold after midnight. We had been given old blankets, which were thin and worn out. Images of Taprandich back in our lives horrified me. I fretted until the first light of dawn and then I fell asleep.

We were woken by Father. After a quick breakfast, I went to the dining room. My father always took a book with him to the table and I found him reading as he ate his breakfast. He did not notice my presence for a long time until I coughed, then he looked up and

Chapter Seventeen

dropped the book on the table.

I asked him if Taprandich was going to live permanently with us. He told me she was and he was going to marry her; I was not to be afraid, we would all be a happy family. We were not to call her Taprandich but Mama – and Mama she was to be for the rest of our lives.

Safia started to bed wet and our bedding was always smelly. Every morning I was made to carry our old mattresses and blankets out to dry them in the sun. Father still taught at Ole Kajiado secondary school and Kazungu was his cook there. I missed Kazungu's cooking and the way he used to housekeep and organise everything the way our father liked it, but those days were over and we were now all under Taprandich's care.

As the days went by, her standard of cleanliness dropped drastically. She brought in her sisters to help her: Borangei, Taputany and Mambili. Taprandich built round huts for them some metres away from our house. These huts were built out of mud, wood and cow dung and roofed with grass cut from the bottom of our farm.

Behind these huts, Taprandich built a *boma* and brought in a few goats, sheep and native cows from Chepareria Farm in West Pokot. Everything changed, including our father; we were all being turned native except for our clothes, which were still modern.

Soon it was announced that Taprandich and our father were married and we started to acknowledge her as our stepmother. Our home was full of her relatives, who continued to visit our stepmother all the way from Chepareria. This change was too much for Safia and me. We hardly met our father. He stayed separately from us, ate English food and we were not allowed to see or talk to him.

A hut was made especially for Safia and me, and we shared this with our stepmother's sisters' female children who were dirty and uneducated. We were not allowed to play the piano or listen to our father's gramophone. Only in the distance some evenings did we hear beautiful music to remind us of days gone by and lost happiness.

Sometimes, as I sat under the shade of the fruit tree in the afternoon and Safia sat beside me, tears sprang from her eyes. She would try to tell me something then go silent and stop to weep. I would take a handkerchief and wipe the teardrops from her eyes. We talked of the old days, of our mother, sister, as though fondly turning the pages of an old nursery book from our childhood. We spent many hours talking; sometimes the talk turned into whispers because we were afraid someone would hear us.

Did we think our father saw what was happening? I do not think so. Father only saw what suited him; he could not have the whole farm under surveillance and still be a teacher at Ole Kajiado. We were anxious about what would become of us. I had long sleepless nights trying to figure out in my child-like brain what had gone wrong. I had hoped that Father would make the effort to bring back my mother.

I gazed into the darkness amid the deep breathing and muttering of the other children in our hut, turning over everything in my mind. I could see no solution and I knew Safia and I were stuck in a miserable situation. A long, sickening feeling was there in my heart.

I imagined how Father must have felt about my mother during those years in Lamu and realised that he had no desire, tenderness or esteem for a once-beloved woman. There was no hope of setting things right. There was nothing that remained except the bonds of law, duty and custom. Father has to take care of us and we had to trust his choices.

I had seen all this domestic tragedy. My mother, in her naive native way, had tried her best to set things right but now she seemed to be a total stranger to whom we were no longer bound. We seemed to be forgetting her and were more concerned by our present problems. Just living and being recognised as children was a struggle

Chapter Seventeen

that we never could win.

Father had an old brick garage; this was quickly turned into two rooms and we were move into one of the rooms and shared it with our stepsister, Florence. Florence was never a kind person; she was very strict and made us tidy our belongings and bathe every day. We had to scrub the floor and the veranda with a brush and soap so it was always clean.

Our stepmother liked attention and she liked to be talked to. She liked visitors best when they paid a lot of attention to her as she sat in one of my father's old armchairs, knitting. She had a very watchful look and treated us like we were not members of the family. Sometimes, Stepmother cooked chicken and rice for the whole family. After we sat at the table, she served each person a piece of chicken but Safia and I always ended up with the legs and the head; the rest of her family always got the best parts.

Safia and I could not stand the mistreatment much longer but we had no one to turn to. We lived in fear and terror.

My stepmother bought a lot of geese and they grew in number. All day they made a quacking sound and chased us round the house; there was no proper place for them to lay eggs, so they just walked into our food store to nest.

One particular morning my stepmother, as usual, sent me to fetch potatoes and carrots from the food store. I found the door open and then I saw it, this loathsome, spitting cobra. It must have sensed my footsteps because it reared up from among the potatoes in the sack. I saw its squat, diamond-shaped head and puffed neck move upwards and sway gently with its tongue darting in and out of its mouth. This is among the deadliest snakes in Kenya. If I had not seen it, I would have walked right to it and would have been bitten above my ankle. I would have had ten uncomfortable minutes left to live.

The cobra moved very quickly towards me and started to strike.

Safari back to Kitale Farm

I jumped backwards just in time for it to miss. It was getting ready to strike again but I dashed out of the door. My stepmother noticed the fear in my eyes and stood up. I could hardly speak but I turned round and pointed at the deadly creature, which had followed me. As we watched, it hid behind a flower bush that grew near the doorway. Half its body was still exposed; the other half, the head part, was hidden by the bush.

My stepmother ran to her bedroom to get her Maasai spear. By the time she returned, the gardener and most of the family members had gathered. This must have made the snake vicious, because it coiled and started to spit in our direction. Its poisonous spit did not reach us but some got on to the wall, all dark in colour.

Our stepmother took her spear and aimed at the snake. She threw the spear at it but missed. Everyone started to throw stones at it. The snake coiled itself around the spear, which was stuck to the ground next to it. Someone threw a bigger stone at the spear, with the snake still coiled around it. The stone hit the spear, which fell to the ground. Finally, the snake had been hit on its head and it did not move. The gardener pulled a large wooden post from the garden and hurled it with a better aim; the post caught the snake in the middle, but it was lifeless except for a slight movement of its tail.

Chapter Eighteen

Change of School

My schooling changed completely because Stephen was too old to join the Jack and Jill Nursery School. My mother persuaded my father that it would be proper, because we were the same age group, for us to go to a school some three kilometres away from home. The school was initially built for the prison warden's children and was near the prison. So, my life changed.

Every morning, Stephen and I had to walk to school and back after noon. Like every other student, we carried boiled maize and beans for our lunch, wrapped in polythene paper. My shoes were worn and torn; no one bothered to mend them for me and my toes stuck out.

Safia continued to go to the Jack and Jill Nursery school. At least they employed a person to take her on a bicycle to school and back. My school was called Prison Primary School; the walls were built from posts, sticks and mud, the roof was iron sheets, which had gone rusty. During the rainy season, the ground flooded and we were always soaked.

The school was disorderly and the children badly dressed. Most of them came to school barefoot and dressed in torn uniforms. We did not have desks or tables, only old benches. The teachers had big sticks with which to frighten the pupils and almost daily someone was beaten for not learning or misbehaving. It was a very rough

Change of School

environment but I managed to fit in. Lunchtime was the worst time of the day. We had to find a tree to sit under but it was difficult as most were already occupied by other pupils and they bullied us. Sometimes we had to sit in the field under the hot sun and eat our maize and beans.

My stepbrother Stephen and I were very light in complexion so everyone called us MUSUNGU (white). Sometimes, Stephen was given better food for lunch than me but I never complained just in case I was beaten up for telling Father 'lies'. I suffered very much and could not say a word.

I only saw Safia at four o'clock. She was always silent; things had changed and she missed me as we had always stuck together. Then one afternoon I happened to come home early, just in time to see my stepmother beat Safia with the stick. I ran in between Safia and my stepmother, who had raised the cane to beat her again, and when she saw me her anger grew. She turned around and hit me across my back. I caught the stick, pulled it from her hands, and threw it down. She stepped forward and slapped me across my face. Her hand was very swift, and it was a vicious stinging blow. She hit me again and again till I fell backwards. Then she stopped as she heard my father's car come down the driveway. I knew if I told Father I would create big problems for Safia and I. Pretending I was alright, I pulled Safia to her feet, still sobbing, and walked her to her room. It was all because Safia had wet her bed and not taken the bedding out to dry.

That night in our room we lit our candles. Tears were flowing down Safia's cheeks and I cried too. It hurt so much, the pain, humiliation, rejection. Safia went to bed and her eyelids slowly closed. As I stood watching her, I heard her whisper. Was it to wish me good night or to murmur a prayer for both of us, or was she remembering the nursery rhymes that our father told us in earlier days that came to her now in the twilight world between sorrow

Chapter Eighteen

and sleep? I stayed awake till I heard her breathe softly and I knew she was fast asleep. Then I tiptoed to my bed next to hers. I lay down but remained awake, deep in thoughts of horror and sorrow.

Soon, Safia was upgraded to primary level and she was called for interview at Kitale School. Father managed to get me a place at the same school. This was an old colonial primary school and most pupils were white. The headmistress took one look at me and enrolled me. I was not given an interview otherwise I would have failed miserably.

That day I cleaned up, then brushed my hair; in new shoes and clothes, I looked like a well-behaved pupil. That night, I heard a heated discussion between my stepmother and father about my change of school. Why had I not been left with Stephen in the Prison Primary School to continue learning, as she thought that was best for me? Stephen would be lonely without me. The discussion took them to dinnertime, lay dormant in the presence of the members of our house, and started again as soon as they were alone when everybody had gone to bed. It lasted long after midnight. Up and down and round the argument circled and swooped like a gull, now out to sea, now circling the patch where it stayed floating.

Next morning, no one talked about it. Father went ahead quietly without my stepmother's agreement. She only knew when the uniforms were bought. The truth about my stepmother – this is my own opinion after I grew up – was that she simply wasn't a complete human being and was emotionally underdeveloped. The changing times were hard for her; she was primitive in her ways but trying to fit with the modern way of life.

Stephen eventually joined an Asian school called St Columban's Primary and from what I gathered later he was happy there. I went into the British-system school; it was still very colonial, every pupil there was white, and all our teachers were English from the UK. Mrs C.I. Evans was the headmistress, followed in subsequent years

Change of School

by Mr G.H. Gilbertson-King. My very first English teacher when I joined Grade Two was Mrs Buckley and she taught me for two years. When I joined the upper grade, Mrs Sloan taught me, and finally Mr Sloan was my teacher for Seventh Grade.

When we first joined Kitale School, we were accustomed to suffering and I looked much older than the other pupils as I was used to a hard life. Constant discourse in the Kalenjin language had worn away the nuance of speech; our spoken English wasn't good and the teachers often told us to speak loudly or pronounce the words clearly.

Every morning, we were driven to school in our father's car, as this was required by the school. No pupils walked to school and parents were responsible for dropping off and picking up their children every morning and evening. The school was run properly, everything in place. It had a big swimming pool, painting rooms and libraries, gymnasium, horse riding, and a room where they held piano lessons. There was belly dancing, and all sorts of games: rounders, cricket, hockey, football, tennis, badminton, squash.

When we arrived at school before assembly, we were expected to hang our hats and coats on hooks on the veranda. Our names were marked against the hook, so everyone knew exactly where their coat was to be hung. After assembly, I had to go for piano lessons. My piano teacher would be waiting for me and I found her very scary and not a kind old woman. I always forgot what she taught me. Eventually I had to drop piano class, but years later I took up piano lessons again and this time I was taught by Mrs Sloan, the wife of one of my class teachers. She was kind and patient. After she and her family left the country for the UK, there was no one to teach piano lessons and the school's standard dropped.

We had ballet classes. The teacher was young, pleasant and relaxed, so I enjoyed ballet but soon I dropped out as the teacher noticed that I was not concentrating and I didn't get the movements

Chapter Eighteen

right. She made me see that ballet was a system of movements as rigorous and complex as any language. Like Latin or ancient Greek, it had rules. Getting it right was not a matter of opinion or taste; ballet was a hard science. It was also, and just as appealingly, full of emotions and the feelings that come with music and movement. It was blissfully mute, like reading. Above all there was the exhilarating sense of liberation that comes when everything worked; if the co-ordination and musicality, muscular impulse and timing were exactly right, the body would take over. One would let go, but with dancing, letting go meant everything – mind, body, soul. That is why, I think, so many dancers who became professionals describe ballet, for all its rules and limits, as an escape from the self. This was held in our hall; there was a stage to display the best dancers to the school audience or parents when they were invited for the occasion.

We had an English teacher for ballet and she was different from the other teachers. Young, pretty, she liked to wear tights that showed off her unusually long and impressively muscular legs. Her movements, even when she was not dancing, were gracious and elegant, conveyed in ways that teenagers could never quite replicate. The teacher was not just teaching us steps or imparting technical knowledge but giving us the culture and the tradition of ballet. The steps we were taught were living, breathing evidence of a lost past. The dancing was on the tips of the toes, known as pointe work. We wore beautiful shirts made of tulle and a short skirt made with many layers of stiffened fabric. The school provided these costumes.

The meals were good and at break time we had tea or cocoa, buttered bread with peanut butter and two biscuits. Lunch was our best meal and we ate good food. There were prayers before meals. Meals were eaten in silence and the only sound was the tap of the spoon, forks and knives. The head of each table made sure our table manners were up to standard. Teachers sat and ate their meals on an upper platform at the end of the building to oversee us.

Change of School

The whole school was grouped into three: Nandi House, Elgon House and Cherangani House. We competed among the houses in swimming, sports, ball games, cross-country races and class performance. Whichever house won, there was a house party held in their honour.

We had a Christmas party at the end of each year and a grand ball was held in our beautiful hall. It was always splendid. After a big feast, we all rushed up to dance. We could hear music floating out among the *nandi* flame trees and the bougainvillea hedges. We sat at the end of the room watching the older pupils dance. We all had fun. Parents were notified to pick their children at ten o'clock.

One of our best festivals was Guy Fawkes Night, which the school held on November fifth each year. There was always a lot of wood to burn as the year came to an end. This night marked the anniversary of the discovery of a plot organised by Catholic conspirators to blow up the Houses of Parliament in London in the year 1605.

A huge bonfire was built during the day. Parents were invited to come in the night at 8 p.m. to take part. Some older pupils were allowed to wear spooky outfits. A dummy of Guy Fawkes was made of old clothes and stuffed with paper or straw. Looking at it, it reminded me of a scarecrow. Guy Fawkes' effigy was traditionally placed on top of the bonfire then set ablaze. Fireworks filled the sky. There was traditional food – parkin cake, sausages cooked over the flames, marshmallows toasted in the fire and potatoes baked in the ashes. We were given plates and everybody was given something to eat. Our father did not come and Safia and I sat beside each other; we did not see Stephen the whole evening of the festivals. He probably walked home and didn't feel free to join in.

We also had a carol service at the end of the year. Parents were invited to watch the service and to participate in singing Christmas songs. There were traditional carols and a reading of the Christmas story as well as songs and bit of humour.

Chapter Eighteen

A choir was specially selected to practise the carol songs for a whole month for this special season. The carol concert was acted to perfection: prayers, hymn and carol songs were included, readings from the Bible, poetry, and a play about the birth of Jesus Christ the Saviour were all part of the event. The hall was decorated with a huge Christmas tree and lit up, and there was candlelight everywhere during the service.

After a year, my stepbrother Stephen joined us at this school. Soon our stepmother gave birth to our half-sister in the bathroom. She refused to be taken to the hospital. Caroline, who was named after our father's mother, was a cute little baby. As she grew up, we loved her and I was made to carry her always tied behind my back like a lump of baggage. I soon got used to it. I never understood why my father or stepmother could not get a wet nurse or maid to look after Caroline. Stepmother made it my duty to do the work and this interfered with my education so the teachers complained about my classwork. My father never understood what was going on; he just thought that I was a thick head and called me a stupid child, which eventually affected me mentally and psychologically.

One day during school holidays, we had visitors from Kajiado District. A young man by the name of Joshua had come with his parents to ask for my stepsister Florence's hand in marriage.

That day everything started well. The visitors sat under a tree to discuss the bride price as my stepmother was very traditional and full of African cultural ideas. No daughters of hers would be handed down for marriage without the exchange of many cows. The young Joshua worked as a clerk with the Nairobi municipality and he earned enough money to take care of a wife; he was very much in love with Florence. They had met briefly during one of her short visits to Ole Kajiado Secondary School where Father taught. In accordance with Maasai culture, they had come all this way to discuss the bride price.

Change of School

Florence was asked to come forward and meet her future in-laws and her husband-to-be. She looked very unhappy. After a long discussion, a number of cows were agreed upon. Florence immediately refused to marry the young Maasai and told everyone that she was expecting someone else's baby. At that moment, the atmosphere changed as if a thunderstorm had appeared on the horizon. My stepmother stood up and looked at Florence for a long time in shocked dismay. There was nothing in the world she wanted more than to give her daughter to young Joshua, her tribesman, in exchange for many cows, bulls and heifers. Joshua's parents were equally shocked by the unexpected turn of events.

There is nothing more important to the Maasai than the exchange of cows for a young lady. This is their culture and the cows have great meaning; rejection was too much for Joshua to handle. Another meeting was held and the conclusion reached that Florence had to be married off to Joshua, who would accept her and her unborn baby. Florence started to cry very loudly then everyone started to talk at once. Florence did not want to marry Joshua. She feared the Maasai tradition of yearly pregnancies; she feared being dressed up in Maasai cow hide with beads round her neck and big earrings made of copper wire. Florence wanted to stay with us and become a modern lady.

Joshua and his Maasai mother and father went back to Kajiado very disappointed. Two days later, my stepmother would not talk to Florence but called her native relatives to prepare a circumcision ceremony for her. Florence disappeared for a week. We later heard that she had eloped with a Kamba (name of one of the Kenyan tribes) man called Tony Maima. My father had to go the police station to get help to bring Florence back home. No charges were pressed on Tony Maima; we found out later that Tony Maima was the father of Florence's unborn child.

My stepmother went ahead with preparing the circumcision

Chapter Eighteen

ceremony for Florence. This was to take place at her Chepareria farm in West Pokot. Some five young girls, who were Florence's cousins, joined her but first the ceremony had to start from our home in Kitale.

The young girls, including Florence, were dressed up for their special dance in full traditional attire, in a red cloth with beads of all colours. This was tied round the young girl's waist, to allow dancing so their beauty was shown off. The necklace was part of the outfit and a nice long *kofia* (hat) made of monkey skin, decorated with beads of all colours, was placed on the head. There was a fly whisk made of a horse tail and a whistle to use as part of the dance. The girls danced and jumped to show off their beauty. On their ankles, they wore tiny bells that jingled as they moved. These girls would take weeks moving from one village to another, inviting friends and relatives to bring gifts and come to the circumcision ceremony. We knew it would exhaust Florence but her mother was a hard woman and would not tolerate weakness from her daughter. Luckily for me, I was not of an age to join these young girls otherwise I would have had the same fate.

When the big day finally arrived, Father drove us down to Chepareria. I never understood why he allowed such savage behaviour to take place but he was dragged into it. The day of the ceremony started with a big dance party at the homes of our stepmother's relatives. Everything reminded me of the Pokot people and their culture; this was similar except here people wore more clothes rather than animal skins. The elders drank a lot of the native drink called *busaa*. Many young girls and boys came to join the final dance as the night approached and to sing songs of praise to the young girls who were being circumcised the next morning, but first the older women had to check to see if these girls were virgins. This checking is done according to their customs. We could only view it from afar. Safia sat next to me because everything seemed to get out of hand as people got drunk.

After checking the virgins, a special leaf called *sinnendeet* was used; this is associated with happiness during weddings and circumcisions. If a girl is found to be virgin, this *sinnendeet* plant is placed on the roof of her hut to announce her virginity. Unfortunately, Florence did not get her hut decorated since she was not a virgin. This brought great shame to our stepmother.

The circumcision started at four in the morning, before sunrise. Older women cut off part of the young girl's private parts. It is a very dangerous process; anyone could die of shock or haemorrhage, or her urethra, bladder or rectal area might get damaged. Luckily, Florence and the other young girls did not die but managed to survive the whole ordeal bravely. Circumcision lasted from 9 a.m. to 4 p.m. Then middle-aged women sang the final songs before breaking into long ululations and shrieks; their voices would rise up to heaven as if to thank their god that the ceremony was over. Their passion for the ceremony could be felt like a great furnace of fire spreading throughout the crowd. Florence and the young girls were escorted to their huts for rest and healing; they were taught for a month to respect elders, respect their husbands, and their role in the community. They wore cow skins and sheep skin for a whole month. They use cow skin as a carpet to sleep on.

I went to join Safia in our hut. We were both weary and slept all morning and afternoon. When we woke up, it was to the sound of late afternoon rain that turned into a big storm. When I went out, there were tree branches and leaves everywhere and the wind was still there. The place seemed quite empty except for my stepmother's relatives.

Father could not stay for too long at this ceremony, which went on for the whole month. He had to leave our stepmother behind and took us, including Stephen my stepbrother, back to Kitale to our farm and to our comfort zone.

Chapter Nineteen

Visit to a Witch Doctor

MY HALF-SISTER WAS with my stepmother and she cried all the time. This upset everyone. My stepmother hated me and made me do all the work without rest; this upset Kazungu, as he did not want to see me cleaning up the kitchen, washing dishes and clothes at my age. Sometimes I had to carry the baby, Caroline, on my back the whole day without putting her down except for meals or to sleep. Our father stopped noticing us; he went to his office, which was in the school compound, to avoid confrontation with my stepmother. We never sat at a table for meals but were made to sit on carpets on the floor. Our meals changed to native food provided by our stepmother.

Kazungu never interfered but did things quietly, without complaint. I knew he would leave if his way of doing things was not respected. He could not work with my stepmother's interference.

One day on our farm at Kitale, Father got very ill. We thought he had malaria but it was not; he had drunk contaminated water. A beetle had gotten into his filtered water and for weeks the filter was not washed out. Stepmother continued to fill it with clean boiled water. Father was the only member of our family allowed to drink this water, so he got really sick.

He was taken to hospital to our family doctor, I.M. Leach, and he had to be admitted at the Mount Elgon hospital for several days.

Visit to a Witch Doctor

We thought he would die. Imagine missing him for a whole week! Eventually he came home, very pale and weak, and had to rest for two weeks under the supervision of our stepmother. Kazungu was ordered not to cook for him because Stepmother was still looking into who poisoned our father; no one but her was allowed near him, not even us children. Every evening, Father was carried out to an armchair under the tree for fresh air. As the days went by, we saw him walk round the compound and we were glad to notice that he had his energy back and was himself again.

My stepmother, seeing that Father had regained his strength, insisted that the whole family, Father included, go and see a medicine man. She knew a *muganga* (witch doctor) by the name of Onalo who lived in Kipsaina, a village fifteen miles away. My father was not strong-minded enough to refuse her and he drove us there in his car. She insisted that we all had to be cleansed, that someone had used black magic on the family; if we did not go to the *muganga* for protection, we could not remove the spell and death would follow.

Kimeli my stepbrother, Florence my stepsister, Stephen, me, Safia, Caroline and our stepmother all squashed into father's Volkswagen and drove down the dusty road in the direction of Kapenguria. Halfway is Kipsaina centre then we branched off to the right, taking a tiny road towards a compound. There were many thatched huts in a circle and in the middle there was a huge hut. Goats, sheep, birds and a tortoise had been fenced off at one side of this hut. Some birds were in a cage. Father drove underneath the trees in the compound for shade, though he had not asked permission to do so.

Our stepmother got out of the car and walked to the big hut. We did not see her for a long time. Then our father was called in and he stayed for an hour. He came out and waited at the car. After about fifteen minutes, our stepmother came out and walked towards the car. We were told to go to the hut.

Chapter Nineteen

I was very frightened. The hut was dark and our eyes had to get used to the darkness. A fire was burning on the stamped clay floor; the heat was suffocating and the smoke was dense. We saw this massive figure of a man dressed in cow skin and round his neck he had a necklace made out of teeth; I didn't know if they were human or animal teeth. There were feathers on his headdress and animal skulls around his chair. The place had a bad smell – tobacco, molasses and incense. It was believed that the smells would attract the genie or spirit.

We were made to sit on the floor. Our stepmother took out a sharp razor and began to cut our nails and some hair from our heads. She wrapped them up in separate wrappings, placed them on a calabash and took them to the witch doctor. I wondered why they needed our nails and hair – maybe to stuff them in tiny dummy dolls and put our names on them? These dolls represented real people – in other words, they were voodoo dolls. They were kept in the witch doctor's hut and a spell put over them, depending on the request.

The way I saw it, all was more to do with placing curses on me and Safia and gaining control over our family. My stepmother never liked our cook, Kazungu; she thought he had brought genies from the coast. She used her witch doctor to overpower Kazungu and tried to make Father resent him.

A woman came in and the witch doctor ordered her to kill a chicken. Blood was sprinkled round where we sat. A goat was tied at the end of the hut and forced to inhale the negative experiences they thought we harboured in our minds. Everybody sat watching, afraid of what was happening. We had never experienced such behaviour. No one dared to run out or talk.

Finally, Stepmother was ordered to take a razor blade and make small cuts on our foreheads, chests and upper arms. Some ash was rubbed in and I saw the baby Caroline faint. Stepmother took her

Visit to a Witch Doctor

out for fresh air. What good would such a 'medical experience', as they called it, bring? At the end, the witch doctor gave Stepmother lots of bundled-up burnt leaves, which had turned into ashes, to put in our meals for a week. Thank God no one got sick.

My stepmother believed in magic and it became part of her life, though she tried to hide it. We all knew when she went to visit this *muganga* (medicine man) to get herbal medicine. We were always frightened of her and scared to eat food prepared by her in case it was poisoned.

Sometimes we started to believe in this magic. I feared she had cast spells on me to lower my intelligence because my thoughts were slowing down and sometimes I sat like a zombie, dumb and stupid, staring into nothingness. Sometimes I cried over nothing and wished myself dead. Sometimes I would wander far away and no one knew where I went, but I did all of this as if I were in a daze.

As the days went by, Father thought I had lost my mind and I was taken to the government hospital for treatment. My mother was called and I was left in her care for two weeks till I recovered my senses and started to feel myself again. Sitting under a tree with Mother, whom I could scarcely recognise, I once again felt the sun and the wind, which had fallen to a soft breeze, gently stirring the blossoms on the lime trees and carried its fragrance, fresh from the late rain, to merge with the sweet breath of drying stone and the shadow of the obelisk that spanned the place.

I noticed for the first time the bungalow where my mother stayed with her friend, Mrs Esther Bedford-Pim, on the neighbouring farm. The bungalow was beautiful and she had a lovely orchard beyond her front courtyard. Most of the fruit trees were in blossom. There was a sweet smell in the air and bees buzzing round these tiny flowers.

My mother was her great friend; they had known each other long before Kenya attained independence. Mrs Bedford-Pim was

Chapter Nineteen

glad to see Mother and me and let me stay at her place to get well.

Mrs Esther Bedford-Pim's husband came and took us to his farm in Cherangani Hills, a one and half hour drive away. He owned a big farm of two thousand acres and kept dairy and beef cattle. In the early afternoon we came to his farm, driving through a big iron gate through open parkland. There was a turn in the drive and suddenly a new and secret landscape opened before us. We were at the head of a valley; grey and gold, amid a screen of boskage, shone the dome and columns of an old house. The garden and the fountain were lovely to look at.

The car stopped and we all stepped out. We were invited into this beautiful place where I was to rest and to be happy for a while. Mrs Esther Bedford-Pim had three children younger than me and they were brought up the English way with a nanny and wet nurse for the very young one, a boy called Norman. The two girls were Cylia and Francisca, and we went to Kitale School with both the daughters.

Their home had many rooms and was very spacious. I was led through a big living room that looked more like a ballroom. The big curtains were drawn back and the late afternoon sun flooded in. There was a vast fireplace, beautiful furniture and shelves with many books. I noticed that the big doors were made of mahogany.

Mother and I were given one of the rooms in the left wing of the house and we climbed the scrubbed elm stairway that led to the upper room. The nanny, after showing us our room, announced that tea would be ready in an hour's time and our presence was required as all members of the house would be gathered.

Dinner that evening consisted of soup, fried fillets of sole with sauce, lamb cutlets propped against a cone of mashed potatoes, stewed rhubarb and sponge cake. The following nights we had different meals: fish, meat and savoury, on others days it was meat, sweet, savoury. Mrs Esther, my mother and Mr Bedford-Pim drank

Visit to a Witch Doctor

plenty of different wines. Did they have a cellar full of wine, I wondered.

That night I did not sleep well, probably because I was in a different bed. I was awake most of the night, restless, hot and cold by turns. Was I becoming sick again with a touch of malaria? I thought my distressing nights were over but now here I was, in this lovely home, still having bad dreams. They went on till dawn. I repeated silent prayers, I tossed, turned and fretted all night till light broke through in the early morning. I walked to the window, opened it and felt the cold air rush in. The rustle of a rising breeze turned me back to bed.

When I awoke, my mother was at the open door. She looked worried but all was well and I felt better and happy. For the first time, I asked my mother about my half-brother, Rotich, and Selina. She just mumbled that they were alright but her face showed concern.

I enjoyed myself so much that I did not notice the two weeks pass by. Soon I was taken back to Father. Mrs Esther Bedford-Pim was very concerned about my health and welfare. She personally took me to Father and advised him that I was not to be overworked or mistreated. During the weeks that followed, my relationship with my father improved and he spent time with all of his children. He took us to the Kitale Club, gave us treats and introduced us to some of his old friends. He ordered our stepmother to bring our meals to his table and we sat with him for meals. It was all thanks to Mrs Bedford-Pim.

This did not last long. Stepmother had a baby girl called Catherine and my father loved her very much. Then our relationship with my father deteriorated sharply. We saw little of him during the day; he spent hours in his library. Now and then he emerged and I heard him calling too loudly for one of the servants. He often stayed late in his library and I saw trays going up to him at

Chapter Nineteen

odd hours, laden with snacks, tea, biscuits, cakes. If we met in the passageway, normally I would be cleaning the house again and he would stare at me as if I did not exist. At dinnertime, he was clean and dressed and sitting alone for dinner, reading his book as he ate. He had a small bell beside him to ring when he needed his next course. After the meal, he would go to the garden room where he drank his tea and read. We did not exist in his world anymore and that was very worrying.

Most Friday evenings, he went out to dinner and he wore his dinner jacket. If he was not at the Kitale Club he would join his friend Bob Weizmann at the Masonic Lodge. Other friends of his were: Bedford-Pim; Dr Belcher; H.M. Bowker; S.A. Dalton; P.L. Davies; C. Grand Court; E.M. Hansen; H.M. Hunt; J.S.H.Meyers; W.R.Millar; Bernard Mills; D.J. Orton, and last of all his very good friend, Williamson.

Chapter Twenty

Encounter with a Lioness at Tambach

ONCE AGAIN, WE had our father to ourselves – except this time Stephen was with us. Stephen was always very quiet and kept to himself. I learnt that Father had to change schools and join a place called Tambach Secondary School and the three of us joined him. It was near the Kerio Valley and the Elgeyo Escarpment, and had the most stunning views when you looked down at the dramatic Kerio Valley. This is called Kenya's own Grand Canyon; it plunges a thousand metres and the opposite wall rises up dramatically. Elgeyo Escarpment is among the most beautiful places in Kenya.

This was where my father was to be head teacher for the next three years. The school was situated on the slopes. He liked this place very much and brought with him his cook, Kazungu, who had been in his service for a long time. Father was given the best house in the school and it had many rooms. Everybody was relaxed and happy and we were glad, especially me, that our stepmother and her relatives were not here; once again we had our father all to ourselves. This was during our school vacation.

Father even came to our room to read to us at bedtime until nine o'clock when he closed the book and said I should go to sleep. He left the room and blew out the candle; it was totally dark except between the window and curtains. I could see the light of the full moon that penetrated our room as I lay there between dream-

Chapter Twenty

ing and waking. I thought about my stepmother and, in my brief dreams, she took on a hundred terrible forms and it turned into a nightmare. I woke up early morning and felt really tired because of the lack of sleep. The whole day I did not feel well.

Kazungu was left to look after us one weekend when Father had to drive to Kitale and back. Father didn't come back as we had expected, so the next day Stephen decided to take Safia for a long walk down the valley without permission. At midday, I decided to follow the direction they had taken. I used the rough road, walking steadily down and hoping to come across them thinking they would be on their way back. This countryside was not populated, so I saw different species of game lurking in the distance beneath the big trees. In the glades and dappled undergrowth, the ever-alert, always-nervous buck, duiker and other small game paused. Luckily, I did not meet any herds of buffalo.

I stopped to look back at where I had come from. I could see great bluffs on either side of the precipitous cliffs. Wind circled constantly to form thermals that blasted up the face of the cliff, across the plateau and through the Elgeyo Escarpment. I kept telling myself to turn back and go home, but I found it easier to walk downwards till I came across a small stream that crossed the road. I decided to sit on a stone by the road and decide whether to turn back or go downhill. If Safia could not make it back up the hill, at least she would have me and Stephen to carry her.

I decided that if I went on looking for Safia, I would never make it home before dark. I had not realised how far I had come. I got up from the stone and started to walk uphill following the same road I had come down. I had been told there were many cheetahs and leopards in this part of the country and just thinking about them frightened me. I stopped to catch my breath and looked back. In the stillness there was silence for a time then, quite suddenly, a lion cub appeared down below at the stream. He must have been five

Encounter with a Lioness at Tambach

or six months old.

I quickly hid behind a tree and watched him put his nose down to the water. One lap and his head was up, looking around. Something else was there. I could make out nothing at first but then there was a sound between a purr and a grunt, and I saw a lioness. At first, I was very frightened and shaky. I even thought of climbing the tree I was hiding behind. Then I just froze; I couldn't move or run or climb the tree.

This was a near-death experience for me. What was I doing here alone away from home? The lioness had been standing well concealed in the shade; that's why I hadn't seen her before her cub. Her cub was very playful; it gambolled up to her and back again. Then I saw her move quickly to the water with strong, determined strides. She did not drink but stopped dead and turned her head towards me. I was so confused that I did not know if she had seen me or not. She thought there was no danger and in a flash the two of them disappeared back into the bushes. I sat down and my body was shaky. I had to wait for a while to steady myself before I started to run up the road towards home.

I kept on walking and stumbled several times. It was getting dark. I followed the rough dusty road I had used while coming down. Then, when I thought I would never get home, I saw the flash of lights from a car ahead of me and heard the engine as it came steadily downhill. I stepped in the middle of the road so the driver would notice me. What a silly thing to do; imagine if this car had not had brakes, it would have run over me. The brakes screeched and it came straight at me, just missing me by inches.

I heard people jump out of the car and voices. The lights from the car still blinded me. Then I heard a voice like my father's calling out my name. Although I was still in shock and frightened, I knew I would be scolded, and I hoped my stepmother was not at home. Stephen, my stepbrother, had never liked me; he had probably told

Chapter Twenty

tales about me trying to run away. I was helped to the car, still shaking from cold and shock. I passed out and didn't know when we arrived home. Sure enough, my stepmother was there. Her eyes frightened me and I knew that the next day she would beat me.

Chapter Twenty-One

Mount Elgon

OUR FAMILY WAS desperately in need of a bigger house and farm, so Father and Stepmother drove towards the Endebess area. This is on the slopes of Mount Elgon and is a very fertile place because of lava from the big mountain. If we could buy land, it would benefit the whole family. Coffee farming would do well here.

From our house I could see the mountain. During the rainy season it was very cloudy and heavy rain came down right across our farm because we were in the rain belt area. Sometimes though, the sky was blue and one could hardly see a cloud. The beautiful indigenous forest could be seen sometimes on a cool breezy day from our farm, as well as the high cliffs of the Endebess Bluffs.

This fertile place was where Father wanted to buy a farm. My stepmother, after our journey to view the farm, turned it down. She made many excuses to turn down all the farms she visited: she did not like the place or the local tribe, the Sabaot. These people lived on the slopes of Mount Elgon and she did not trust them. My stepmother was also afraid of the Pokot and the Karamojong, who were the neighbouring tribe, as she was tired of the cattle thieving that continued in those areas.

My father was very keen to settle here. Mount Elgon had a national park and part of this park was in both Kenya and Uganda. He took me on a camping trip before he gave up on buying a farm

Chapter Twenty-One

on the slopes of the mountain. The park was established in 1967 and gazetted in 1968. It lies on the eastern flank of the massive volcano, its boundaries some distance beneath the summit. The mountain is ancient beyond comprehension. Mount Elgon feels like a link with the beginning of time; it burst out of Trans-Nzoia plains more than fifteen million years ago.

My father did not have a four-wheel drive vehicle so his good friend Alistair Burn lent him one of his vehicles. My stepbrothers Stephen and Kimeli accompanied us. Safia was too young to come. It all sounded exciting. Our four-wheel drive had to be left behind and the game warden advised us to hire police who were in charge of the game park. They were armed with rifles, as there were leopards around.

We had to carry camping gear, and Stephen and Kimeli complained all the way because the climb was hard. This is the most beautiful unspoilt place in all of Kenya's national parks. We laboured up the trail through the glorious forest, walked onto the moorland heights. Here we saw different specimens of game lurking beneath the centuries-old trees that rise for thirty metres or so. In the glades and dappled undergrowth, the ever-alert, always-nervous bucks or *duikers* and the small game paused, frozen in the panic of discovery as we continued. We never encountered elephants.

Before we arrived at the peak we had to visit Kitum Cave, one of the largest caves deep inside the mountain. The Elgon elephants came here during the night and mined the cave salt by gouging it out, sometimes making the cave roof fall and trapping an elephant or two. The Kitum Cave was the inspiration for Rider Haggard's great adventure drama; it also inspired a television documentary about the Elgon elephants.

The main peak is Wagagai on the Ugandan side, which has a fantastic view of the Caldera. The highest peak on Kenyan side is Sudek, followed by Koitoboss where one can see the Suam gorge

Mount Elgon

on the Kenya/Uganda side of the mountain. The gorge forms the Suam River, which flows to the Turkwell Dam. At the Caldera, there were no huts or campsites so we had to use our camping gear. At night the air was very cold; if we had gone right to the top, there would have been ice that, it was then believed, never melted.

The next day we did not stay long because the cold was too much for us. Stephen and Kimeli kept on complaining so, after breakfast of coffee, bread and boiled eggs, we climbed down. Lower down we saw lava and more caves. We saw black-and-white colobus monkeys swinging through those trees and caught a glimpse of the Mandarin-faced De Brazza monkey, which I believe were very rare in this place. We came across other rocky peaks on the lower side and the views were excellent.

It was late afternoon, just about sunset, as we arrived at our four-wheel drive. We saw more antelopes and other animals as they came out to graze.

We drove home. For weeks the subject of the farm was never brought up till one day our father and stepmother visited another farm, Machungwa Farm on the Kitale–Eldoret Road, seven kilometres away from Kitale Town.

Chapter Twenty-Two

Machungwa Farm

Father and Stepmother visited this farm; at this point we thought it was just another family property. We were not aware that this would be our stepmother's farm and the land title would be in her name.

Stepmother seemed very cheerful and happy; her drinking had reduced and her kind nature, which we rarely saw, was back. There was much talk in the evening when they came back and I assumed it was plans for this farm. Both Father and Stepmother seemed very happy.

Eventually we moved to the farm. Some of our furniture was carried there in a hired lorry but the farm already had a lot of furniture.

My first visit was very memorable. We had to pass a thick, five-acre eucalyptus forest. The driveway was beautiful; it reminded me of fairy tale in a book Father had read to us. Both sides of the driveway were lined with palm trees. Nandi flame trees were everywhere and the orange flowers were blossoming on them.

We arrived at the compound, which had a lovely car parking area with bougainvillea hedges. In the middle was a pond with lilies floating on top of the water. These lilies are amazing plants that flower all year round with large white, pink, purple and yellow blooms that give out a wonderful aroma.

Machungwa Farm

This house was massive, had creepers all over the front and had many rooms. There were towers each on either side, each with a stairway. The first thing we children did was climb the scrubbed-elm stairs. The stairways were gated at the end and the doors were locked, so we never got to see inside.

Immediately we started to choose our rooms. I fancied taking one of the tower rooms but Father thought it would be too lonely at night for me, so I took one with Safia near a bathroom and toilet. I thought it best for us to stick close together.

This house was initially owned by H.M. Bowker; he was the earliest settler who came to farm in Kitale. This farm was more than three-thousand acres but the family had been selling it off in big pieces and only one hundred acres or so remained, ninety-five acres of which were land, ten acres of indigenous forest and a beautiful dam. Everything was in order; all machinery worked, and the Lister engine and a generator gave light to the massive house.

We were told that water flowed continuously and a rain-water pump engine was in place to pump twenty-four hours round the clock. We had pineapples on five acres of land and we grew tangerines, oranges, guavas and grapefruits in the orchard. Most of these fruits were under irrigation all year round as the dam pump was always working and never needed any repairs, except for cleaning the waterway and removing dead leaves. There was another patch of land that grew macadamia nuts. In the orchard we had one pecan tree that was well over fifty feet high and fifteen feet in width. Pecan nuts are good for the heart; they contain 87% unsaturated fatty acids and nineteen vitamins and mineral types. These became part of our diet and were delicious. It was the only pecan tree on the farm; for pollination to occur it would require another variety. Self-pollination is possible but for years to come this tree just stood alone in the middle of the orchard.

Not too far away was a huge jackfruit tree. There was bamboo

Chapter Twenty-Two

everywhere and twelve acres of irrigated fertile land with vegetables growing. By the dam, there was a pump with its attendant piping and storage tanks. Cattle troughs were placed in between the driveway on the way down to the river.

I walked down to the dam. Usually I liked to be on my own but this time Safia followed me. The virgin forest around this dam was mostly indigenous trees. It was mysterious and quiet. In other places the trees grew so tightly together that I had to bend low while looking for a path through them, always looking behind me to see if Safia was still there. She seemed very scared. Some places were dark with green shade. Once inside, we could not see the sky but the rays of sunlight penetrated in many strange ways, falling through the foliage. Grey fungus was everywhere, like long drooping beards on the trees. It gave a secretive air to this beautiful little forest.

I made up my mind that this would be my place to come when I felt lonely. I would wander round the little winding paths that abruptly ended at the edge of the dam. I looked down at the water, saw my face staring back at me, and wondered what life held for me.

There was a quick movement through the dry leaves; it was not Safia because she was right behind me. I started to be afraid. A frog jumped into the dam gave me a fright. The air was cool and the creepers entangled everything. I had to be careful in case a green snake was in them; I could not see clearly as everything was green in colour.

The forest was full of the scent of plants and, when these creepers flowered, they had an overwhelming sweet perfume like lilac. We ran down these tiny paths that ended at the edge of the dam. The lilies were beautiful; they give off another attractive smell and there were bees buzzing everywhere looking for nectar round these pretty lily flowers. The flower shape is cuplike; their pods are green and bronze speckled with a wavy margin and a very pleasant fra-

Machungwa Farm

grance. On one side a neat structure had been built. The surrounding clearing looked like a picnic place with benches and a table. Near it was a springboard, one end hanging over the water and the other firmly fixed.

I saw four small boats; this place was used for fishing or a picnic site. Safia walked too close to the edge of the water and nearly slipped in. I gripped both her hands to lift her up. We stood still in the middle of this beautiful place and felt happy in the silence. We could hear the birds speak in a multitude of small clear noises. It was getting late and we had to find our way back to the big house.

Safia's eyes were bulging; any movement scared her – even her own shadow could scare her. We did not go as far as our waterfall and the bridge was not safe as it was half rotten. As we came into the open, the sun had sunk beyond the upper side of our farm. The shadows grew long across the pasture as we ran up the hill towards our house.

We saw the moon come up. We walked round the house under the lime trees and paused. Safia idly snapped off one of the long shoots and stripped the leaves as we walked, making a switch as children do. I snatched the leaves and crumbled them beneath my fingers. I peeled the bark, scratching it with my nails; we had a happy feeling of belonging. Maybe one day we would play hide and seek here.

We turned towards the house. We came to the lighted passageway that led into all the other rooms. We could figure out where Father was; we always knew where he was.

We had dinner in the smart dining room. No one had noticed our absence and the other stepchildren were late. Stepmother came in and sat down. It was the first time in many years that I had seen her sit down for meals.

Kimeli, my stepbrother, amused everyone with a silly tale that his bed was full of bedbugs, saying he had been given the worst

Chapter Twenty-Two

room. Everyone was tired. After our meal, Safia yawned and then whispered to me to take her to our room. I took her. We had a small dressing table. She sat at it, head bowed, her hair over her face. When she looked up, I saw her in the mirror. Her face was dazed with weariness and beside it my own stared back looking worried and tired.

In the coming week, our other furniture was transported to the farm. All the rooms had decent furniture and for a time everyone seemed content. Every evening, when it was getting dark, I went to my favourite spot, the lily pond. I would sit on the log next to it and watch the millions of fireflies. These tiny insects flashed their signals till they matched the countless stars overhead. The fireflies seemed like another canopy of stars beneath me, as if they had fallen to earth. I was told this was part of the mating ritual; these tens of thousands of insects find their mates, each one a pinpoint of brilliance.

A man named Abraham, who had worked on the farm all his life, asked to stay and look after the sheep that Father had bought off the owner. Abraham looked very old and I wondered where he got the strength to control so many sheep. His house was right at the bottom of the farm at the edge of the indigenous forest. The sheep had the paddock near his house. I remember him well. He reminded me of the Abraham in the Bible, wandering round the farm with his flocks. Abraham had given the sheep names and they knew him well. He lived a very lovely, secluded existence. Father had instructed him to come each morning to the house to have breakfast and take food for his midday and evening meal. It was mostly *posho* (maize meal) milk and vegetables and fruit. I saw him around nine o'clock behind the kitchen, sitting on an old log, waiting to be given his ration of food. After that he would go off to the sheep.

Abraham was a rare person; he seemed utterly isolated from

everyone and kept to himself. He could leave the sheep to graze in the paddock and it was funny how they obeyed him and would not move very far away until his return. The sheep were his companions and they listened to him alone.

Chapter Twenty-Three

Selina Came to Stay with Us Permanently

ONE AFTERNOON IN November, Safia and I stood at the big window in the far end of our father's favourite sitting room. Father loved to rest here, have four o'clock tea and read his book as he lay on the long settee. Here was his piano. Now it was his, not ours any more. Stepmother would not let us play it in case one of us ruined it and it got out of tune.

The big window faced the driveway. It was a windy day and the wind stripped the leaves off the trees, sweeping them up the lawn and driveway, leaving them in a pile against the stones near the front steps. We heard a car; it was our father's Volkswagen. We ran out as always; we loved our father very much and wondered if he had got us any chocolates or sweets. Beside Father was our stepbrother, Kimeli.

As the car stopped, Kimeli stepped out and behind him was a little thin girl. At first we could not make out who she was. Safia stared, not knowing it was our sister Selina. It took me a long time to recognise her; I had not seen her for many years and the last time she was left behind she was about six months old. It was just instinct that made me recognise her. She looked very frightened. She must have had a hard life living with different relatives of our mother. Selina held a small bundle of clothes tightly, the only possessions she

Selina Came to Stay with Us Permanently

had in the world. She looked tired and wore old clothes; she looked accustomed to suffering. When she said hello to me, it sounded like a grunt of an animal returning to its basket. She looked down all the time. She was the saddest little girl I had ever seen.

We walked behind them and I carried her bundle. Stepmother was under the mulberry tree as usual, knitting or decorating her Maasai dress with colourful beads. This way she escaped the realities of the world and dreamed of the Maasai people and her traditional past.

Father and Kimeli stood in front of her. Selina looked like a scared rabbit caught in a trap. She was introduced and Stepmother looked up, startled. I heard her say very slowly that this was not part of the bargain; that she only agreed to look after two daughters not this third one. Her words hung in the air between us, like a wisp of tobacco smoke.

That evening the subject of Selina was still not cleared up. She was called into the living room and I trailed behind her. We sat in the shadows beyond the lamplight, beyond the warmth of the burning logs in the fireplace, where Father, Stepmother and Jimmy, my stepbrother, were still discussing Selina's fate. Tea had been cleared away and the curtains drawn. My eyes were heavy with sleep. I had been working very hard to clean this massive house and having lots of thoughts about the future of our family and my mother.

Selina looked totally out of place; she had pouches under her eyes, her movements were listless and jumpy and her hair had grown very long. There was weariness in her eyes.

Father and Stepmother reached a deadlock, not because they failed to understand one another, but because they understood too well what it meant for a third child of my mother's to come to live with us permanently. Stepmother feared that if we grew up together, our father's love and affection would turn towards us. Kimeli never said much, only stammered, finding no reason not to have

Chapter Twenty-Three

Selina as a family member.

In the following week, the subject was discussed among the other stepchildren and Stepmother's relatives; it was like a fire deep in the hold of a ship, below the water-line.

Selina seemed a total stranger in this home; it was a different world to her. She was put in our room to sleep and that night again I woke in the dark and lay, turning over in my mind the conversation I had overheard between Father and Stepmother.

The next morning, I stood outside. Although it had rained all night, the rain had ceased but the clouds hung low and heavy overhead. I noticed that one of the family members had lit the kitchen fire. As I looked up, I saw the smoke from the chimney rise straight to the leaden sky. I cleaned up Selina and took her to the kitchen for breakfast. There was nothing much for us except two slices of thin unbuttered bread with a cup of tea that hardly had any sugar, but all in all this was good enough for us.

I wanted to show Selina the farm to cheer her up. I had to take two Mackintoshes with us; I borrowed Safia's for Selina to wear as the weather was unpredictable. I wore my rubber boots; Safia's rubber boots were too big for Selina's feet, so she used her flip-flops. They got stuck in the mud till we had to carry them and then she walked barefoot. We walked towards the dam, my favourite spot. It was bright but still the clouds hung heavy in the sky – it could rain at any minute. That morning, we saw lots of monkeys but as soon as they heard footsteps they rushed off. I was used to them now and they never frightened me.

It started to rain heavily. It was stupid of me to bring Selina out here. The weather was really bad. What if she got sick? We were soon drenched, as if we had waded up a stream. The heavy mist came suddenly from nowhere. We could hardly see each other – and then it drifted off. When we got home we were very wet and I sneaked Selina back to our room to get her warm clothes. I told her

Selina Came to Stay with Us Permanently

not to tell anyone where we had been. She nodded.

That night Selina suffered so badly, with her teeth chattering, that I could not get her to sleep. I crept to my father's office, knocked and walked in. He was clasping a quill pen, which he continued to dip into the ink container, then stopped to see who it was. He sat on his comfortable office chair writing letters to old Oxford friends and his old colonial friends who lived in the UK. He spent a lot of time in this room writing letters, as though he were reliving colonial times. Sometimes I wondered if it surprised him to live as part of history and remember people and events as if they had happened yesterday. The British Colonial period in Africa had ended some nine years back but Father hung onto his memories and escaped reality by reliving his past.

This is how I see my father and how I saw him that night, lost in his own world. I told him Selina had malaria. For once he stood up very quickly and followed me to our room; Selina was very shaky and hot. Father dressed her to take her to Kitale Town but the car battery was low. Stepmother suggested that Selina should sit naked in a tub in the draughtiest place available on the veranda, and sponged her continually with cold water. Selina's teeth chattered. I was standing doing nothing, looking on. Her temperature had to be brought down. This was what they called the cold-water cure, based on the theory that the parasites that cause malaria and other fevers thrive only at high body temperatures and perish at normal temperatures. We did not have ice cubes then. The method worked because by morning Selina felt better but very weak. Someone had to take the bicycle to town get a taxi. The car battery had to be charged so we could get Selina to hospital as soon as possible. After a week, we were told that she was lucky to have survived. Malaria normally kills very quickly.

Things on the farm went on well for a while and then started to go downhill. I discovered that the workmen were not being paid as

Chapter Twenty-Three

Stepmother could not keep farm accounts and they left without notice. This farm needed strong men and machinery. Probably Father did not sleep well at night but meditated upon improving the farm. He bought more dairy cows but that year the rains did not come on time. Normally the rains came in the last week of March and went on till the middle of June.

Before the rains, the atmosphere grows hot; sometimes the neighbouring people set fire to their land to reduce the bush and the fire accidentally came to our land. Part of the forest round the dam caught fire and from our house we could see the flames. The air over the forest danced with the mighty conflagration. The smoke rolled along the grass and the heat and the smell of burning drifted over our land.

Father was furious as we would have less grazing for our cows but he could not complain as there was no culprit to accept responsibility for the fire. So, we waited for the rains. Some days we saw gigantic clouds gather for a long time overhead, but they quickly dissolved. The evenings grew cold and we thought it was going to rain as we saw the stars at night had disappeared. The night air was often deeply cold. Then we would hear a quick rush of wind in the trees, shrubs and long grass. Sometimes it would continue for hours and we believed that at last the rains had come.

Finally, the rains did come, pouring down, a lover's embrace. We children ran out, excited. We got wet, felt the rain pouring on our faces and we screamed with excitement. We were happy; the crops would grow on time.

Chapter Twenty-Four

Real Work

LATER IN THE morning, I sought my father. The wind outside was too much and we stayed indoors as it was raining. Father was at the fireplace in the living room. Someone had lit the fire and the room was warm. He was bent over his books as usual. I could hear the creepers outside on the windowpane as the rain splashed against them.

I never spent much time in my father's presence, maybe because I feared Stepmother who never allowed any of us children to stay in his company. She was following African native culture; female children were not allowed to be in their father's company especially when they got to a certain age. It was at such moments like this, alone in the living room, that he was lost in his books or writing letters. He was a great correspondent and this showed his need for admiration and applause. The same singularly proud and reserved nature, which meant he would turn away sometimes with disdain from popular notoriety, was capable of being moved by praise from friends and family.

Father commented on my stepmother's horrid behaviour towards us and especially Selina. There was nothing happy about our conversation. Father was definitely unhappy. I thought he would be able to control the situation. When finally I was through talking, I quietly closed the door behind me, shutting out the massive sitting room, the high ceiling, the old pictures hanging on the walls, the

Chapter Twenty-Four

piano, the gramophone, the books; the modern world.

As I walked through the corridors past the kitchen and towards the outer store, I found Selina alone on the bench, her hands folded in her lap, so still that I nearly passed by without noticing her. What was she doing here? She opened her hands on her lap, still shaking with fright; of late she had been wetting her bed badly and today there would be no sunshine to dry it for her and she needed to bathe. I sat by her and she started to speak to me. Here we were again re-joined by life. She spoke as though we had been together all our lives. We had parted as children when she was just a baby. We had now connected and we had to stick together. She kept looking at me for protection. My mind went back to the years on Siyoi farm. There was nothing but humility in the way she spoke but still her eyes were full of fear. I sat for a long time with her and spoke to her to give her confidence. But I too had spent my life in fear and there was not much to share at that moment except to talk about the farm, the dam, the jungle and the butterflies.

Her mood changed fast; she was not paying attention to what I was saying and our talk came to an end. We both sat frozen as we heard our stepmother call out our names.

Later that evening, I was called in to see Stepmother. I could hear all that was being said though I pretended not to hear. Father was also present. Stepmother wanted Selina to be sent back to my mother; the farm was in Stepmother's name and she had the right to get rid of Selina. I looked to Father for support. He stood there, alert, almost scared. Selina had quietly come in to hear all that was said and I saw that she was in tears. She turned round and ran off. Afterwards, it was decided that she would stay until the school holidays were over.

Later I looked everywhere for Selina. I went out towards the orchard, but I could not find her. As I was going through the living room, looking through the open window as the light streamed across the terrace and the lily pond, I caught a glimpse of a white blouse against the stones. I found her in the darkest refuge. I could do nothing much as the situation was beyond my power. I felt adrift in a strange sea; my hands were cold and stiff on her tunic and my eyes were dry. I was far from her in spirit as she sat beside me in the darkness. Her weeping stopped. She sat up, away from me, then rose to her feet. I followed her to the house and to our room. She went straight to bed without supper that night and no one cared if we starved.

The following morning, all that remained were the sad situation and memories that were my life and are always with me. My soul revisited these memories, including many images that never went away. Our stepmother's relatives stuck their noses into our affairs and it was very annoying; it made me angry to think they felt important around this big house. They tried to boss me around and make me do servant's work.

My stepsister Florence had taken charge of the whole household once more. She walked around with a bunch of keys and everywhere was locked up. No one was permitted to enter the food store. With a girl's curiosity, I peeped through keyholes but I was never able to see more than one side of the room, in which the tinned food was kept, as well as some china cups and teapots. Florence was disliked by family members and surrounding neighbours; she had a hidden temper and a foul mouth when she got angry. She never mixed with society and had hardly any female friends. She would get into a fight with the other young ladies over men friends. Dressed up to go for dinner and dance parties at the Kitale club, she was never up to standard. We were terrified of her. We never refused her orders because they were so defined and given with such a quiet air of mastery, especially in the presence of our father. I hated her hypocrisy, pretence and lies.

I was not surprised to hear that the new cook was leaving Fa-

Chapter Twenty-Four

ther's employment; even if he were offered higher pay he would not stay. Florence frightened everyone and was always very mean when giving out the food rations. I caught her on several occasions hiding foodstuff in cardboard boxes in her room. She caught me and accused me of poking about her room without permission. She could turn violent, her grim mouth loosened into a false laugh, which was more menacing than her frown. She watched me rush away until I went round the corner out of her sight. We loathed and feared her more than anyone. We couldn't say a word to Father about her as he was always away on school duties. The best we could do was to sneak into the orchard and eat the pineapples, tangerine, oranges and nuts. No one caught us, as there were plenty of them growing.

Our stepmother sided completely with her daughter Florence. If it were not for the fruit, we probably would have starved. My love for my stepmother had completely died. There was nothing remarkable in the manner of its death, though it had been dying gradually over the years. Many nights I lay awake in the room I shared with my two sisters, gazing into blackness, turning over in my mind what I had to do the next day. As I lay in those dark hours, I was aghast to realise that something within me, long sickening, had quietly died. I felt sorry for my father; he was too soft and weak in nature to put things right. Sometimes I wondered if my father's marriage was for convenience rather than anything else. He stayed away in the school's head teacher's staffroom and seldom came home. He found no pleasure in running the farm, no curiosity about my stepmother's Maasai culture and farming methods. He had no self-reproach for the whole drab marital disillusion, which he did not want. Nothing remained, no love except the bonds of law and duty and custom.

We were all in this domestic tragedy. The quarrels that we overheard at night stopped as we tiptoed round the dark corridors to our room. They engendered a mood of aloofness and cool criticism and a growing conviction in me that all this was because of us three girls. Father had to take the blame.

This particular afternoon, Father had just come back. I was called to the living room. He was sitting in his favourite armchair; he was very silent, with his head sunk forward towards the red glow of the fire. Then my stepmother walked into the room, her cigarette lit. I watched blue smoke-rings as they chased each other up to the ceiling. We were silent while she finished smoking. To tell the truth, I felt helpless, like one of those poor rabbits when the snake is writhing towards it. I seemed to be in a grasp of some inexorable evil, which no foresight and no precaution can guard against.

This was not the time for despair. Someone must have reported me to Stepmother. Some lie, some wild story from the mad relatives, especially Florence who did not like me. I caught deceitful notes in my stepmother's voice when she falsely accused me of laziness and stealing fruit. I listened and recognised that resentful, hateful stare of incomprehension in her eyes and the selfish hard set of the corners of her mouth. I looked up in Father's direction, hoping he would support me. This time he was different; he seemed to listen more to stepmother and totally ignored me. I walked out of the living room feeling very sad and lost.

A rainy night was followed by a glorious morning. The bushes were neat and the flowers were beautiful. I inhaled the morning air and rejoiced in the music of the birds and the fresh breath of the early morning. I noticed Selina had followed me but my sister was compelled to fall behind. I was very energetic in the morning and seemed to have inexhaustible stores of nervous energy. I didn't slow down till we were three hundred yards away from the front door of our home.

We continued towards the forest, which seemed deserted. The hedges had been cut back; palm leaves which grew on either side provided shade and the flame trees had orange flowers. I felt alive

Chapter Twenty-Four

and happy just to be outside. We paused by the roadside at the junction to look for the baboons that lived there but the place was empty. I saw a great change on the neighbouring side of our farm. Most shrubs and trees had been cleared away to make way for new homes. I saw endless tin roofs spread over the valley as they twinkled in the sunshine like bangles spread out on a pale cloak. These tin roofs were used to catch rainwater.

We continued our morning walk. The road seemed deserted, but then I saw a cyclist and recognised Stephen, my stepbrother. Right behind him was Safia on a bicycle. She struggled to keep it balanced. Stephen cycled very fast towards me then turned his machine and cycled fast after Safia. She turned round and cycled away, trying to get as far away from him as possible. They both disappeared in a gap in the forest and were hidden from my sight. I hoped that Safia would not fall off her bicycle because it would mean trouble with Stepmother.

Selina and I went back home. I left her scrubbing the veranda floors, while I took the wheelbarrow, axe and machete to chop up some wood in the forest. Most of our workers had deserted their duties so I had to keep the kitchen in order and find enough wood to cook the meals and heat water.

One day, after Father came back from school, he did not feel well. Everyone thought it was the flu that goes away in a couple of days but the next day he was pale and shivering with cold and I knew that it was malaria. Stepmother did not call the doctor at once, so Father stayed in bed and the weeks of his illness wore on. The life of the house kept pace with the faltering strength of our sick father on whom we all depended.

The house was hushed as he sat in bed, I propped up his pillows and tried to spoon-feed him with soup but he did not have much appetite. I often sat for hours at his side to keep watch. He was given quinine – was it the correct dose, I wondered? After some

Real Work

days, Kemeli, my stepbrother, decided to call the witch doctor. Father did not have the strength to resist this decision; his illness had got worse and we were all frightened. I felt I could not object to such nonsense. Witch doctors brought great comfort to all native people. Stepmother and my half-sister, Florence, also believed in magic.

Kemeli came early the next morning; behind him he had the witch doctor who lived five miles down the road. He had come to perform his magic ceremony. I saw him sit under a tree while waiting for a white goat to be caught and brought to him. The ceremony involved sickening cruelty.

All four of the goat's legs were broken and its stomach was slit open to extract the undigested contents, which were believed to have magical properties. It was essential that the goat remained alive while this was done, and even then it was not put out of its misery. The cruelty was not acknowledged by Stepmother, who seemed to derive sadistic pleasure from it. The witch doctor found it normal practice because the object was not to inflict pain on the animal but to drive out the demon that was believed to cause father's sickness. Horrified as we were, as young children we soon learnt that pain was endemic in African life and there was no way to avoid it. Pain had to be endured; it was a stoicism that constantly amazed us as we grew up.

The contents of the wretched goat's stomach were mixed on a banana leaf that had been cut from a tree in our orchard. Other nameless and unpleasant-looking substances were added to it then the witch doctor dipped a goat's horn into the concoction, thrust it into our father's mouth, recited various incantations and marked our father's upper body with chalk, which he had mixed with other powders. He assured Stepmother that the devil had been expelled. It was all was very distressing.

The weeks passed and Father's condition improved slightly. Our

Chapter Twenty-Four

stepmother's moods had changed drastically; especially as Father's condition was not improving as quickly as she had expected. She behaved like a caged animal, pacing up and down aggressively and becoming short tempered and irritable. Our father gradually got better but he took little interest in events outside his room. We took him the paper daily and I raised the pillows behind his head so he could eat his meals comfortably. The doctor was brought much later on and Father got better. Then he took to sitting by the window in the open air and breathed more easily in the morning sun that warmed the room.

Safia and Stephen went off again on dangerous adventures on the farm. Safia fell off her bicycle and hurt herself so badly that she nearly dislocated her left hip. She ended up getting a good beating from Stepmother. Safia and Stephen had rushed off early that morning towards the fruit orchard and far beyond, right down towards the dam. They were missing the whole day so I decided to look for them. Halfway down the farm, I heard shouting and a shriek and ran towards the noise. I noticed a boy running towards me; he was one of Stepmother's distant relatives on a short visit. He looked as if he was running for his life to announce a catastrophe. He stopped by me and I slowed down. He pointed towards the bottom end of the farm and started to speak. He stuttered as he spoke but after a minute or so, I learnt that a tragedy had happened near the dam. Safia was dangling from a high broken branch and any minute she would fall down.

On hearing this, I ran very fast. I heard the shouts get louder as I got closer and I saw Safia dangling in the tree. Stephen was desperately climbing up the tree but the branch snapped. Safia fell, but miraculously she managed to grab another branch halfway down. Stephen got to her, grabbed her hands and helped her climb down to the ground. I discovered that the right side of her stomach was badly grazed. Luckily there were no deep wounds but she was bleeding badly.

Stephen and I managed to get her home. We were all in a panic. We took her to our room. Safia clung to me and cried in the greatest anguish. I left her with Stephen as I rushed to get hot water and bandages to dress her wounds and stop the bleeding. When Stepmother came back in the evening from her usual drinking, she punished Safia for climbing trees and locked her up for hours in the cold store, a small room used for keeping vegetables. I could hear her crying. I did not want to get involved in an endless discussion of the tree-climbing tragedy in case I was implicated and punished as well.

Honey hunting at the bottom of our land near the dam, and below the cliff and the forest, was common. The young boys went out to steal from the wild bees that bred in crevices among the rocks; they would take the dark honey full of grubs. The boys wore no protective clothing and sometimes got badly stung but it was a point of honour not to retreat but be stung. Hives were made of hollowed-out logs, which were wedged in the fork of trees. We had many flowers all over our forest and they were ones that gave good nectar and produced the best-flavoured honey. These flowers gave rise to lavish quantities of honey. Many boys from our neighbourhood never left them alone but constantly robbed the honey.

This particular morning, we went looking for honey. Soon after leaving one end of the forest, we ended up in the swampy part of our dam, slowly moving and sometimes getting stuck in the mud. The water was very high. Safia was behind me; she always wanted to be by my side. She was slightly shorter than me and I got scared when I realised we had gone too far into the swampy water. We moved slowly through to the far end where papyrus was growing and we could feel the mud, the roots and reeds with our feet as we passed more floating vegetation. It was like some slow random vegetal pavane, conducted in a moist oppressive heat amid a smell of

Chapter Twenty-Four

rotting reeds and turgid mud. Plops and gurgles disturbed the water – a fish; a gurgle or croak from the other direction – a bird dipped and dived. Mosquitoes rose in clouds as I continued to move slowly, one hand holding Safia as I led the way across to the other end.

We got out of the swampy water and ran through bush vegetation then across a narrow wooden bridge, which was a crossing at the edge of our farm. A swift river flowed beneath the bridge and dropped like a waterfall some metres away. As we moved away from the sound of the river, we heard the birds chuckling around us. Still dripping wet, we sat at the campsite where the lilies grew. The place was lively with herons, ibis, kingfishers, quail and a dozen varieties of wild geese and ducks. We watched these birds dart over. The swimming birds have a purposeful flight, unlike the other birds. Some are on a journey going from place to place, while others are amazing to watch, especially the wild swimmers, the ducks included. They swoop noiselessly into the dark water like so many arrowheads let off backwards by a heavenly archer.

We moved away; every step was as an adventure as we picked our way through. All my senses were tight as a bowstring, eyes alert for the quiver of a twig or the warning call of a bird. Then, behind me, Safia screamed when she saw a tiny mouse shoot across the path, visible only for an instant. Did she think it was a snake? I noticed that Safia's dress was torn. We went back along the narrow path leading home. The sun was dropping in the sky but it was a hot and windless day. That day, we never found any honey hives. It was our lucky day; we were too young to handle wild bees as they stung viciously.

Chapter Twenty-Five

Our Uncle Visits Africa

WE HEARD THAT our uncle had flown in and been picked up by Father's friend from Jomo Kenyatta Airport and given a lift to Kitale Golf Club. We sat in our father's Volkswagen Beetle car while he went to the Kitale Club to collect our uncle. It was very uncomfortable, as we had to sit on wooden planks; the seats had been removed to create more space for us children to fit in.

It didn't take long for Father to come out with his brother. Uncle Kenneth was much taller than Father; he had Father's hazel-blue eyes. He carried himself extremely erect, had a fine physique and neatly combed short hair. He was dressed in a grey suit and he carried his luggage and his hat, which he placed behind his seat. He said hello and he knew all our names. Within hours of arriving at our farm, he was awash with perspiration. His jacket had been removed and his white linen shirt and trouser and waistcoat hung from his body like a wet dishrag.

We were told that a new maid and a cook had been employed. The house once more was kept to high standards. Father played his gramophone and the piano and things were cheerful for a while. The meals were of the highest gastronomic standard in contrast to what Father usually ate, which was tough mutton or scrawny fowl. The cook made delicious meals – shepherd's pie, rice pudding, magnificent chocolate cake – and we were given treats. I had not

Chapter Twenty-Five

seen Father buy large quantities of champagne and wine for a long time. The best glasses and the china teacups and cutlery were used; these were normally locked up.

One night, Father and Uncle were seated by the fireplace in the living room having a last glass of wine and talking about the English weather in comparison to the Kenyan climate. The day had been exhausting as we had been planting young trees to commemorate our uncle's visit to Kenya. Everyone took part. I was just going to my room when I heard the sound of the doors being locked, a signal to tell everyone that the cook had retired.

Father and Uncle continued to talk late into the night. Father's relatives and friends in England missed him. He had come during the final years of the colonial period; maybe he felt left out. Kenyan society hadn't thrown Father out but times had changed and he did not belong here. He was a product of the English but his was an earlier England, a world that no longer existed. I wondered if Father sometimes felt guilty about not living in England. Did he feel he was a self-imposed exile here in Kenya? He bore his exile with a good grace but he was lonely.

His friends in England wrote to him, telling him to sell up and leave Africa, but Africa kept him here because of his instinctive attachment to us, his children. Stepmother would not move to England and would not fit into the society; the cold climate would be too much for her. As children we would have adapted to the climate but Stepmother surrounded herself with her relatives and never let go of her Maasai culture.

Father and Stepmother decided that we must take Uncle to Chepareria Farm in West Pokot. This is where Father was posted as an Agricultural Officer from 1957 to 1959, and that particular farm had been allocated to Stepmother. We had made several visits there and everyone was looking forward to the long journey. Since Father's Volkswagen was not big enough to carry the extra luggage

Our Uncle Visits Africa

and camping gear, Father rented a four-wheel-drive Land Rover.

That morning we were soon on our way to Kapenguria, West Pokot. This road was very familiar and the years seemed to slip away. Nothing seemed to have changed as we passed the little shopping centre at Chepareria; it was only a small market place where people came to exchange and buy foodstuffs or animals. Small children shouted as we drove by, '*Mzungu, mzungu,*' meaning 'white people'. These children were herding their goats and sheep.

We arrived slightly later than expected and our two vehicles bumped to a halt near a two-room, tin-roof house that belonged to Stepmother. Circling this house, which had mud walls, were six round thatched huts, presumably belonging to Stepmother's relatives who came out to greet us. The older ladies grinned from ear to ear.

The evening sun had fallen behind the dark crest of the Pokot hills. The valley below was still flooded with long purple shadows. A thorn *boma* was not too far away, where all the sheep, goats and cows were put at night for protection. The cook was with us to provide meals, drinks, clean laundry and fresh water from the river several miles off, with the help of the many relatives.

Our tent was made out of strong canvas and was brand new, purchased specially for this occasion. The tent was erected in an open clearing; underneath was an open-sided shelter to act like a small veranda. Here whisky and soda or brandy was served for Father and Uncle. Both of them enjoyed the evening breeze and sunset, when the doves called and weaver birds chattered from nearby thorn trees behind the tin house. We could hear goat-bells tinkling in the distance as the flocks were driven into their *boma* for the night. A bonfire was built in the centre of the compound and the fire kept ablaze all night; this reminded me of old times, camping and safaris. Safia and I occupied one of the grass-thatched huts which our step-aunties' daughters used. It was not very comforta-

Chapter Twenty-Five

ble but we did not mind as we knew it was only for a week.

Next day we walked and ran round this farm. Stepmother had many relatives and some used this land to graze their animals. Each morning the smaller boys drove the goats and sheep into the bushes to graze. The women arrived in the evenings with loads of sweet potatoes and cassava tops to feed the cattle. The young girls fetched the water using traditional gourds. Collecting bundles of firewood was part of their duty. The meals were cooked using soot-blackened pots. It was always a busy scene and orderly, each person going about their work in a leisurely way like bees in a hive.

My stepmother had allocated them small *shamba* (plots) fenced with thorn bushes, so everyone knew their lot. Stepmother's relatives were numerous and they knew each other as individuals. Sometimes they stole from each other and arguments arose but the older males solved the problems like in the olden days. Polygamy and female circumcision were still practised here. The little children giggled and pointed at Father and Uncle and ran away; they were not used to white people. In the evening we loved to sit round the campfire. We enjoyed our time there and felt free from restrictions and work.

Our visit coincided with the time when female circumcision ceremonies were being practised. There was much dancing and traditional singing; the throb of drums and sounds of chanting and stamping lasted half the night around our campfire. The government had tried hard to do away with such practices but this was a backward part of Kenya. The only hope to stop circumcision was to educate the girls.

At dawn on the day for the operation, the men were banned. The girls were taken to the nearby river and made to stand for several hours in its cold water to numb their nerves, then told to step on the bank of the river to an appointed place. By then the sun had started to come up. The numbness wore off but I am sure the psychological effect remained, accompanied by shock. We children were equally shocked; though we were chased away, we managed to sneak back and peep. My stepmother's married relatives were there, the girls lined up in semi-circle, each sitting on an ox-hide with their legs outstretched with other two ladies holding them down and whispering moral support.

This operation was conducted by a grey-haired old woman. She dressed in normal clothes, not animal skins as in past times. She was professional in operating on young girls; her payment was a goat per girl.

This circumcision poses danger to young girls, making their future life dangerous especially during childbirth, but these relatives cling stubbornly to this practice; there is no compassion for the girls. As the old toothless lady continued her operation, the girls looked very frightened. The old lady had a razor blade but no antiseptic. None of the girls flinched or cried out and the old lady worked swiftly.

The girls were taken to their huts and the whole place went quiet. The morning sun rose. Uncle thought these practices were barbaric but Father was used to these ceremonies. Then, as the campsite went quiet before tea was served, we heard a bird call, the first pleasant sound we had heard. The sun's beams gilded the tree trunks on the horizon. Then came the tinkling of goat bells as the sun's strengthening beams fell upon a bush full of flowers. A flock of green-winged parrots passed overhead in search of breakfast. Doves dropped their melodious notes like water poured from a bottle.

A farewell gift was given to Uncle, a large ram with a fat tail that hung to the ground. It would be prepared for a feast before he went back to England. The circumcised girls were asleep or maybe struggling with the pain; the world was dead to them at this particular time.

Chapter Twenty-Five

This was still the wet season; in a few weeks, heavy rains would come. The roads to Chepareria Farm were non-existent. The grass rose up above a man's head and the ground was strewn with rocks that could easily puncture the tyres. When the rains were heavy, the cars could not cross the dangerous rivers, which were full of sand, and the rain could swamp the luggers, which made it difficult for cars to cross, so we had to go back to Kitale on time to avoid the heavy rains and not be caught in such danger.

Chapter Twenty-Six

Back on our Kitale Farm

SOMETIMES THE HEAVY rains fell while Father and Uncle were on their evening walks round the farm. When they entered the sitting room, where I had just lit the fire, I watched their streaming umbrellas and their shining waterproof coats which told of the fierce weather through which they had come. They brought some traces of the storm into the sitting room. Both drew chairs close to the fire to get dry and pushed their wet feet towards the flames.

My father loved Kenya. He told Uncle lots of stories about the pioneers who had come out to Kenya in the early 1920s. Uncle listened to these stories curiously. Most early settlers were Anglo-Saxons, since the colonists' rough-hewn democracy seldom embraced the members of another race or nationality. They were almost pathologically proud of their stock. Kenya's immigrant Britons viewed all lesser breeds, Americans included, with attitudes ranging from good-humoured tolerance to aloof condescension to loutish bigotry.

Uncle found it difficult to understand how a white family could cast aside the security of England and come out to Africa to spend the rest of their lives in a land that seemed to breathe hostility. But then he saw my father, who came out and liked it out here. Maybe Father would finally wish to lay his bones in African soil.

This country had its challenges. Most people thrived on risk and

Chapter Twenty-Six

savoured physical hazards; some even went bankrupt while trying hard to farm the beautiful fertile soil. It was an experience to witness some of Kenya's challenges.

The day Uncle left to go back to England, we were all sorry. Things had been different for the short while he was with us; we were cheerful and happy. He brought some good luck and happiness with him, and everything on the farm seemed to work again. For once our father had been in control of the farm; the wages were paid on time, no one left work. We knew the sad atmosphere would return once our Uncle was gone, and that day was now. Our performance at school had improved during his short stay, but soon it would drop because of too much work on the farm.

The day Uncle was to be driven to Nairobi, I felt the tension return. It was a cool bright morning; the sun had just come up and Father was carrying the last of Uncle's belongings to the car. He looked pale and we thought the malaria was back. All our other sisters, stepbrothers, cook and maid came out to say goodbye. Uncle said goodbye to each of us, shaking our hands lovingly. The car drove away and the little boys, mostly our stepmother's relatives, ran after it while waving goodbye. It disappeared round the corner of the driveway out of sight.

Chapter Twenty-Seven

Punishment for Food Stealing

CHEPKEMEI WAS A very dark, scrawny girl with moist black eyes. She had a lovely smile but she always looked gloomy. She was not unfriendly, at least not towards me, but unfortunately she was a thief.

Chepkemei was my age and she was one of our house helpers though she was related to Stepmother. She was given duties in the kitchen. I caught her stealing food, particularly meat, cheese, sugar. I found her in Stepmother's bedroom where she stole cigarettes; I knew she took them to her mother's hut, which was built outside the main house near the servants' quarters. I never told anyone about this.

One day, at around ten o'clock, just after finishing the cleaning and opening the windows, I heard a loud scream from Stepmother's bedroom. Chepkemei had been caught stealing.

I ran towards the noise and found Chepkemei tied by the wrist with a rope. She begged to be released as Stepmother took her whip, which was made out of strong rope fixed on a birch handle; we called it a snake whip. Stepmother lashed at her while uttering all kinds of words. I could not hear half of what she said as Chepkemei cried while every stroke from the whip landed on her.

Chepkemei's shrieks were dreadful. I looked on in horror as the whip slashed at her back, shoulders, arms, head and legs. Luckily her jaw did not break or her teeth get knocked out. This went way

Chapter Twenty-Seven

beyond punishment. She was dragged to the dark store room, and spent the night there in the cold without supper. This was our jail room, for those who did not work or took food from the kitchen or store without permission or stole fruits from the orchard.

Our father was not around; he was on school duties. I was horrified and afraid of Stepmother in case she turned the whip on me. After she left, I looked through the holes in the wall of the dark store. Chepkemei begged me to let her out. Her black eyes looked very scared. I thought she would run away during the night. From that day onwards, food was never stolen by relatives or us children. Two weeks later, Chepkemei and her mother left the farm and went back to the West Pokot farm.

Our stepsister Florence was in charge of the farm once more. She tried to be farm manager but she did not have the experience or skills. Many young men came to the farm asking for her hand in marriage but she refused all of them. She wanted a white man for a husband.

She had no interest in anyone; she lived apart in her little world, distant from reality. All her friends had been married off. Florence had a disadvantage – the scandal of having had two children outside marriage. This was a barrier to her goal to get a white husband.

She tried to draw them into her world; she used to seek them out, contrary to Nandi custom. She attended the ball at Kitale Golf Club to mix with the white settlers. After a while she started to sneak off to Kitale Hotel, or make long trips to Eldoret to a place called the Wagon Wheel Hotel, where most white people went for parties or dances.

I learnt all this about Florence from guess work and from what she let slip in dreamy monologues. Sometimes I saw her sneak out during weekends, dressed up pretty, never to be seen till late Sunday evenings. Others noticed but we were scared to report her to Stepmother. Florence was getting past the zenith of her loveliness

Punishment for Food Stealing

and what remained was a haunting sadness. The lonely years had made her sad.

Florence was very tricky at times and had her mother under her thumb. She sneaked into Father's office, which was right at the end of the building near the driveway, found lots of documents and read through them. She stole whatever she thought was important, taking some documents to her mother; most documents got lost or disappeared completely. Farm title deeds, my original birth certificate and Selina's birth certificate were never traced.

Chapter Twenty-Eight

Tower on Fire

THE LEFT TOWER on the farm had recently been repaired. New windows and doors had been put in, and the old uneven stone steps had been repaired. This was the farm's guest wing. Standing on top of this tower, the scenery was very lovely and one could see a good distance.

Everyone retired to bed early this particular night and the generator was switched off. Soon everyone was fast asleep. It took me longer, as the wind whistled round the main house and I could hear the iron sheet rattle and shake. The wind was trying to lift off the roof. Then I heard Safia utter, 'Good heavens!' The cry was sharp and loud. 'It's fire!' she continued, looking out through our window, which overlooked the left tower. I saw bright light and we ran out and saw fire burning at the side window. We could do nothing by ourselves.

We ran to Father's bedroom and banged on the door, screaming. We ran to get help from relatives who lived a few yards from the main house. Some family members rushed out to cut down branches and bushes with axes and they tried to climb up the stairway to put out the fire but the wind was against us; it made the fire burn in a hundred flashing tongues of flame.

One man ran into the smoke with a wet blanket wrapped round his head and body. He rushed back, nearly choking to death with smoke in his lungs. Still those tongues of fire shot in all directions, nearly setting fire to the nearby cypress hedge. What a disaster it would have been if the fire had spread to the building below, which belonged to Florence. Everyone worked hard to get buckets of water to stop the flames spreading in that direction and to save the main house.

The fire continued to creep forward. It seemed as though nothing could stop it until it had burnt its fiery pathway, destroying everything in front of it. No one could slow it down or get it under control. The wind started to lose some of its force but the fire roared as loudly as ever. We, the firefighters, kept retreating down the steep stairs.

I wiped the sweat off my face. It was very hot and I was too close to the fire. I felt the smoke in my eyes and the heat burning my cheeks. Some of the family members had tied cotton clothing over their heads to protect their hair.

Our clothes were covered with dirt and black marks from the floating ash. After what seemed like hours of hot and back-breaking work, the fire slowed down as the wind dropped. We stayed there all night, bewildered, amazed. The remaining fire started to smoulder and die except for the smoke drifting upwards.

When the morning came, we saw huge smoking heaps of ash. What remained of the building was still smouldering. We were all hot and dirty. Could this fire have been started on purpose? It was such a waste, a terrible danger to everyone. Who could be guilty of such a crime? I heard some say it was an accident and a candle burned through the curtains.

A week after this fire, Chepkemei left the farm. She was not seen again for a very long time.

Chapter Twenty-Nine

Stepmother became Alcoholic

TRADITIONS, CULTS AND taboos were strong in Kenya, and my stepmother, born into such an environment, could not rid herself of them. She was stubborn even in these modern times. She would disappear and reappear in the evenings with bundles of herbs and roots. She would kill a goat, boil the intestines and mix them with the herbs and roots and we were forced to drink the soup. It was very bitter and Safia would always become very sick – but the sickness was blamed on malaria or a stomach upset. Everybody else managed to drink and swallow the disgusting stuff and no one dared complain to our father. Probably he too had to drink the stuff.

Stepmother was wife to a white man so she was lucky; no one took notice of her visits to the herbal man. In previous years, she would have been marked as a person who practised magic as she had a habit to go to a muganga (a person practising magic). Culprits in those days were believed to bring calamity to the society and burning the person was always the solution. For instance, if the rains did not come on time, they believed the black magic had caused the crop to dry up. The people would go out witch-hunting and round up some people, mostly women, and burn them in their huts. From 1940 to 1963, the British government had problems with such behaviour and found it difficult to stop the natives from

Stepmother became Alcoholic

carrying out such savage practices.

People seemed to have no explanation of such deeds and reported them at the police station as an accident or tribal clashes. Of course, immediately after these murders, the clouds would cover the sky and torrents of rain would fall over the district. It was very mysterious and upsetting. The natives were no doubt puzzled that the white men wanted to stop these practices, which they believed were part of their day-to-day life. But with education, these practices eventually came to an end.

As we grew up, our stepmother saw Safia and me as a threat to her. She was unhappy whenever she saw us playing happily in the back yard. She started to drink the local beer behind our father's back and, when drunk, she would shout and chase us out of our home to sit outside under a tree till darkness. Then we went to bed without supper. This happened most of the weekdays when Father was away at Tambach Secondary School.

Stepmother got drunk to escape her disappointments, which no one understood. She drank more each day even though she knew she had to stop drinking, as it would ruin her. Father could not leave her. He was stuck as he had children with her. It was very difficult – the only option was to make the situation work at all costs.

Stepmother drank hard for a week in a nervous, surreptitious way. I noticed that she hid her drink behind a cupboard and kept slipping away at odd moments during the day. All the time she was never quite sober but she escaped attention by staying silent.

Stepmother disappeared for the whole afternoon. Father arrived and asked for her. No one dared tell him that she was down at the bottom of the farm in the servants' quarters where they brewed local native beer. Then we heard her arrive; she raised her voice and started to complain about Safia and me. She said that we must be taken back to West Pokot to our mother. I recognised the drunken thickness in her voice. She went to Father's drinks' cabinet; she

Chapter Twenty-Nine

knew he had brought some gin and tonic.

Her hands still not steady; she slopped gin and some tonic into a glass and carried it out of the room. I dared not follow her but wished Father would notice this drunken behaviour. Then Father came and asked where she was. I pointed in the direction of their room and he followed her but she shut the bedroom door in his face and turned the key.

Father returned to the drawing room, full of dismay and foreboding. After some minutes he went to their room and this time he found the door open. At the dressing table there was a half-empty bottle of whisky and Father picked it up. She spun round, snatched it from his hand and started to scream at him using all sorts of absurd language.

There would have been a fight if Father had not controlled himself. Stepmother went to get her Maasai spear, which she normally kept propped up by her bedside. Father snatched it from her hands and quietly put it down and made as though to reach out to calm her. Then suddenly I saw she had a Maasai sword and was about to pull off the sheath. Father grabbed it from her hands and there was a struggle. She would not let go; both Father's and her hands were still on the sword above her head.

I heard her scream in pain. Although the sword was still in its sheath, it had cut her on the top of her head. It was a fairly big cut because blood started dripping down her face. Both of them dropped the sword and Father was in a panic, looking for the car keys to get her to hospital. The stitching of her head went well but she dragged me into the whole affair as a witness. I was forced to go with both of them to the police station to make a statement.

My father looked very worried as he drove us there. At the police station, luckily for my father, the crime officer knew him well; Father taught his son at Tambach. He heard both sides of the story but Stepmother was sober by now and she told her story in a femi-

Stepmother became Alcoholic

nine, flirtatious way, blaming Father. She made up stories and tried to force me to back her statement with lies. It took two hours before it was all was over.

Florence, my stepsister, appeared just as we were about to drive away. I wondered why she had come – probably to tell lies to the police officer to get Father into trouble, to blackmail him later on as she usually did. Florence had destructive qualities, making sure she told as many lies as possible to bring war to peaceful homes.

After the hospital we went home. Everyone was waiting for us and the atmosphere of tragedy had vanished except that Caroline and Katherine were crying all the time because no one had fed or washed them. They looked scruffy, untidy and hungry. Safia had Katherine tied to her back. Katherine looked heavy and Safia struggled under her weight. What a mess everything looked! Kazungu our cook was leaving us; he could not stay any longer under our stepmother's drunken state. He was worried about my stepmother being deceitful and that she would tell lies to get rid of him. She was envious that Kazungu had known Father from the late 1950s; Kazungu had been very close to my mother, Safia and I, and was very protective towards us.

Our stepmother's drinking stopped for a while. Father asked for a transfer from Tambach to a school in Kitale, the Kitale Day Secondary School. At least from there he would be able take charge of the situation.

Kazungu went to Lamu for a while. Since there was no one to cook, and Stepmother continued to sneak off to the worker's camp whenever she could to drink the native brew, Florence was left in charge of the kitchen. Things got worse. Florence was a very selfish and mean person and we were underfed. She locked up all the food; the only thing left for us to eat was guavas and wild berries.

Florence had a second child, a son called Peter. We all knew that the child's father was a Kamba (Kenyan tribe) man named

Chapter Twenty-Nine

Tony Maima. Florence's daughter (first born) called Dina was a year younger than Katherine and she doted on her. She used all the money given to her by my father for the house to buy nice clothes for her baby. The rest of us nearly starved. Stepmother never noticed as she continued to drink and get depressed.

Our stepsister would be taken by our father to Kitale Club, a colonial set-up for the settlers, with a golf course and more than 300 acres of land. Kitale Club had a discrimination policy and only very rich white men who had married Africans were tolerated, like Mr S.A. Dalton and Mr Bedford-Pim. Stepmother was way below standard and she could not speak English so no wonder Father took Florence out instead. She knew how to speak English. My father hoped Florence would find a nice person to marry. So, off they went to Christmas and dance parties. Stepmother was left behind because she was a disgrace. She disappeared most afternoons and we knew she was on a spree again. She had hiding places in the house where she kept her bottles of whisky and took a swig now and then on the sly. Things went from bad to worse. Florence was not doing her job properly and I wished I was grown up to take charge of our home.

Probably Africa had gotten to Father; he seemed to forget his upbringing in the UK when he ate his food using silver forks, knives and spoons. I heard him complain that some of his silver utensils had disappeared and no one could trace them. Father used to use his silver cutlery while we used the ordinary forks, knives, and spoons and sometimes our fingers to eat like our African relatives.

Our stepmother's relatives swamped our home like bees. We lost count of them visiting and our standards of living dropped drastically, never to be recovered. The problem of relatives never went away. Father asked Stepmother to turn them away and they talked it over until it became an annoying and very sensitive subject. Father could not accept these relatives anymore; they were thieves.

Stepmother became Alcoholic

Everything was locked up but the stealing continued because the female relatives were given charge of the foodstuff stores.

My stepmother was very controlling and we all suffered. The best my father could do was to get a transfer to Kitale and take charge of his farm and work at the same time. One day, I walked into his living room where he was sitting alone before the fire. He was reading his book and he did not notice me. I thought I was quiet but I stepped on a magazine that had been dropped on the floor. He put down his book, took off his spectacles and looked at me hard as if it were the first time in months that he had seen me. I started to talk to him, mostly to complain of the way Safia and I were mistreated and neglected. He did not answer me but looked at me for a long time; even with me, he made excuses as though he had rehearsed his story over and over again. He said the situation would improve and I was to go play outside. Was he scared to be found talking to me by Stepmother? As I stepped away to leave the room, he picked up his book and searched for his page. He was completely dead to his surroundings as if he only existed in books and not in real life.

I realised I had to take care of Safia and myself because I could not get any help from our father. After a week, he told me he would be gone for two weeks to transfer his belongings from Tambach to our house in Kitale; I was to be strong and to take care of my sister while he was away.

I started to hate my stepmother; I hated my childhood and all its misfortunes. Father had built a pigeon house down near the cattle shed and I liked to sit and watch the pigeons. I would sit under the tree and reflect on my memories. I looked up at the pigeons and they were everywhere, under my feet, singing in pairs in little honey-voiced congregations, nodding, strutting, winking, rolling the tender feathers of their necks. If I stood up swiftly the place was bare; with a flutter and sweep of wings, the sky above was dark with

Chapter Twenty-Nine

a tumult of fowls. Thus it was this morning.

The following day I got really ill and had to have lots of check-ups. Father had no alternative but to take me along with him to Tambach Secondary School to have me examined at a hospital in Eldoret for blood tests in case I had malaria or typhoid. Leaving me behind would have been unwise.

Once again I found myself in his company and, although I was sick, I was glad to be with him without our stepmother's interference. Luckily Kazungu had arrived from Lamu and I was happy to have our old cook back again.

At Tambach, I spent the first afternoon in the house, wandering from room to room, looking through the plate-glass window, which faced the garden, the hillside, in a mood of vehement self-reproach.

My father was in his study packing his books. He dined at home and wore his smart suit. At dinner, my father took a book with him to the table then, for the first time ever, remembered my presence and dropped it under his chair. Then he took the book once again and propped it against the epergne. For the rest of dinner he was silent, save for an occasional snuffle of merriment that could not, I thought, be provoked by the words he read. Presently we left the table and sat in the garden room and he put me out of his mind. His thoughts were far away in those distant days when he moved at ease. He sat in an attitude that to anyone else would have been extremely uncomfortable, askew in his armchair, with his book held high to the light. Now and then he made an entry in the margin with his gold pencil. The room was very quiet except for the ticking of Father's old clock, distant voices in the school and my father's regular turning of the pages.

I left for a while and returned but Father did not look up. I did not go to bed early. I was still feeling ill and walked around for a while. The evening passed. Eventually all the clocks chimed eleven; my father closed his book and removed his spectacles and saw me.

Stepmother became Alcoholic

He told me to go to bed; we would talk tomorrow or before we went back to Kitale.

Chapter Thirty

Farewell to Tambach

THE NEXT MORNING everything was packed and loaded on to the school lorry to transport Father's furniture to Kitale. The school staff helped. Some schoolboys came down to the house to see my father off; they felt sad that he was leaving. The morning was cool with little colour in the air and on the landscape. To the east, the hillside before us was a little floating grey mist in the creeks; it would survive through another moment of its many thousand years. I suddenly felt cold looking up at those hills and thought I would miss this place.

Kazungu sat in the front seat of the lorry with the driver and I sat in my father's car. Father drove ahead of the lorry very slowly at the pace of a riding camel. The lorry followed us at the same speed. At the school gate, some boys had run ahead of us; others ran after the car as fast as they could as if whirled on the dust by the wind. They ran past the gate and waved goodbye. My heart filled with love and gratitude for these students who had known Father for three years; now they were saying goodbye, probably never to meet again.

There were two in particular that father liked to invite to his house to carry exercise books, by the names John Kiplagat Rutto and Simon Kiplimo Mutai. These two boys started to run faster than the others to where the school road joined the main highway. I

Farewell to Tambach

looked back at them, thinking they would continue running after us along the main highway, but they stopped. One took off his pullover and waved till we could only see tiny figures behind us as the car climbed up the escarpment road.

I felt sad and loneliness crept over me as I reflected on my good memories. As we drove upwards towards Item Market, I saw the great view of the north where the virtually impenetrable Tugen Hills lie. The Kerio Valley was down below and clouds covered part of the view. I grieved and wept. I was sad to leave this place. It is as if I was going through the same events again and again; all I had was my memories to take with me – sad ones and happy ones.

The mist returned. Looking back to see if the lorry was following us, I could only see the flash of its headlights coming steadily behind us. It started to rain. Father drove very slowly in case an animal crossed the road. Everything was dripping wet, the leaves, the trees, bushes. Then the mist parted and the rain subsided. Looking down the valley, I saw a stretch of indigo blue land below us, like a slate, then I saw one of the tall peaks far off. In a moment it was covered by the drifting rain and mist.

We stopped at an inn in Eldoret called the Wagon Wheel. This was where all the Boer settlers came for drinks and meals. Father ordered eggs, bacon, pickled walnuts and cheese, and we drank our tea in the parlour where an old clock ticked in the shadows and a cat slept by the empty window.

We drove in silence to Kitale. Father did not say much except when we passed a place called Soy Club, where the giraffe cross the road and we had to stop and admire nature at its best again. We have two types of giraffes in Kenya: the Maasai and the Rothschild giraffes, with their distinctive white 'stockinged' forelegs – the ones that roam in this spot.

Most trees here have no common English names. Of the many species of acacia, two stand out: the yellow fever trees – *acacia xan-*

Chapter Thirty

thophloea – and the stunted, shrubby whistling thorn acacia – *drepanalobium* – on the open plain, home to a species of ant. They drill their nests in the twigs, leaving one or two holes as entrances. When the wind blows across these holes, it makes a tinny whistling sound. When an animal brushes against the tree or browses its leaves, the ants rush out to attack. While defending their nests, the ants also protect the tree.

I have watched a giraffe browsing on whistling thorn; it will eat only a few mouthfuls before moving on. The plain is full of many species of trees and shrubs. As I watched, the giraffes moved, some crossing the road with their young ones. They are not afraid of cars or people. I hoped that these giraffes would not be poached, killed by humans who were greedy to take over the land for themselves. The question was, would our government be strong enough to control human encroachment of the animal grazing spaces? Kenya is rich in wildlife, a treasure that many could not see or acknowledge.

Soon the giraffe crossed the road and most cars, including ours, continued our journey to Kitale. Other cars proceeded in the opposite direction to Eldoret.

Chapter Thirty-One

Death of Abraham, the Sheep and Goat Shepherd

As I mentioned, Abraham lived down at the bottom of the farm; he had no helper or company to stay with him. Once in a while I visited him. Very early in the mornings I used to meet him halfway from the farm with the goats and sheep following him as they spread out to graze. He had lived on the farm for many years before we moved there; he did not have a family, so whoever bought the farm became his family.

He was the most pitiful object you could set eyes on. Moving round the farm, herding the sheep and goats, he looked extraordinarily lonely. His coat had worn out and was torn in many places. He had no shoes and no one bothered to buy new ones for him. He kept on scratching his body and head and I could smell him from far off. He seemed to be suffering but he was used to it, as suffering was part of his life. When I spoke to him, he pointed to his toes. His feet were full of jiggers. I told him I would tell Father and asked him to come to the house next morning before Father left for school.

Abraham was isolated from the world and, by a sort of deadly resignation, completely closed to all surrounding life; he had no wish for contact with the world around him. He was too used to being alone and he was, by his philosophy, prepared for the worst.

Chapter Thirty-One

The next morning Abraham came to the house earlier than normal. Father was not around so I went to the cupboard where he kept medicine and brought out the cotton wool and disinfectant to cleanse Abraham's wounds. I made him put his feet in warm salty water. I did not know how to treat jiggers. For a long time, I washed his feet but the jiggers were deep and I could not get them out.

Abraham's skin was flaky, pitted and covered with nodules from burrowing fleas. Jiggers had burrowed deep into the fleshy part of his feet, laying pea-sized eggs and multiplying. They had caused swelling, itching, ulceration and infection. If he was not treated in time, he could suffer blood poisoning, gangrene, tetanus or other diseases. Sometimes this could lead to amputation or death.

Cutting the jiggers out of his foot and soaking it in disinfectant was the only way I could help. It was a painful process and there were too many to remove. I took a sharp pin to cut out the jiggers. Jigger bites are treated with bleach to try and suffocate them. Sometimes this method does not work.

Abraham's only hope for relief of the itching and inflammation was that Father would buy him calamine lotion or corticosteroid creams. I did my best and he walked away slowly. I told him to come the next day as I hoped Father would take him for proper treatment. Father did not turn up, however, so I repeated the washing, trying to remove the jigger eggs from Abraham's feet.

Sometimes I got scared that I would get the jiggers too but I was always careful to wash my feet with disinfectant after I had finished with Abraham. Abraham bore his treatment stoically. He came to me every day for nearly a week then Father took over until Abraham was taken to hospital.

Abraham was very unlucky for he never fully recovered. His toes and fingers were badly affected and it was difficult to control the gangrene. Father told us that Abraham's backside was jigger-infested too. Abraham was an old man and all the wounds had gone

Death of Abraham, the Sheep and Goat Shepherd

gangrenous.

A lot was done for him; the affected areas were washed with clean water and soap and his feet and hands soaked in potassium permanganate for more than fifteen minutes. But his house where he slept with the sheep was not thoroughly disinfected and the sheep carried the fleas, so Abraham got re-infected.

That week Father drove him to the district hospital. Abraham was unable to walk so a couple of men brought him up on a stretcher. I went down to his hut to see him being brought up. As we neared his hut, there was a strong smell of sheep droppings. Abraham was placed under a tree; he looked extremely ill. His legs had turned a bad colour and were so swollen that you could not distinguish his knees. The helpers put him on the stretcher but I saw his eyes were getting dim. He was in terrible pain. I knew this man would definitely die. I looked on with a heavy heart as I followed them.

My father drove him to the district hospital but it was too late and Abraham died that same night. My father made the funeral arrangements and a week later we all went down to his hut as they had chosen a hill next to it to bury him. Our area chief attended the burial. They lifted Abraham's dead body, which had been wrapped in a white sheet and put in a coffin. There was no service; the chief spoke and someone said a prayer, then the body was lowered into the ground and covered. I felt very depressed.

Driving away from Machungwa Farm to go to our smaller farm next to Kitale town was another memorable time.

Jimmy Kimeli, who sometimes seemed archaic with the face of an Aztec, came to see us off. He promised that he would come to see us twice a week as he liked to cycle for exercise. But not Florence; not her, she never seemed happy for us, she always thought we didn't deserve the best in life. She had packed a lot of suitcases and boxes ready for the journey to the small farm. She sat there on the back seat of the car with the face of a flawless Florentine

Chapter Thirty-One

quattrocento beauty; almost anyone else with her looks would have been tempted to become artistic. How anyone else could not see the hypocrisy behind her beauty left me wondering.

My mood lightened. The further we drove from the big farm, the more Safia seemed to cast off her uneasiness and the restlessness and irritability that had possessed her. The sun was behind us as we drove so that we seemed to be in pursuit of our own shadows.

Everything was unpacked on arrival on the farm, at least what we needed to live decently on our small farm, which was now our new home. Dinner was served and that night we ate a proper meal at the table. I spent the first afternoon at home wandering from room to room, looking from the plate-glass windows. Then I turned into the garden and walked to the bottom of the farm. Memories flooded back and with them self-reproach.

Afterwards, we sat by the fireside with our father who was spending this one night with us; he had accompanied us to pack the rest of his books to get them out of the way to prepare more space for us to put our belongings. But we were under the supervision of Florence.

Father sat warm and cosy in his armchair by the fireside. He wasn't thinking of us but living in the past where he moved at ease. The evening passed peacefully and soon Father left us in Florence's care.

During the sultry weeks that followed, my relationship with Florence deteriorated sharply. I saw little of her as most weekdays I had to go to school. Stephen and Safia accompanied me each morning. I had a very exhausting day and looked to a little conversation with my sister to cheer me up. I particularly wanted to tell her about the things that happened at school, particularly in my class.

Our menu kept changing. Florence's cooking was good but she did not spend much money on food. We were handed very small portions and I could imagine licking the plate. Dinner sometimes

Death of Abraham, the Sheep and Goat Shepherd

consisted of green vegetables and what we called *ugali*; *ugali* is made out of *posho* mixed in boiled water and left to cook for a while. When Father came to visit, Florence cooked mashed potato and lamb cutlets for us and she tried to make a three-course dinner in the middle-class English style. But when Father left, we went back to our third-class native food. We didn't mind and were used to it. We were strangers in our father's farm but we accepted it without question. It would only last for a year.

We lived there during our school term. It was convenient because school was walking distance and now we were big enough to walk there alone.

Some weekends Father came to the farm. He dressed for dinner to go to the Masonic lodge in a black waistcoat, high collar and narrow white tie; this was his evening dress. He wore it with an air of melancholy, as though it were mourning dress that he had assumed in early youth and, finding the style sympathetic, had retained it. He never kept other dinner jackets here on this farm; most of his best clothes were on the other big farm. I thought his dinner jackets were outdated but Father liked to wear these jackets; it reminded him of the old days. His closet was full of old riding boots and World War II army coats, all neatly stored. I never touched them; only on occasion would we see him wear them.

Some nights Florence invited guests to the house. This time it was an Englishman who worked in Eldoret down the Kerio Valley. Florence was happy to make dinner; she could cook and the food was delicious. This time all of us were present at the dinner table. Manners were up to standard. Father asked his guest, whose name was Jonathan Brown, if he was here on business. No, he said he was working at Fluorspar in Eldoret down in the Kerio valley. They talked about England. We giggled and Father looked reproachfully at us until we fell silent.

My father was master of the situation. He had made a little

Chapter Thirty-One

fantasy for himself and imagined that Jonathan was an American. Throughout the evening he played a delicate, one-sided game with him, explaining peculiar English terms that occurred in the conversation, translating pounds into dollars, and courteously deferring to him with such phrases as, 'Of course, by your standards...' All this must have seemed very parochial to Jonathan. He was left with the vague sense that there was a misconception about his identity, which he never got a chance to explain.

I saw that Florence was very nervous and a little worried that Father would not approve of her guest. Again and again during dinner, Jonathan sought my father's eyes, thinking that this was an elaborate joke but was met instead with such a mild, benign look that he was left baffled. Once I thought Father had gone too far, when he said, 'I am afraid that living in Eldoret you must sadly miss your national game.'

'My national game?' asked Jonathan, sensing that here at last was the opportunity to clear the matter up. My father glanced from Florence to Jonathan and his expression changed from kindness to malice, then back to kindness again as he turned once more to Jonathan. 'Your national game,' he said gently, 'cricket,' and he snuffled uncontrollably, shaking all over and wiping his eyes with his napkin. 'Surely, working in Fluorspar in the mines supervising the company, you find no time for cricket?'

That evening was uncomfortable for our guest and Florence. I wondered if Father had taken too much wine.

Next morning, Father asked Jonathan Brown if he would be back again but Florence, not pleased with how the evening turned out, told Father that Jonathan would not be back for weeks.

The outer rooms had a corrugated iron roof and no one had made any effort to put ceiling boards on the inside. When the sun shone on the roof the room was very hot. All day long the heat made us sweat. The other top room had been made into a junk

Death of Abraham, the Sheep and Goat Shepherd

store, filled with broken wheelbarrows and other discarded tools; it made this room look like some ancient, gruesome place of execution. Our old clothes were worn to threads and no one seemed to notice. We wore them and pretended to be happy.

The air at midday was burning; us walking around the farm again and running down the valley. I was grown up and I had no fear of these bushes and forest vegetation. Safia was right behind me doing exactly as I did, jumping, running and rolling in the grass.

We all went to Kitale School and we had to walk each morning so as not to be late for assembly or else we would be punished. Stephen always took the lead, walking very fast, half running. Stephen failed all the exams and had to repeat them, although other successes and honours, especially in sports, came his way later. But those early failures impressed themselves on him. I also failed and slipped into less august academic fields. We had lived a hard childhood and the school system added a grim strain, although Safia coped well and excelled in her class work and Father was proud of her. But all in all, we enjoyed our school.

Memories of our stepmother started to fade; the cruelty of that time was like the spirit they mix with the pure grape of the Douro, heady stuff full of dark ingredients. These ingredients both enriched and retarded our adolescence in the same way that the spirit checks the fermentation of wine and renders it undrinkable. It must lie in the dark, year in year out, until it is at last fit for the table. I wished I had the courage to tell Stepmother that to love other human beings is the root of all wisdom.

During the night we had no generator; we used pressure lamps and Safia, Stephen and I used kerosene lamps. Our rooms were on the outer side, so at night sometimes it was very scary. But here on this farm, Safia and I were happy; the sense of sadness due to overwork had vanished and we were gay and free as we were the first time we were brought to live on this farm.

Chapter Thirty-One

We still missed the other farm, the lily pond, the dam, and the fruit in case we got hungry. Florence hardly cooked and if she cooked we were given very small portions. We knew Father gave her money to buy food but we never saw much of it so we went to bed most nights with little to eat and next morning we had no breakfast. By the time we arrived at school we were starving and during morning classes I couldn't pay attention to the teachers, so my grades got worse. I disliked Florence; it was unfortunate that she was in charge here. She reminded me of a monster with a sightless face and thrashing tail, thrown up from the depths of the sea. We went to the bushes in search of berries or climbed guava trees – these trees were full of birds that liked to eat the fruits as well, and each time we neared the trees, the birds flew off. It was funny to see them all fly off at the same time.

Safia was very afraid of darkness in our room, it made her feel lonely, so I was always beside her and the kerosene lamp burned all night. I imagined shadows like figures walking sometimes in the middle of the night. The kerosene smoke smelled bad but we were never poisoned because the window was left open, although the mosquitoes buzzed round all night and bit us. Safia gave up the struggle and let them bite her but I could not sleep and fought the mosquitoes off. When I woke up every morning, I always hoped that this day would be better.

When it rained heavily I sheltered myself from the cold winds. When the rains stopped, no wind stirred outside our room and we saw a change in climate; bees slowly sought their hives in the heavy afternoon sunlight. I would sometimes leave my bed and open the windows, let in the fresh air and breathe more easily.

It would all be better tomorrow, when the fresh wind blew down the valley and I could run along with it and feel it push me ahead. I could turn to meet it and fill myself with air, like a beast coming up for air from the depths of the sea.

Chapter Thirty-Two

Visit to Big Farm to see Selina (Machungwa Farm)

EVERY MORNING I woke up to Safia's glum face. I should have encouraged her but I could not help her in any way. I was usually tired in the evenings from the long walks to and from school. We were supposed to be given a glass of milk each night after dinner; instead we got used to drinking water and went to bed at eight o'clock. I was always awake and fearful an hour before falling asleep and sometimes sleep did not come. I lay awake gazing into complete blackness; I had to turn off the hurricane lamps because their fumes gave me nasty coughs and red eyes.

Our father came that weekend to take us to visit Selina and we had to spend the weekend there, which was not at all exciting for me. As we arrived at the last turn before the house on the driveway, the phantoms of those past years returned.

We finally arrived at the parking area near the lily pond and looked round. There were no lily flowers on the pond; things had been left to dry up. Outside the front entrance I stood awed and bemused; everything around me was familiar. From where I stood, I could see the whole house. I knew all corners and rooms and verandas that I had laboured on for so long. I knew this home very well.

It was a day of peculiar splendour, the sort that is given to us once or twice in a lifetime, when the leaves and flowers and birds

Chapter Thirty-Two

and sunlit stone and shadow seem to proclaim the glory of God. But I did not enjoy the beauty of it because my mood changed on this visit; I was expecting to see Selina and my heart was very sad.

No one came to greet us, so we made our way through the corridors till we arrived at the side where the tower house had burnt down. Father had planted a mulberry tree in memory of that occasion. The tree had grown with fruit on it, ready for picking. Stepmother sat under this tree; she was making a traditional marriage ceremony shirt for a young girl.

I walked towards her and said hello with a handshake; there was no cheek kissing. Safia did the same. We were made to sit beside her as Father went to find Selina. I sat there looking at Stepmother and wondered if she ever missed anyone or just thought of herself, planning in her head how to humiliate someone to weaken them, make them feel worthless, useless. Today she looked different, slightly sad. Her pierced, stretched earlobes were decorated with metal hoops, which made her look like a Maasai woman. She was making a traditional dress of animal skin which had decorative beads round it; a necklace was one of the items she had made and it looked huge, with many round metal beaded loops attached together to form one great round huge necklace.

I looked around, feeling the aura in the air; it had lost its beauty, its splendour. I felt more like a visitor than a family member.

After a while, I noticed that Selina had not appeared and I got up to follow Father. Stepmother cried out to stop me but for once I ignored her. I found Father and Selina in the kitchen. Selina was sitting on an old chair that looked as if it could collapse at any minute. She looked very fatigued and thin and her complexion was dark; her clothes were very dirty.

As I looked round the kitchen it looked very dirty and disordered. I knew this kitchen well – I had scraped the floors, cupboards and shelves. We moved to the living room and sat by the window

Visit to Big Farm to see Selina (Machungwa Farm)

overlooking the lily pond. Safia came in and sat on the sofa.

Caroline and Catherine were not around and I wondered where they must be on a weekend like this. My father sat in the armchair, his favourite place. We were alone together. Father was having his ten o'clock tea. We did not talk much, just kept each other company.

Selina was very nervous and she did not feel at all at ease with us. She wanted to run along and do her usual work and she seemed very scared of Stepmother. Maybe she was listening for footsteps in case Stepmother suddenly appeared in the doorway. I was not here to protect Selina but I knew she was suffering a lot of cruelty and overwork. It had happened to me and now been passed down onto her shoulders. She was too young to handle such tasks on her own and she was not like me; I loved to work, no matter what. Stepmother had seemed calm but she hated Selina the way she hated us; she was a volcano of hate. The hatred on this farm had driven everyone away.

We kept very much to ourselves on this short visit. I helped out with the duties of the house and the basic cooking. We had to stay there the whole week because it was half term. We had time to run around and remember our past – the walks, the dam, the forest, the valley. Everywhere there were memories.

In the morning, I saw strange faces around the house – maybe they were Stepmother's relatives, I did not pay much attention because I needed to keep Selina company. We felt very close. The place seemed different; there was no Florence locking up food stores and hanging the keys round her neck on a long chain. The place looked gloomier. The farm lacked someone to take proper charge. Since there were few family members living here, there was no strong bond to hold us together; we had grown and behaved differently now.

Stepmother's importance diminished. I noticed she had lost her

Chapter Thirty-Two

power to bully people, except for Selina or her other relatives, who congregated in our room to stare at us. They found out we had changed and our lives were better in every aspect. We spent a cosy evening with our father in front of the glowing fire.

I was touched by Selina's behaviour. She was very quiet and distant and she always looked dirty and mistreated. She worried me; I saw her as being threatened though I did not yet know just how bad the threat was. She looked as though she was in constant despair. She wanted to be alone so she could escape into her dreams. Human contact and affection frightened her. I had known her well in this mood of alertness and suspicion, like a deer suddenly lifting his head at the sound of the hunt. I knew she had grown wary of Stepmother and the whole farm. She was afraid to keep company with us. She was not used to such luxury and, when I called her in, she was shy and she made straight for the fire and crouched over it, shivering. We spent the evenings playing the piano or reading our book in our father's living room. For me, this was a tranquil time.

We hoped Stepmother would make us dinner and all the children would sit at Father's big mahogany dining table, which we all could fit round. We were very hungry; we had been starved the whole day. Stepmother kept using Selina as a servant girl, treating her not like a family member but her slave. Halfway through dinner, Selina was sent to fetch Stepmother's cigarettes from her room and once or twice, when she tried to settle down to finish her meal, she was sent to the kitchen for additional food. I looked on with shock; Stepmother had not changed.

Later we retired to bed, very tired. Next morning I awoke with the puzzled feeling of being in a strange room. In the first moment of consciousness, the memory of the previous evening returned. This was Selina's room. A spare bed had been put in for Safia and me. Unlike Safia, Selina had not stopped bed wetting, and there was a sour smell. We opened the window to let in fresh air. Selina's

Visit to Big Farm to see Selina (Machungwa Farm)

bedding needed washing and leaving out in the sun. Selina had to go to her Sirende primary school, two kilometres on the way to Kitale town, and this morning I saw her rush to go to the kitchen to prepare breakfast first. I followed her.

Selina was growing up scared, being made to work for Stepmother and the two half-sisters Caroline and Catherine. In fact, Catherine was much gentler. She was the smaller sister but Caroline did not get on with Selina, and everyone expected her to do the housework, clean rooms, cook, and wash clothes. In fact, she had the nickname of Cinderella.

She went to school without shoes sometimes and I wondered what had happened to them. She always looked very untidy and dirty, as if she had not washed for a long time. Maybe this made life at school difficult for her; a light-skinned girl appearing dirty with hair that was not combed and kept clean. The children teased her and life became more unbearable for her as the days went by.

The next day we had to leave. I found Selina to be the saddest person ever. The previous evening Father had packed his books and some old letters and put them in several boxes ready to take them to the other farm. Father took some of his china teacups and plates. Stepmother had locked up all silver utensils – forks, knives, spoons and the silver tea kettle. The piano was too heavy to move to the other farm, although we needed it for piano practice as we were still taking piano lessons at Kitale School.

The grass on the lawn had started to grow long. Hardly any labourers were around, just a few cows grazing round the lawn to keep the grass short. That last night I walked outside just before dark; the stars were out and when I walked out in these familiar grounds, I felt as if the ground fell away beneath me and the stars fell from the sky too. I reflected on many things, trying to get a clear picture of the meaning of life. I knew I must look for a sign. Looking for a sign takes a particular state of mind. Not many people find

Chapter Thirty-Two

themselves in such a state, but I was out there, surrounded by stars, looking for a sign.

For a second, time stood still. I felt afraid. Was it bad luck that I had experienced or was this an unlucky place for me? I knew my luck would come back one day and happiness would be within arm's reach. Still frightened, I walked back to the house, stumbling on some stones as I found my way back by twilight. I dared not look up in case I got a sign; I did not want any more signs. I would go with the flow of events and hope an angel was nearby, guiding and protecting me. I had had a difficult life and become flint hard, like the old mules that bite you if they have to so as to survive.

The next day we went home. The time I had spent on this farm had taught me that strange things happen, which we cannot possibly imagine. The only thing to do when such things happen is to keep in touch with what is going on, like a blind person who is being led and places one foot cautiously in front of the other.

I met Selina round in the shadow of the veranda to say goodbye. There was little time to talk. I told her that I knew they treated her like Cinderella. I asked her to be strong and to pray to God so she didn't shut herself out from His mercy.

As we were leaving, Selina threw her arms round me, tears running down her cheeks as she said goodbye. It was sad for her to see the only comforting person she had leave. As Father drove away, I could see her sad face and I wished I could have stayed one more day to give her courage to overcome the hardship that might prevail in my absence. She needed support. There was so much work, all on her shoulders and I whispered, 'Poor Cinderella.'

Chapter Thirty-Three

Father Transfered to Chewoyet Boys' Secondary School in Kapenguria West Pokot

The Ministry of Education transferred our father to Chewoyet Secondary School in the lower Kapenguria area, West Pokot district. He was given a big house to live in. He retired from being headteacher because of too much work and he found it hard to discipline the teenage boys; some of them were much too old for the class. Most of these boys were too old to be in school. I think Father was much happier to be a teacher with less pressure from the parents who expected free education from government secondary schools.

I was glad too that he was now only a teacher as this would give him more time for us and we would spend all our holidays with him at his home at the school.

Our first drive to Chewoyet Secondary School was pleasant and brought back memories that I still remember. Normally we saw no mountains on our way to Kapenguria except the Cherangani Hills far away. There were always clouds that travel with the wind and stick round these hills for a while, caught on the top ridge before going higher as they drifted towards the Kitale area. Moving with the wind they would break into rain. Other clouds sailed higher over us and met the clouds from Mount Elgon to create big thunderstorms. Sometimes the clouds from Mount Elgon would change

Chapter Thirty-Three

their character many times as they floated down the mountain. Many times they seemed to be close but other times they were far off. And many times in the evening, as it got dark, the sun dropped behind them to form shiny silver line across the horizon. Gazing at this beauty, we could see the peak of Mount Elgon shining very brightly as if it had snow on top.

Kapenguria is on a higher level than Kitale but Chewoyet Secondary School was situated on a side of the steep valley. It was a very cold place at night. This valley was full of forest planted by the government during the colonial era, when my father used to be an Agricultural Officer.

We drove over an old wooden bridge with thick planks strong enough to handle the weight of the cars or lorries that drove over it. Underneath, the river flowed crystal-clear along the river banks. Broad mimosa trees grew alongside.

It would be a different experience in this school. Maybe Father would let us have evening walks in the valley. No more walking bare footed or in simple shoes, he would buy us proper boots so we could walk through the indigenous forest. I wouldn't go catching butterflies any more; I was grown up and I no longer kept up the hobby. Hard work on Machungwa Farm had destroyed that for me.

We finally arrived at the school grounds. The school was more than one hundred acres and we did not drive to see the school buildings but on a narrow road that had a neat cypress hedge alongside it, cut back to maintain its beauty. We arrived at our father's house with its big backyard compound. Father had a garden where he grew his vegetables.

Father's cook opened the gate, received us and showed us our rooms. The place looked very beautiful and it reminded me of old colonial times when Father kept his house in order and meals were on time. We would have a normal life till the school holidays were over.

Chapter Thirty-Four

My Mother's Visit

ONE EVENING I was in the kitchen; my father had gone off for evening classes at the school. I heard someone knocking on the outer kitchen door. I opened the door and saw a dark lady standing on the steps. I said hello and at first I did not recognise her – it was my mother. She looked very different, thin and dirty. I remained standing at the doorway for a while, not letting her in, in case my father did not approve. We would await Father's approval but, as we continued to talk, it became clear she did not expect to be invited in for long. Maybe she had no faith in any kind of welcome but just wanted to see us. She was shaking so much from cold and fright that eventually I let her in as she looked very lonely and worried. Anyway, I was glad to see her. It was a long time since I had last seen her; so much had changed for her and we had grown up.

As she came through the kitchen corridor, I saw her in the bright light. She wore a dark dress, an oversized sweater and flip-flops. Her nails had not been cut for a long time and her feet looked dirty. She wore an old headscarf round her head so I could not see her hair.

I gave her a chair by the kitchen fire to warm herself as we waited for Father to come back. She did not say much, just stared at me. I did not wake Safia as this particular day she was sick and I did not want her to see our mother looking so untidy.

Chapter Thirty-Four

As I watched Mother, I wondered what she had been doing and what her life was like. I asked her how she had got here from the Kapenguria shopping centre and she told me she got a ride on a lorry that was delivering goods to the school. She told me she had no money to buy food and her only option was to come and beg my father for money. I had no idea how Father would receive such news. She sat in total silence looking into the fire.

The kettle was on and it whistled away while the water boiled. I tried to make her a cup of tea. Her eyes seemed unnaturally dark and large, taking in every detail in the kitchen and me. I wondered what her life was like.

I looked at her and tried to remember the days we had lived together as a family. I pulled a chair close to her. What had happened to her? She seemed distant, different.

I was close to tears but I held them back. I could do nothing; I was drifting in a strange sea of misery as we sat in silence. I knew I was far from her in spirit as she sat there like a total stranger.

Before I could make her a cup of tea, I heard Father's footsteps at the door. He walked in and headed straight to the kitchen looking for the cook who was late and had not prepared supper on time. I met my father halfway but he walked past me into the kitchen as if he knew my mother was there. He had been told at the school by the watchman that she was here. Father was angry that Mother had come to see us; this was unacceptable and unexpected.

Father immediately switched to Kiswahili when he spoke to her, anger in his voice. Was he quarrelling with her? Father did not need a translator; he spoke Swahili very well for he had taken Kiswahili as a subject at Makerere University in Uganda before Kenya acquired its independence. Not only that, he had done Kiswahili in grammar school and taken written lessons after independence so he could become a teacher in Kenya. These were the requirements to becoming a teacher in Kenya in the early years of independence.

My Mother's Visit

This talk between Mother and Father nearly turned into a heated argument. Mother threatened to come back every afternoon till she was given enough money to buy food. Father's worry was not her buying food but that she would spend the money on beer and make a nuisance of herself in public. My mother insisted that she be given a weekly allowance and she would be no trouble then she asked where Selina was. A settlement was made for her weekly payment and my father quickly whisked her away to his car to drive her to Kapenguria Town to stay with her relatives. I did not have time to give her a farewell handshake or a goodbye kiss but she came towards me swiftly to say goodbye, went to the car then came back to say goodbye a second time. I stood at the doorway, staring as the car pulled out of sight round the corner.

For the rest of the evening I thought of my mother. At bedtime I put on my pyjamas and settled down to read a book to improve my spelling and pronunciation. My spoken English was not up to standard; Father had complained and had a habit of correcting every word I spoke, which embarrassed me. My thoughts got in the way and I kept wondering about the events of the evening, seeing my mother after a very long time and the shock of it all. I felt no love, no affection towards her; she was like a stranger to me.

I kept on turning the pages of my book and trying to concentrate. I did not sleep much, just dozed off, but within an hour was wide awake and restless. My mother's pathetic state bothered me. Her face, as she sat by the kitchen fire staring at me, raced through my brain throughout the wakeful hours. I could still see her sad eyes. I got out of bed and went to the window, opened it wide for a second to let in the air. I bent my head to see the many stars above me and the full moon, which gave out enough light to see faintly around the room. I fretted for a while till the breeze became bitter cold. I closed the window and tried to get some sleep.

Father had not spoken about our mother to us before; he thought

Chapter Thirty-Four

it best to leave things as they were as they might upset us and interfere with our schooling. Next day he tried to explain to Safia and me so we would not grow up hating our mother.

During this time, my father's sister came over on a short visit to Africa. She had never seen us before, only in photographs; we wrote letters to her and that was all. As usual, our family was delighted to meet Father's relatives. We all enjoyed a change, things were done differently; more servants were employed to give the impression that the farms were flourishing and making money. But the farms could not pay wages and Father had to use up his savings to keep the two farms in running order.

Aunt Mary was happy to see us and knew us by name. She preferred to stay with our father at the Chewoyet Secondary School house, which was better maintained and had a cook to serve both her and our father. She asked Father to bring all the girls, including Catherine who was three years old. Our Aunt Mary noticed a lot of difference in our relationship with our stepmother and our step-family; straight away she complained about Stepmother, her constant drinking, her untidy living standards. The farm had been completely run down and most of the labourers and servants had left.

Stepmother liked to enquire about my education. She still liked to sit underneath her favourite old mulberry tree with a teapot that was black from the constant heating up of her tea using the old Maasai kitchen she had made for herself. At that time, she was making a wool rug. She got wool from the sheep. She was lucky that she had money she could spend but she refused to spend it to improve the farm and got stuck in her old traditional ways. She still kept a small gang of relatives who she treated like servants, Selina among them.

The feeling of oxygen being pumped out of the atmosphere felt like the energy was being sucked out of their bodies. Some relatives

My Mother's Visit

stayed around pretending to work but nothing was improving. They were stuck in this situation, a circle which was hard to come out of.

Our Aunt Mary noticed everything and advised Father that if he did nothing about it, we would be just the same as these relatives – especially me as I was the grown-up, thirteen years old, and could easily go wrong at this age. If things went on the way they were, I would miss out on my youth. I would lose the zest, the generous affection, the illusions and all the traditional attributes of youth.

Thank God Aunt Mary came to Africa to visit us. Her intervention saved me from missing out on youth and becoming someone totally different, forgotten by the modern world, left behind in misery in the Maasai tradition. My aunt insisted that I be put in a boarding school so I would improve in my schoolwork.

We arrived back in Kitale at our farm on the day before the term began. We were expected back at school and we looked forward to it. Unfortunately, the headmistress called my father and told him that I had made a very bad start that term; improvement was required otherwise they meant me to change school. This worried Father so much that Mrs Sloan, my class teacher, offered to give me extra lessons in Maths and English. She also taught me music and gave me piano lessons. These lessons took place after four o'clock and I enjoyed going down to her house to take my lessons; both husband and wife took a great liking to me and treated me like their own child. They had a daughter, Sheila, and a boy who was three years younger called Norman.

Our aunt did not stay long and she finally went back to the UK.

Chapter Thirty-Five

Our Holiday at Mombasa

During one Christmas holiday, the Sloan family asked Father if they could take me with them for four weeks' holiday to Mombasa on the coast of East Africa. I was so excited when Father accepted the offer. I would be tutored during this holiday in English and Maths, which was dragging me behind in class, and I ran the risk of being removed from Kitale School if I did not improve.

I remember the morning we drove out of Kitale Town. It was bliss for me to get away from my family, who reminded me constantly of backwardness. Father was always telling me that I had no brains and I would continue to be a stupid girl all my life. He was always negative, they all were – no wonder nothing improved on the farm. Stepmother had turned my father against me.

I was made to sit on the seats in the back of the car between Sheila and her brother. Sheila was much older than me while her brother was three years younger and always up to mischief and in trouble with his parents. In the middle seat I did not have the best view so I just gazed to the left if there was something interesting or exciting to look out for, or stared straight in front of me, which didn't bother me at all.

We spent one night in Nairobi and the next morning we were soon on our way to Mombasa. The last time I had made this long journey was when we went by train. Every time I have flashbacks

Our Holiday at Mombasa

on my journeys to Mombasa by train, I love to revisit my past.

As we neared Tsavo we started to see animals, first a herd of buffalos. We slowed down at a safe distance as we watched them cross the road. Buffalos do not, as a rule, take the offensive unless wounded and then they are the most formidable of African wild animals.

Everything looked familiar as we drove through a stretch of dry land, only shrubs here and there. From far off we saw the dim shape of animals but we did not have field glasses. The sun was rising steadily and, as we drove by, without warning we saw two rhinoceros about to cross the road. They sensed us and stopped. My teacher, Mr Sloan, drove past a few yards and we watched them at close range from our car. At first I thought it was a hallucination, but the two animals stayed where they were; they were motionless in the bright sun. Mrs Sloan tried to take a snapshot but could not get the right angle.

Very soon we had to start the car in case these animals ran after us. Rhinos can outrun a car. Black rhinos prefer areas between grassland and forest and they have excellent hearing and smell to compensate for their poor eyesight. They charge when they perceive danger, which gives them a reputation for being temperamental. We sat quietly but soon we had to move as they could sense us; the engine noise would definitely attract their attention and maybe they would charge towards us. It did not happen but Mr Sloan started the car swiftly and soon we were driving away from the two big animals. What an experience – a very dangerous and exciting one.

We came across herds of elephants and as we watched they came close as if to charge at us and we realised they had young ones. It was only their protective instinct. The leopard we saw was free and wild. I looked on, knowing I would miss all this: the massive Tsavo Park – truly a paradise, the brilliant birds, the giraffes,

Chapter Thirty-Five

the zebras on the side of the road, Mount Kenya with its iced top, the brilliant colours of the landscape. Maybe I would come back one day for a proper tour when I was old enough and not miss out on the pleasure of camping out under the bright stars and sightseeing during the day round the game parks.

Driving to Mombasa was the same. I was among people I had known when I was a child; I could see no changes in the people as we drove by but there were changes in Mombasa's buildings. Modern Swahili architecture had mushroomed everywhere. Mostly the outer colours depicted sand and sea colours.

We had a late lunch at the Mombasa Club then drove straight to the North Coast Kikambala village and the beach house which would be home for six weeks. It was twenty-eight kilometres from Mombasa. The drive took us thirty minutes. There was a huge house with a breath-taking view of the Indian Ocean; weathered grey stones acted like steps going down to the beach.

The place was neat, with fruit gardens; mangoes grew on one side. I was allowed to run down the steep steps towards the sea and look at the blue ocean. At that moment the tide was out; I could see that it would be wonderful to pick the cowry shells, other shells and starfish. Far off I could see caves and grottoes that would give shade when the sun got hot. When the tide came in, these caves would be full of sea water.

I knew I would enjoy my holiday here, forget my past and embrace the future. The sun shone, the water was warm, and I imagined tropical fish dancing in the sea. Maybe the Swahili fishermen would catch them to make a supper-time dish for us.

How beautiful that evening was when, after sunset, I walked the full length of the beach. The air was warm, moist and salty. Over to the west I could see a single star, which grew and radiated through the night. As I walked back to the house this star was so bright, like a topaz stone placed up high. The night winds whispered through

Our Holiday at Mombasa

the palms that overlooked the Indian Ocean. They swayed and whistled in the soft breeze, which continued and gently stirred the blossom of the white and pale-yellow frangipani flowers that grew near the house and carried their perfumed fragrance into the air.

Sloan's son, Norman, loved to catch butterflies and here in Mombasa there were so many of them. I no longer kept butterflies but I went out each morning with Norman to catch them. There are so many butterflies along this coastline and around Arabuko Sokoke Forest in Kilifi and the Kwale-Shimba Hills Forest in Kwale. Butterflies, like bees, play an important role in plant pollination and indicate a healthy environment and ecosystem. Seeing all sorts of colourful butterflies was a very good sign.

One day, I found a butterfly cocoon in a place that no one visited. Each morning I watched this cocoon, which hardly moved. One day, a small opening appeared. The butterfly inside was struggling to force its way through that little hole. It seemed to make no progress so I decided to help it out. I went back to the house and took a pair of scissors to snip the bit which seemed to prevent the butterfly coming out. It emerged easily; it had a very swollen body and small shrivelled wings. I sat there watching, hoping to see its wings enlarge to support this great body. Nothing happened for days. Every morning and evening I came to see what development I had missed. This butterfly spent days crawling around with its swollen body and little shrivelled wings but it was never able to fly.

What I did not understand till later was that the cocoon and the struggle required for the butterfly to get through the tiny opening were life's way of forcing fluid from the body into its wings so that it would be ready for a flight once it achieved its freedom. I was very sad to have interfered in its process of survival and I never told anyone.

I see myself as that poor butterfly in a cocoon, struggling to emerge as a full-winged butterfly. We need no interference to

Chapter Thirty-Five

achieve our freedom. Nature will take its course.

We visited friends at Watamu and Kilifi who had sold up their farms in Kitale, retired, and were involved in the tourism business here. Upcountry Europeans and package tourists from Germany, Italy, France and the Scandinavian countries came over to tour the Samburu and Maasai Mara, expensive tourist areas, and dominated the waterfront sports in Malindi. Watamu has a national park with limestone cliffs and sandy beaches. There is also a bird sanctuary. At high water we saw divers visit underwater caves where *tewa*, giant rocks weighing up to four hundred pounds, hang suspended upside down. It was not very safe as the currents of water were unpredictable so we never attempted a dive in case we drowned.

We did not miss out on Malindi, the old town with its large and busy markets. One of our family friends, the Daltons, who had sold out in Kitale, had set up a hotel business on the beach front. Here deep-sea sports anglers flew in to joust with the giants of the deep. From Dalton Hotel one could view the wide bay where the ocean swells over the broken reef; surfers visit all year round. This was a beautiful tourist spot. The Daltons were my father's old colonial friends, so visiting them was welcome and I got to meet their daughter, Helen, and son, Geoffrey, with whom we used to go to Kitale School in Kitale.

The day passed quickly and sweetly, perhaps too sweetly. We were invited to stay overnight at the Dalton Hotel. We sat on the balcony in the cool evening and had hot cheese sandwiches. Mr and Mrs Sloan drank champagne cocktails at the bar. We dined and mingled with the tourists. Afterwards there was dancing and we all joined in, although I was only thirteen and a half. I joined the other children my age.

There was a show that we watched, then entertainment with three musicians who called themselves the Strolling Minstrels. One had a fiddle, the other a guitar and the third was the soloist. The

Our Holiday at Mombasa

fiddle squeaked, the guitar twanged and singer sang. It was a love song, not a native tune, mournful, wailing, and miserable. We sat politely although we would have loved to have seen the local *ngomas* (traditional dances), which would have been more interesting.

I slept until the hotel girl called me. I rose wearily, dressed in silence, my mind going back in time to when I was a small girl. This place, though built in a modern style, still had an ancient feeling. It felt strange, and haunted me with flashbacks. Then, through the open window, I caught a glimpse of Norman walking down to the beach, a butterfly net in his hand, and I realised I had missed breakfast. I must have slept very late.

Going to the breakfast room, I was told that the Sloans had gone to Mombasa Town and I was alone. I spent the morning walking by the sea, looking for cowry shells and pondering my past.

While walking, I came close to the cliff's edge. I saw what appeared to be a clam shell. I had read of giant clams – bivalves big enough to close on a man's foot and hold him in a trap – but I had never seen one alive. I scrambled back down to the sand and sure enough I found a real whopper. It was the top half of the shell, over two feet in width. I turned it over. I imagine it must have weighed between forty to fifty pounds. The shell had obviously been washed ashore during the high seas. When I showed the Sloans the shell they said these big clams were sometimes seen on these reefs. I was glad to have the shell as it was in good condition.

I was told that giant tortoises roam this place and many of them weigh three hundred and fifty pounds or so, but I never saw one.

The coastline is full of weaver birds. These excitable, noisy little yellow birds provided some fun in our garden and sometimes they would fly very close. I clapped my hands and shouted good morning to them and a tremendous twitter was the reply. Of course, it was the sudden clap of the hands that disturbed the birds but it was pleasant to think that they might be answering my greeting.

Chapter Thirty-Five

That particular day, as I walked back to the house, I saw hawks slowly descend in a wide spiral. Down through the crows they came and one, in a final dive, attempted to take something from the tree. I could not see what it was but the crows' patience was at an end. One excited black bird made a wild dart at the hawk and together they wheeled and turned until the hawk flew away. His companion followed.

Then the crows split into pairs and imitated the battle they had just seen. In their pairs they chased one another, tumbling in revolutions I had never thought possible. A crow looped the loop by dropping its head and turning over once or twice. It turned over on its back in flight and pecked upwards at an adversary. I saw one bird dive and catch another's wing in its beak. Then howls of protest turned the fun into a real fight. I had an amusing morning watching these birds.

One weekend, the Sloans decided to sail beyond Makarungu (a village on the hill top) before dark and anchored in midstream. The next morning, we sailed on until noon. The coast disappeared until we saw the Vilima Vitatu (three small hills). The three hills loomed over us at one point and the further we went, the more undulating the terrain became. At noon we ate lunch on a beach and then climbed a hill to get our bearings. The wind had sneakily blown us off course and we found that we had sailed for an hour almost in a circle. The trip had taken us nine miles or so. Then the wind dropped; we were drifting peacefully when there was a tremendous whoosh over our bows. A kingfish had broken water. We watched it rise up right over the mast, which was more than twenty-four feet high. We did not watch the descent because from the great height the silvery monster seemed to be falling straight down on top of us. It landed a foot from Mr Sloan's back. It was a strange feeling to know it could have landed on anybody. After a while drifting along, we returned to the island at sundown.

Our Holiday at Mombasa

One afternoon when the tide was out, I persuaded Norman to accompany me right out to sea to collect more shells. He gladly accepted; it would be our last chance to get more shells and starfish as our holiday was coming to an end. Norman kept yelling and warning me to be careful where I trod. Too late, my foot came down on the sea snake. It gave a convulsive wriggle and I jumped very quickly. The snake chirred off through the seawater. Looking round, we saw other sea snakes so we were careful to watch our step as we went back to the shore. As we walked back we could see these snakes on the reef, their little heads looking like mice peeping from holes in the coral. The fishermen had told me some of these snakes were edible but I didn't think it would be a good idea to eat sea snakes.

On our way back, we decided to stroll round the bend of the sandy beach since we had lots of time and nothing to do that afternoon. We had walked for three miles and were getting tired and ready to turn back home when we came across a group of people who were looking at some performance. We went to see what it was.

In the middle was a local man; he looked like a *mganga* (magician). He was performing his tricks, starting with a battle between a snake and a mongoose. I wondered if there was anything phony in such fights. When the mongoose had killed the snake, the old magician asked for some water in a bucket. He threw the snake into the bucket for a moment or two then took it out again, alive. He popped it back into its box and I've no doubt it lived to fight another day.

The *mganga* looked up at the crowd of people then picked Norman out of the crowd and asked him to cup his hands. He told him to close and open them again. Looking self-conscious, Norman did so. To our horror, a little green snake rested in his palm. We all jumped with fright. Norman threw away the snake and ran off.

Chapter Thirty-Five

I followed and we went home, half walking and half running. We had been told there were many snake charmers on this island and the mainland, but we did not care to visit them. We saw them from afar, with crowds watching them use snake-charmers' pipes which, when put to the lips, produce thin, spindly music. When the tempo of this music increases, it makes the snake rise up from the bucket. The snake charmer, cross-legged and clad in a dhoti and turban, plays his music. I found them very frightening so we never saw one at close quarters.

When the day came to leave Kikambala, which had been our home for six weeks, I felt a slight sadness. I had come to love this place that had given me a different kind of freedom. I had grown up and was no longer a child but a brighter Susan, ready to face the world in a different way and try to put my past behind me. Here I had got back the balance of my mind and gained courage.

The girl carried our suitcase and bags to our car. She gave us a beautiful smile goodbye, her eyes shining at me. The cook came out to say farewell. As we drove away, I looked back at the house then beyond to the blue Indian Ocean. I watched the long coastline of pale grey and yellow coral-rock till it was out of my sight; a tear dropped from my eyes to my cheeks and I felt very sorrowful to have to leave this place where once I had found comfort and rest from my past miseries. One's past is commonly supposed to induce melancholy. I sat there gloomily like some lone, battered spirit struggling against the malign, hostile universe. I was so sunk in my misery that I hardly spoke all the way home.

'You're looking very sad today,' said Mrs Sloan.

I nodded and wiped my tears and tried to smile and look forward to what the world had to offer in the coming years.

www.ingramcontent.com/pod-product-compliance
Lightning Source LLC
Chambersburg PA
CBHW031101080526
44587CB00011B/770